Parent Survival Training

A Complete Guide to Modern Parenting

Marvin Silverman, Ed.D.
David A. Lustig, Ph.D.

MJF BOOKS
NEW YORK

Published by MJF Books
Fine Communications
322 Eighth Avenue
New York, NY 10001

Parent Survival Training
LC Control Number 2002102485
ISBN 1-56731-535-6

Copyright © 1987 by Dr. Marvin Silverman & Dr. David A. Lustig

This edition published by arrangement with Wilshire Book Company,
12015 Sherman Road, North Hollywood, California 91605

Manufactured in the United States of America on acid-free paper ∞

MJF Books and the MJF colophon are trademarks of Fine Creative Media,
Inc.

BG   10 9 8 7 6 5 4 3 2 1

DEDICATIONS

To my sons, Peter and Victor, who bore with me during the months that I was glued to the word processor. To my parents, Hyman and Betty, who struggled to provide my university education, which eventually enabled me to help in developing PST.

Dr. Marvin Silverman

To my wonderful parents, Charles and Evelyn, who first demonstrated to me that the goal of perfect parenting may not be elusive after all. To the rest of my family, who illustrated that love and support can indeed be limitless. To all of my many friends, who understood when I placed this book before all else and who proved that real friendship endures forever.

Dr. David A. Lustig

FOREWORD

There are many good books on parenting and on the management of children that use behavior therapy approaches, and this book, *Parent Survival Training,* is one of the very best. Not only does it show parents specifically what to do about their difficult (and not-so-difficult) offspring, but it does so in a remarkably clear, precise, and down-to-earth manner. The situations that it presents are truly typical, and they are handled in an exceptionally effective way that provides mothers and fathers with fine models of what to do—and what *not* to do—about scores of everyday child-rearing problems.

Best of all, Dr. Marvin Silverman and Dr. David A. Lustig's manual is one of the few parenting books that consistently mentions the principles of self-control and child management that are advocated in rational-emotive therapy (RET), and one that my associates and I have employed successfully since 1955. In many ways, it is an up-to-date version of the book that I wrote with Janet L. Wolfe and Sandra Moseley (*How to Raise an Emotionally Healthy, Happy Child*), which is also published by Wilshire Book Company. It nicely supplements this earlier volume in many important ways.

Dr. Silverman and Dr. Lustig particularly include the basic principles of RET in *Parent Survival Training*, and they explain throughout its pages the ABC's of rational-emotive therapy, which are re-worded as the "three R's": Reality situations (such as a child lying to his parents); the emotionally disturbed Result (such as the rage and upset of the parents); and the Response or irrational beliefs that contribute to and especially produce these Results ("You absolutely must not under any condition act in the way that I forbid you to behave!"). Where other forms of psychotherapy and child training wrongly explain that Reality situations (especially during one's early life) directly cause emotionally and behaviorally disturbed Results, the authors of this book, following the principles of RET, correctly show how parental Responses or irrational beliefs are the main cause of poor child-rearing Results.

In addition, this book specifically shows parents how to change their irrational Responses when they are confronted with the various difficult Realities of child rearing and precisely how, by doing so, to achieve much better Results. In its own right, *Parent Survival Training* is a remarkably good volume for parents. I recommend it enthusiastically and feel quite sure that, if its directions are actively practiced, it will bring most parents unusually good results!

Albert Ellis, Ph.D., *Executive Director*
Institute for Rational-Emotive Therapy
New York

ACKNOWLEDGMENTS

Any given philosophy, such as PST, evolves over many years and represents the culmination of countless hours spent developing myriad hypotheses and techniques. PST was influenced by our professional and personal experiences, as well as by academic training, the work of many different behavioral scientists, the hundreds of patients with whom we have had the opportunity to work, and the thousands of participants in our PST workshops around the country. We wish that we could express our gratitude to each one of the multitude of people who has had some influence in encouraging us to develop PST, but since such an acknowledgment would be impractical, we will say "thank you" instead.

In particular, we wish to recognize the following individuals for their special assistance and to thank them for showing tolerance during the year in which PST seemed to occupy our lives completely, especially since our absorption affected some of them, as well:

Dr. Richard Schaeffer (Barry University, Miami), Jay Woolfstead, Doug Mann, Dr. Paul Kulscar, Dr. John Foreyt, Dr. Karen Lickiss, Judy Dmyterko, Carlos Zaragoza, Ada Young, Rosemary Russo, Lorri Kellogg, Al Rantel (WNWS radio, Miami), Mike Miller (WIOD radio, Miami), Lynn Allison (The Globe), Kitty Oliver (Miami Herald), Dr. Tracy Levy, Bruno Lis, Robert Mulder, Conchita Herrera, Lawrence Rosenthal, Colossal Video (Sal) of Miami Shores, and Sister Jean O'Laughlin, Sister Agnes Louise, Father William Messick, and Pat Minaugh (staff members at Barry University).

We are deeply grateful to our publisher, Melvin Powers, who believed in this project from the beginning, and whose encouragement and support were an inspiration to us. We would like also to express our appreciation to Karnie Starrett for her editorial expertise.

Finally, we wish especially to thank colleague Dr. Albert Ellis for the influence that his work has had upon rational thinkers everywhere.

Dr. Marvin Silverman is a licensed psychologist in private practice in Pembroke Pines, Florida. He is a single adoptive father of three sons, and he has two granddaughters. He is the Adoption Program Director for Universal Aid for Children and the author of numerous professional journal articles. As an expert in child behavior, Dr. Silverman has lectured internationally and has appeared on more than four-hundred radio and television programs, including Sally Jessy Raphael, CNN, the CBS Morning Show, and others. Dr. Silverman is an expert in the field of psychoeducational assessment, ADHD, and child behavior.

Dr. David A. Lustig is a licensed clinical psychologist in private practice in Pembroke Pines, Florida, where he specializes in working with children, adolescents, and families. In addition, Dr. Lustig has been an adjunct professor of psychology at several colleges, including Barry University in Miami. He hosted a talk show on CBS radio and has appeared on more than 600 radio and television programs, including Oprah Winfrey, the CBS Morning Show, Sally Jessy Raphael, and Nightline. He has conducted workshops for professionals and parents throughout the United States. Drs. Lustig and Silverman, together with Dr. Janie Kondell, and co-founders of *Koala Learning Centers*, in Pembroke Pines, Florida. This innovative center provides supplementary education services to children in grades K-12.

CONTENTS

Parent
Survival
Training

Chapter One

What Is PST?

Congratulations! Upon opening this book, you have taken the first step in learning proven and effective child-rearing techniques. *Parent Survival Training* (PST) will show you how to take charge of your relationship with your children and how to create a home environment consisting of love, warmth, respect, and minimal conflict. PST techniques will enable you to help your child to control his own behavior, so that you can focus on the more positive aspects of your relationship.

What Is PST?

Behavioral psychologists who work primarily with children have discovered effective strategies for changing behavior, including the elimination of fears, tantrums, and school problems, as well as difficulties in following directions, in attention problems, in sibling conflicts, in harmful habits, in parent-child communication, in motivational shortcomings, in insecurity, in peer pressure, and in a variety of other common childhood troubles. Psychologists have also discovered that there are ways of helping parents to keep from becoming angry when dealing with their children and have used these strategies in therapy sessions with great success. Many of these strategies, however, have been difficult for parents to learn because they require training in psychology when they are presented in textbooks, in lectures, and even in other "academic-sounding" books on child rearing. PST presents these principles in a clear fashion, which permits them to be implemented easily into your household. Everything is written in a jargon-free style, with long-winded psychological terms left behind.

PST: The Child-Rearing Approach of the 1990s

The past several decades have seen a plethora of books purporting to help parents by promoting equal rights for children, as well as by suggesting that communicating with children only about their feelings is sufficient to help them become independent and responsible people. These philosophies have been reflected in the classroom, as well as in the media. In the 1960s, many schools developed open-classroom approaches, where the curriculum permitted the child to determine his own rate of learning, often with disastrous results. In the 1980s, many of these schools rebuilt the walls and went back to traditional methods of teaching. For the 1990s, there is PST.

Milk Cartons Are Not Really Dangerous to Your Child

Not realizing the strength and resiliency of the average child, the American media continues to focus on the detrimental effects that real-life events are supposed to have on children. For example, many people have expressed concern about the appearance of missing children's photos on the panels of milk cartons, worrying needlessly that scores of children will be terrified by exposure to these pictures. Instead, kidnapping is now a part of the real world, and, as such, is a fact with which children must be helped to deal as adaptively as possible. Sheltering children from the knowledge that they need to survive in the world is not really in their best interests. For that reason, the underlying philosophy of PST is "helping your child to survive" —while you do the same thing.

The Skills That a Child Needs to Survive

A great many skills are needed for a child to survive outside the home, and teaching these skills to the child is a fundamental part of the role that parenting encompasses. By using PST techniques, you can help your child to prepare for the real world by eliminating maladaptive behavior as soon as it appears. You can teach your child to develop a sense of responsibility, to think before he acts, to accept the differences between himself and adults in positions of authority, and to realize that appropriate behavior leads to pleasant consequences, while inappropriate behavior results in his experiencing discomfort or inconvenience of one kind or another. For example, we have discovered eight common ways in which parents help to create problems for the child.

The Eight Ways to Destroy a Child

1. Tell your child to do something two or three times, so that he will learn from experience that it is not important for him to follow directions on the first request.
2. When your child misbehaves, yell and scream in an angry manner. This will reward your child's misbehavior. He is likely to get pleasure out of seeing that he can control and manipulate your emotions, and will enjoy seeing that *you* suffer for *his* misbehavior.
3. Do things for your child that he is capable of doing for himself.
4. Call on your spouse to be the disciplinarian when the child misbehaves instead of handling the problem yourself.
5. Allow your child to see that he can make you feel guilty because of the things that he says.
6. Give your child money or buy him things as he asks for them, instead of using an organized allowance system.
7. Argue with your child.
8. Get involved in fights between brothers and sisters. Then, play district attorney by questioning them as to who started the fight and by taking sides.

Parents Aren't Responsible for Everything, Though

In any child's life, there are many individuals who assume positions of influence, including teachers, peers, relatives, television personalities, sports figures, and neighbors. Although you may not be able to control all of these areas of influence, PST works by helping you to take control of those aspects of the child's life over which you can have impact and responsibility. Behind the logic of PST lies a set of basic principles, and adherence to these concepts is necessary if you are to succeed in utilizing the techniques in this book to their fullest.

Parent Survival Training: The Basic Principles

1. *Always be consistent.*

   Children react swiftly and negatively to any perceived inconsistency in the actions of their parents, seeing them as easily controlled.
2. *Parents have greater rights than children.*

   By virtue of their position, parents can and should exercise privileges (e.g., decision making) that they have not yet granted to their children.

3. *Don't permit manipulation.*

   Never allow your child to "play" with a situation. As the parent, you must maintain control.

4. *Don't feel guilty when you're right.*

   As a parent, you should not feel guilty for doing what is right for your child's well-being, even if the child doesn't like it.

5. *No arguing.*

   Do not argue with a child, or you risk legitimatizing his right to call the shots in decision-making situations.

6. *Behavior that is rewarded will be repeated.*

   Reinforcing any behavior will make it more likely to occur again.

7. *The reward must be worth working for.*

   No child can ever be expected to work hard for a reward that isn't significant to him. Find something for which the child will be willing to work.

8. *Occasional rewards work best.*

   Rewarding an appropriate behavior every time that it occurs means trouble the first time that a reward isn't given. Occasional rewards make the behavior more likely to persist without reinforcement.

9. *Behavior that is punished without anger will occur less frequently.*

   Parents who can punish a child without anger will retain control while teaching the child to act appropriately.

10. *Punishment must be an unpleasant experience.*

    For punishment to be effective, it must be unpleasant enough so that the child would not want to have to go through it again.

11. *Past behavior is the best predictor of future behavior.*

    You can gain a fairly good idea of what to expect in a situation by examining similar situations from the past.

12. *Anger isn't the loss of love.*

    Help your child to understand that just because he has misbehaved does not mean that you will be angry with him or that you will reject him as a person.

13. *Educate whenever possible.*

Take every opportunity to explain to the child exactly what he did that was "good" or "bad," what the consequences will be, and (if improvement is needed) what he should do the next time a similar situation arises.

14. *Accent the positive.*

When your child has done something well, don't hesitate to reinforce that behavior (so that it will occur again).

15. *Don't be intimidated by your child's anger.*

When you try to help your child to change his behavior, he may react at first with anger and resistance. It is important that you stick to your guns, so that he eventually will see that he has no choice but to change.

16. *You are always a model for your child.*

As your child observes the way in which you act, he will pick up your behavior and your reactions. You must always be aware of the example that you are setting.

17. *Adolescents should not be treated like children.*

Expecting a teenager to react to the same strategies that work with younger children is unrealistic. Be ready to change your techniques as your child matures.

18. *Attention-seeking behavior should never* get *attention.*

Whenever a child is obviously doing something inappropriate as a way to get your attention, make sure that you don't give it to him.

19. *No child can* make *you feel anything.*

It's not your child's fault that you become upset; your feeling is present because you have chosen not to maintain control.

20. *Change doesn't occur overnight.*

It has probably taken your child years to develop certain habits or behaviors. It may take time to change them.

You'll See These Points Again

The above principles will appear repeatedly within the chapters of this book, but they cannot be emphasized too often. Since repetition is an effective learning strategy, we have found it helpful to present major points in more than one chapter. We hope that this will aid you in making these principles an integral part of the way in which you deal with your children.

How to Use This Book

Although the techniques presented have been helpful to most families, they are not a cure-all for every problem that may arise with a child. There are times when more intense help may be needed than can ever be provided in a book, and professional assistance may be an option to be considered in such cases. In Chapter Nineteen, we have provided information that can help you in making such decisions.

It is important that you read all of the chapters in the book before using any of the techniques; in many cases, points that are made require knowledge of concepts that were presented in previous chapters. By reading the book from cover to cover, you can make the most use of the information contained inside.

Chapter Two

How to Teach Your Child to Follow Directions on the First Request

Many parents feel that raising a responsible child is one of their goals. However, in order to learn how to deal effectively with responsibility, your child has to be given responsibilities and then be allowed to face the consequences of his or her own behavior. It is only through such opportunities that a child can learn how the concept of responsibility works.

One of a child's first steps in learning to be responsible is compliance with directions that are given by authority figures (e.g., parents, teachers). Therefore, when a parent gives a child a direction or a request, the child should do what the parent has said to do the first time or be punished for his non-compliance. *There is not one child on the face of this earth who cannot follow a parent's direction on the first request.* Exceptions, of course, have to be made for any child who has a neurological problem or a hearing deficiency, or who cannot realistically understand the directions being presented. When a parent tells a child something two or three times, the parent is *teaching* the child, "It is not important to follow directions because you will always be given another chance." Your child will learn that the worst thing that will happen to him for not doing as he has been asked is that you will get upset, but that nothing will happen to him.

Taking the First Step
The first step in setting up an effective behavior management system within your home is to help your child to learn that *directions must be followed the first time they are presented*. To reach

that goal, you must get into the habit of telling your child something only once. If the child does not follow directions as you requested, there must be an immediate consequence for his inaction. This consequence should be related to whatever the child did that was inappropriate. For example, let's imagine that you've asked your child to wash his hands and his face for dinner and to be at the table in 5 minutes. After 15 minutes, your child still has not followed through on the task. Yelling at your child or repeating the directions would only serve to teach him that he really doesn't have to listen to you. At this point, you must calmly inform the child that he did not comply, and then announce to him exactly what consequence(s) will occur. In this example, an obvious consequence would be that the child miss dinner that evening, since he did not follow the directions given to prepare for dinner. Of course, in a two-parent household, one of the parents should not display sympathy for the child or permit him to eat his portion of the dinner later. Instead, if the child were hungry, you might offer him something that would nourish him without providing pleasure (a sandwich, or just toast and milk). Rather than feeling guilty or sympathetic for the child, you would be better advised to tell yourself, "I'd rather see him be a little unhappy tonight than have to argue with him or coax him for the next ten years."

Matching the Consequence to the Behavior
Another example of a consequence related to a particular misbehavior might be that of a child who is told to come home promptly at 6:00 P.M., but who returns at 6:15. The parents in such a situation should tell the child that he did not follow the directions that were given and, as a result, he will not be allowed out of the house to play the following day. Thus, the child will learn that non-compliance with directions results in an inconvenience to him but not in an inconvenience to the parent.

Once, we counseled a family in which the mother constantly complained that her son would never get dressed on time, thus making himself late for school (and the mother, late for work). We pointed out to the parent that the child was probably feeling powerful, as he was able to see that his behavior created anxiety, excitement, and inconvenience for the parent. We suggested to the mother that she throw the problem back to the child. The child was told, "We will leave the house at 7:45 A.M., whether you are ready or not. If you are not dressed, with your teeth brushed, your hair combed, your hands and face washed, and you have not finished with breakfast, we will leave anyway. I will not remind you or yell at you to 'get ready!' " The next day 7:45 A.M. arrived, and the child had not even put on his pants, socks or shoes. The parent pushed the child out of the door, while throwing his shoes, pants, socks, and jacket behind him. The child ran behind the wall in front of the house and got dressed there. If you were the parent in a situation like this, the message to your child would be "You will leave the house on time, and I will not play games with you. If you are embarrassed, it's your problem, because you had enough time to get ready." Of course, discretion should always be used (you couldn't handle the above situation the same way with a well-developed adolescent girl, for obvious reasons). If the circumstances were to warrant it, you could drive your child to school with a blanket around him or her and have the child finish getting dressed in the car. The concept behind this is that the child must learn that *the parent will not play games with him* or become upset, and that the child is expected to have certain tasks completed on time.

Be Specific

When giving a child directions, it is very important for you to be specific. A parent has to pretend that he is an attorney (writing a contract) whenever he is presenting a direction to a child. If a direction is vague, the child will develop some strategy for getting out of it. Dr. Silverman learned how important it is to be specific when giving directions shortly after adopting his 7-year-old son from El Salvador. "I would ask him each night if he had brushed his teeth, and he would always say 'yes.' After a few days, the odor from his mouth made it obvious to me that he hadn't been brushing his teeth. When I confronted him with this, he pointed out to me that he was telling the truth because he had brushed his teeth last week. The error that I made was that I did not ask him *when* he brushed his teeth. Because my question was not precise, my son's answer was honest and correct, and I could not punish him."

A parent can almost never be too specific when giving a direction. For example, instead of telling a child to "clean your room," the parent would do better to say, "Go to your room, empty the trash can, make your bed neatly, pick up the toys and books from the floor and put them on the shelves or in the closet, and then vacuum the carpet." By giving such specific directions, the parent can then go to check the room, knowing that if one of the tasks were not completed, he could then say, "I told you to make your bed, but you didn't do it. Because of your failure to follow directions, you will not watch television tonight. Now, go make your bed."

The Stubborn Child

Many parents respond to such suggestions by saying, "But what if he says that he won't do it and becomes stubborn? What do I do then?" The parent must be stronger and more stubborn than the child. One technique that has been very effective is that of "packing up the room." The parent can go to the child's bedroom with a box or a big bag and say, "I am going to start putting all of your toys and games in this box. I will keep doing this until you have made your bed. If you refuse to make your bed, I will have packed up every toy and game that you have. Whatever goes into the bag will be given to a charity so that poor kids who don't have enough toys will have a chance to have something to play with." When using a technique such as this one, you must, of course, follow through. If you have packed up several of the child's toys before he starts making his bed, you must give the toys away.

Education Is in the Eye of the Beholder

It is usually best for the parent to take the child with him to the Salvation Army or to other such thrift shops so that the child can watch his toys being given away. The parent should request a receipt for his taxes and then explain to the child that the charitable tax deduction will help to offset some of the cost of the things that were given away. If you were to put the toys in a closet instead with the idea of giving them back to the child a month later, the child would never believe that you will take such promised action if it becomes necessary in the future.

A Parent's Guilt

Sometimes, when a parent has to take such actions, he or she feels guilty about how miserable the child is feeling. As a parent, you occasionally will have to sit back and watch your child feel miserable. If your child felt happy all of the time, he would not be prepared to deal with the real world. In the real world (e.g., school, work, friends), the child is frequently faced with frustration and stress. If you were to try to protect your child from feeling anxious (or "bad") in these circumstances, he would never have an opportunity to learn how to manage stress or how to resolve his own feelings of discomfort. Under certain circumstances, allowing your child to feel bad is actually an important learning experience for him.

No Reminders

When trying to get a child to follow directions on the first request, it is important that you do not give the child any suggestions or hints, such as "Don't you remember the rule? Didn't I just tell you something? If you don't do it, you know what is going to happen." Statements such as these are the same as repeating directions a second time. The child should be told something once, after which he complies or he experiences a consequence for non-compliance.

Of course, positive actions must also be emphasized. When the child is asked to do something and he does follow directions, it is important that you recognize this compliance and praise the child. You might say something, such as "I asked you to tie your shoelaces, and you did it right away. Thank you, I really appreciate the way that you listened so well."

A child must learn through experience that before he can do pleasurable activities, such as going out to play or participating with his sports team, he must first fulfill requirements, such as homework, household chores, or taking care of his pet.

Why These Techniques

If reading about these techniques disturbs you, please take

note of just how important it is for children to learn to comply with directions presented by an authority figure. Outside the household, others expect a child to follow directions and to "listen." For example, if a teacher asked a child to work on page 53 in the math book and allowed 30 minutes for the task to be accomplished, the child would likely get an "F" for the assignment if he just sat there because he felt that "putting my name on the paper is enough work for the day." The teacher certainly would not beg or scream in order to get the child to do his work.

As a child becomes older, other authorities (police, employers) will expect the child to comply readily with instructions or the child will face severe consequences, such as being arrested or being fired. If an adolescent impulsively goes into a convenience store with a pistol and robs the clerk, it is unlikely that the police will tell him that he shouldn't do that because he would be arrested if he did it again. Obviously, the adolescent would be arrested immediately. Although this is an extreme example, it is important to realize that a child's compliance is something that must be taught.

When a child learns that he can get away with little things, he will try for bigger and bigger things until he reaches the parent's breaking point. If a child had to miss an activity, television, dinner, or any other event for one night, it would be well worth it if such deprivation meant that in the the future the parent would not have to beg the child to prepare for dinner, or to follow through with a chore. When provided with the proper contingencies, any child can learn rapidly that the parent is not joking when he gives directions.

The parent who says, "My child does not finish his work at school, and he does not listen to the teacher" (assuming that there is no learning disability or other problem that would interfere with school performance) is almost always revealing a history of having repeated directions consistently to the child at home. Such a child has not learned to listen and thus cannot concentrate adequately on instructions presented by the teacher. As you can see, by teaching a child to follow directions on the first request at home, he is more likely to be compliant with authority figures in other settings.

Be Consistent

It is extremely important for parents to be consistent when they begin to teach a child to follow directions on the first request. If the child knows that one out of five times the direction will be repeated to him, he will know subconsciously that he has a 20 percent chance of getting away with something and will continue trying to "get away with things" by beating the odds. Therefore, consistency in *not* repeating a direction to a child is extremely important. There is no way that a child will learn to follow directions if you enforce only occasionally the rule, "You have to follow directions the first time that I tell you to do something, or there will be a consequence." Note, however, that such assertiveness on your part will be ineffective if you yell and scream so that the child sees that he has the power to make you feel angry.

In Chapter Eleven, we discuss how to set up an allowance system for your child. This allowance system can often be used to help your child learn to follow directions, since a portion of the allowance will be deducted each time that he does not comply on the first request.

Poker Chips As Tokens

Another effective way of setting up an organized program to help a child start following directions is to use a system with poker chips. The logic behind the system is actually one that helps *you* to become more consistent. Poker chips have been used effectively with children as young as 3 years of age, and with children in their early teens. You can buy a box of poker chips in most toy or card shops, and the chips usually come in three colors. If you have more than one child in the house, you can assign one color to each child (e.g., Johnny gets the blue chips, and Susie gets the white chips). Such a color scheme helps to avoid the problems inherent in having the children stealing chips from each other. In most cases, the system has to be set up for all of the children in the family who are of an appropriate age. If this system is used only with a child who is considered to be a problem, then jealousy can occur very rapidly among the other siblings because of all the attention that the problem child is getting.

For the first week, the rules should be written out and posted in a conspicuous place:

> When I tell you to do something, you will do it the first time that you are told or you will lose one chip.
>
> Whenever I ask you to do something and you do it immediately, you will win one poker chip.

This system forces the parent into reacting to the child at times when he does not follow directions, as well as at those times when he does, so that the child has the opportunity to learn the difference between the responses that he gets when he is compliant versus those that he faces when he is non-compliant.

What to Do with the Chips

It is important for you to note at this point that the poker chips are of no value unless they can be made to be worth something. So, what can you make the poker chips worth? It has been found effective to have the child use the chips to purchase things that he wants to have or to trade for things that he likes to do. Make up a list of the things your child does on a regular basis and finds enjoyable. The list might include television, going out to play, having a friend in the house, going in the swimming pool, eating "Doritos," using the video game, and playing with the cat. Then, assign each of these activities a specific chip value. For example, going out to play might cost three chips. Watching television might cost one chip for every 30 minutes. Most children are given 20 or more directions per day by their parents. To determine what values will become part of the system, think about how many chips your child realistically could earn on a typical day. Assign the number of chips needed for each of the activities in such a manner that the child will have just enough chips if he does everything that he is supposed to do during that day. You can also set up a bonus, such as "If I save forty chips, I can go to the movies." Of course, you should specify in advance which movie the child would be able to see. It becomes the child's responsibility to decide whether he wants to use the money to watch television, to go out to play, or to skip some of those activities to accumulate enough chips for the bigger activity. In addition to dealing with the child's behavior, this system is giving the child an opportunity to make decisions, as well as a chance to deal with his own values in determining what is important to him.

Sample Poker Chip System

Rule: Do what you are told the first time.

+1 chip when you follow the rules.

−1 chip when you don't follow the rules. After you lose a chip, you still have to do what you were told or you will be punished.

Chip Values:

Watch TV — One chip for every 30 minutes
Go out to play — Two chips
Use bike — One extra chip
Go to friend's house — Three chips
Use video game — Three chips
Go to "Burger King" — Twenty-five chips

After one week, the chip system can be phased out and replaced by the allowance system (to be discussed later). It is a good idea to use the chip system for a week or two so that everyone in the household gets into the new habit of following directions on the first request.

The Child May Get Upset
Some children become so angry and upset when they learn there are going to be rules in the house that they go into a tantrum. Most children get very upset the first time that a chip is lost because they didn't follow directions. The more upset and angry that a child becomes about such structure in the household, the

more spoiled and over-indulged the child probably has been. The child who goes into a tantrum and screams when he loses his first chip is really showing the parent that he needs the structure. If he says, "This whole thing is dumb and stupid," and then adds, "and I'm not going to do it and you can't make me do it," the parent should look at the child and say, "You are going to do it; you have no choice. If you leave the chips that you threw on the floor where they are, that's okay, but you can do nothing that is on the activity list because you won't have chips to pay for anything. You have sixty seconds to pick up the chips, or I will take them back and you can't do anything on the list until you earn more chips." At that point, as the parent, you can just walk away without arguing and without making false statements to yourself: "This isn't working, because my child doesn't seem to care." *It is not important whether the child wants to participate in the program or not; it is important only that the child learns that the parent is in charge and that he is going to do what he is told, whether he likes it or not.* Don't hesitate to say to the child, "Whether you like the system or not, you are going to do it. You have no choice."

Some children are quite accustomed to a parent's inconsistency; they've seen the parent constantly trying out new techniques. For example, if Phil Donahue were to have a guest to talk about assertive discipline techniques, the child viewing the program might anticipate that things will be rough for a couple of days. However, such a child probably has learned over time that if he resists the parent's efforts to improve things, the parent readily will give up the system. At this point, the parent must "out-stubborn" the child. It is time for the child to realize finally that if he wants to make his own life miserable, he can; but the parent is not going to give up the techniques.

Question:
    "You said that there might be a time when a child would go to bed without dinner. Isn't this a negative thing to suggest, especially since our society has been remiss in the custom of families eating together? Why would you now suggest that a child be made to miss a meal completely?"

Answer:

The example that we gave about a child who might miss a meal because he was late for dinner is something that would happen only occasionally. After the child has suffered the consequence of missing a meal because he was late, it is unlikely that he will continue to engage in this type of behavior. Although some of the examples that we cite may, at first, seem quite strong, please keep in mind that once a child has learned the rules and knows that the parent will not play around with him, he will comply more frequently and there will be less and less of a need for punishment. Of course, it is appropriate for a family to eat together and to be together; however, it would be more damaging for a child to be allowed to eat with the family when he has disobeyed the parent's directions to be home at a set time. It would be better for the child to miss one meal than for the parent to have to argue and yell at the child for a few years because he never comes home on time.

Question:

"I have tried to punish my child for not listening to me, but he always says 'I don't care.' What can I do when he seems to take the sting out of punishment with statements like that one?"

Answer:

Just about every child we know says "I don't care" when a punishment is assigned to him. The child will feel better if he knows that you think the punishment is not bothering him. "I don't care" does not mean that he really does not care, but is a way to make you think that the restrictions you are placing on him are insignificant. It is extremely important that you do not respond to the child when he says "I don't care." If you do respond or challenge him, the child will get satisfaction out of knowing that he was able to disturb you. Always stick to the issue at hand and disregard these challenging statements. If you pretend that you did not hear him and continue with the problem being discussed, eventually the child will stop making such statements because he knows that they do not bother you.

Question:

"The rules that you put forth in PST sometime seem too rigid. Isn't there a risk that such rules will make my child behave like a puppet?"

Answer:

The rules may seem rigid as you are reading them, but when you apply them, you will see that they really are not. It is very important for you to understand that once the behavior management program in your household is well organized and consistent, there will not be many challenges to your reasonable requests of the children. Outside of the household, others will expect your child to comply with directions. As a parent, it is your responsibility to make sure that the child learns to follow directions from authority figures. No one else is capable of teaching this important survival skill to your child. If you want to prepare the child to deal with the real world, prepare him to follow through with required tasks. There is a crucial difference between following directions from authority figures versus behaving like a puppet.

Question:

"I tell my son that he has to brush his teeth when he gets up every morning, but I always have to send him back to do it before he leaves for school. How can I get him to brush his teeth without having to remind him?"

Answer:

As in similar situations we have discussed, a child learns through experience. If your child does not brush his teeth in the morning and you just send him back to do it, he will not be concerned about remembering it. Why should he feel motivated to remember to do it when you always will remind him? When you discover that he has not brushed his teeth in the morning, establish a consequence for this behavior. Any consequence that you feel is appropriate and meaningful to your son should be considered. For example, you might say to him, "Since you forgot to brush your teeth this morning, you cannot have anything sweet all day. You will drink water, and you will not have any punch or soft drinks. You will not be allowed to have any snacks or dessert. You will have only the main part of your meal. If you remember to brush your teeth tomorrow morning, you will be allowed these special treats again." Of course, if you make such a statement to the child, you must enforce it fully. If you fail to do so, your child will see it as a mere threat. As with other behaviors, do not keep reminding your child about what he must do; he will learn to brush his teeth on his own when (and *only* when) he realizes that failing to do so results in inconvenience to him.

Chapter Three

Tantrum Control: Eliminating Your Child's Ultimate Weapon

If the average child were able to describe the purpose of a tantrum, he would probably state that it is a child's *ultimate weapon.* Faced with what he perceives as "no other choice," an angry or frustrated child will lose all apparent control and, by doing so, will actually *gain* a great measure of control. If you're somewhat confused by the last sentence, it's no wonder that you have difficulty controlling your child's tantrums.

Tantrums Are Really a Control Problem

When a child engages in tantrum behavior, he is actually taking control away from the parent. He does so by calling the shots: screaming, kicking, pushing, pulling, crying, and, if at all possible, attracting the attention of passers-by (any child knows that tantrums work best in public places). It's as if the child is saying, "Go ahead and hit me, but I'll scream even louder. Lock me in my room, and I'll kick the walls. Try to reason with me, and you'll frustrate yourself to tears." The child takes control away from the parent by putting the parent in a position where he or she feels utterly helpless. The louder, longer, and more intense the tantrum, the greater the degree of pleasure the child is able to experience as a result. After all, in how many other instances is a child so capable of inducing a sense of helplessness within his mother or father?

Most Parents Fail to Take Control

Parents who have learned to deal successfully with tantrum

behavior understand the secret: You must take the control *away* from your child if you hope to end the tantrum. The difficulty that many parents have is in trying to develop an effective method for taking control back from the child, and that is why public displays of parental helplessness are so commonplace. The next time that you're in a large toy store, take a careful look around, but this time, not at the toys. Do some people watching, and you'll discover quickly that your peers know no more about terminating tantrum behavior than you do.

> *Child:* I want it. Gimme!
> *Parent:* Now, Sean, you know that we agreed you could have the hockey set today, but that you'd have to wait until your birthday next week for the Monster Mash Superhero Incandescent Light Ray Device.
> *Child:* No, now! I'm getting it now!
> *Parent:* I'm sorry, Sean, but you'll have to wait until next week.
> *Child:* Aaaaaaahhhhhhhhh! Gimme!
> *Parent:* Stop it. I said, 'Stop it, right now!'
> *Child:* Aaaaaaahhhhhhhhh! I hate you!
> *Parent:* Okay, young man, I've had enough. Now, shut up or you'll get a spanking right here, right now.
> *Child:* Aaaaaaaaaaaaaaaaaaaaaaahhhhhhhhhhhhhhhhhhhh!

Like most parents, the one in the preceding example has allowed her child to manipulate and to control her. To begin with, she made a fatal error by arguing with her child. Any time that you argue with a child, you are legitimizing the child's right to disagree. Adults can argue with each other because they have the right to express opinions and beliefs of their own. While a child most certainly has the right to hold his own opinions and beliefs, it is against the basic principles of PST to permit the expression of those beliefs to be made in defiance of parental wishes. To permit your child to decide when he is going to receive a new toy is an error for which you may pay dearly later on.

Parents and Children Have Different Rights
Instead of promoting equal rights in the household, work on

teaching your children that their rights and privileges are different from yours; as an adult, you can make decisions by which they, as children, must abide. You will decide whether that stray dog in the back yard can join the family; you will decide whether the child *really* has to go to school on Fridays; you will decide whether your child's future actually depends upon the purchase of a $3,000 home computer. Just a decade or two ago, child-rearing books stressed the idea of equal rights for parents and children. Such ideas are hopelessly outdated today, because it's obvious that such concepts simply do not work.

Beware of Other Mistakes in Controlling Tantrums

The parent in the preceding example made other mistakes. Note that the child was not the only one acting childishly. Whenever you display anger at a child with such minimal provocation, the message that the child receives is an inadvisable one. He learns that he can wreak havoc with his mother or father's emotions: Just a little word here, a quick behavior there, and the parent's emotional state is right in the palm of his hand. PST involves learning how to control your emotions: Don't become angry without good reason, and don't display anger at the drop of a hat. Above all, don't abdicate control to the child by illustrating how easily you can become upset. Children have an inherent respect for strength: Utilize this concept well.

Perhaps, at this point, you realize that there is yet another problem with the way this illustrative situation was handled: the threat of physical force. The last thing in the world that any parent should do with a tantrum-throwing child is to hit him. If the child is already crying and carrying on, does it actually seem possible that he will stop doing so while he is being hit? There are far more effective ways of controlling a child's behavior than by inducing physical pain. In fact, parents often hit their children as a release for their own frustration rather than because the child is going to learn anything from it. Remember: Children learn from the behavior that goes on around them. Therefore, hitting a child who is engaging in tantrum behavior is the same thing as explaining to him that you want to hurt him so that you can feel better, and that bigger and stronger people are always right. Instead, try a little education: Let the child know that he is acting inappropriately and that you will not tolerate it. Don't argue, don't raise your voice, and don't become angry. Follow the PST principles illustrated here, and put an end to your child's tantrum behavior.

Using PST: The Tape-Recorder Technique

Because tantrums basically represent a control issue, you must take that control away from the child. By far, the most effective way to do this is to take the fun out of tantrums, and here's how to do it.

Explain to the child that if he wants to have tantrums, he is free to do so. However, he must have at least one every day, occurring at a pre-determined time and place, and it will be tape-recorded. Tell the child that each day his tantrum must be *better* than the one he had the day before—louder, longer, and more intense. Explain that he will be punished (e.g., loss of TV privileges) for any day on which his tantrum does not show improvement. He will be forced to sit still and listen carefully to the daily recordings of his tantrums, and he will have to explain any lack of success in evidencing "improved" performance. What you will achieve through the use of this PST technique is a complete regaining of control over the child's tantrum behavior. Whereas before, tantrums were fun (i.e., spontaneous, wild, and free), they are now another obligation—another daily chore. Even worse, they've become boring. Within days, most children begin requesting that they not have to perform tantrums anymore. You must resist the initial temptation to cancel the assignment. Instead, have the child continue engaging in tantrum behavior for several days more (after the complaints have started), not permitting him to stop until you are certain that he never wants to have another tantrum for the rest of his life. At that time, you can be relatively certain that you've regained control. It will help to say things, such as "Okay, Ross, if you're *sure* that you don't want to have any more tantrums, I suppose that it'll be okay for you to stop."

Backsliding Is Rare

Experience has shown that few children will revert to tantrum behavior once PST has been employed. If such an event were to occur, however, the likelihood is that you would have only to take a tape recorder, turn it on, and the tantrum would cease. One of the most important principles here is that the child is learning that the parent is not playing a game; when a child knows that his limits have been reached, he will typically resist the temptation to test the same limits repeatedly. Naturally, most children will attempt to get away with as much as they believe they can, but when the limits are held consistently and clearly by the parent, the child is likely to accept them.

Why Positive Reinforcement Doesn't Work with Tantrums

Many parents attempt to alter tantrum behavior by using the principles of positive reinforcement explained earlier in this book. Unfortunately, there is a significant risk associated with such an endeavor. PST skills include understanding that any behavior that is reinforced is likely to occur repeatedly. If you were to reward a child for *not* having a tantrum or were to reward him for ceasing one, you would, of course, be creating a situation in which the child would seek to be rewarded by beginning a tantrum. Consider this: If you worked late one night and found that your boss gave you a large raise the next day, wouldn't you be likely to work late again, expecting perhaps to receive another raise? There is no reason to assume that a child would see tantrum behavior any differently. In fact, any intelligent child who is rewarded each time he stops a tantrum will, in all likelihood, start and stop tantrums with great frequency. By the same token, mere punishment is unlikely to have great impact on tantrum behavior because the child is expecting it and has actually accepted its inevitability by engaging in the tantrum behavior (no child would throw a tantrum if he were worried about the punishment). It's as if the child is letting you know that punishment is okay; it's worth it, as long as he can have his tantrum.

Ignoring the Problem Will Make It Worse

On another level, it is important to note that every tantrum a child is permitted to get away with is actually making the problem worse. Once a child is accustomed to throwing tantrums, the behavior is less likely to change easily. Resistance to change is a hallmark of behavior that is permitted to take place repeatedly. If the tantrums succeed in reaching their goal, they become still more difficult to change. The point is a simple one: The sooner tanrums are eliminated, the less likely they will be to occur again, and the happier the child will be in the long run.

Using the "Tantrum Control Check List"

Your PST book contains a *Tantrum Control Check List* which will help to ensure that all of the major concepts behind the termination of this behavior are met. Once again, don't fail to remember one of the most basic tenets of PST: You do not have to feel guilty about doing something that will actually help your child. If you feel at all uncomfortable about forcing your child to have tantrums every day for a while, simply consider the alternative.

Question:

"If refusing to reward tantrum behavior is so effective in helping to stop tantrums, why do so many parents give in to the child's wishes when he has a tantrum?"

Answer:

Given a choice, the average parent would rather avoid a scene or refrain from arguing with his child, so giving in to the child's wishes is the path of least resistance. What many parents fail to understand is that rewarding tantrums actually makes the tantrums more likely to occur, and makes each one more likely to last awhile. The reason for this effect is that the child has been taught that persistence pays off, so he continues to engage in tantrum behavior as often as is necessary to get what he wants. At the same time, he will maintain each individual tantrum for extended periods, if necessary, believing that he will win if he refuses to give up the fight. Failing to note these facts, many parents instead decide that it's easier to give a child what he is demanding, as long as it shuts him up.

Question:

"When you suggest that parents and children should not be awarded the same rights and privileges, I'm wondering what distinguishes such thinking from that of a dictatorship. As the saying goes — 'Kids are people, too,' but you seem to be ignoring that concept altogether."

Answer:

Would you permit your 9-year-old daughter to decide whether you should have a variable-rate mortgage instead of a fixed-rate one? Unless you say "yes," you and your child have different rights and privileges. What is suggested in PST is that such a distinction be extended to more than just the major decisions facing a family, because failure to do so will prompt a child to believe that he can determine things first and then expect his parents to abide by his decisions. Children have less knowledge, less experience, and less thinking ability than do their parents, and to suggest that they be permitted to enjoy the same rights is to suggest that the only difference between children and adults is that children are shorter. An individual must be 18 years of age to vote, 21 (in many states) to drink alcoholic beverages, and at least 35 to serve as President. There are many good reasons for such rules, but the underlying logic behind all of them is that children are not yet adults, and, therefore, cannot be expected to think or to behave like adults. Encouraging children to believe otherwise will create vast problems within a family and will erode the control that a parent must maintain if he is to succeed in his role. If you still feel at this point that children must have rights equal to those of adults, I suggest that you stay home for a while, think about it, and have your 10-year-old son take over for you at work. Maybe you can even have his younger sister drop him off in the car.

Question:

"What if I use the PST tape-recorder technique, but my child also throws tantrums at times of the day other than the times that I've selected? How do I stop these unplanned tantrums and still use the strategy that you've described?"

Answer:

In cases such as this, it is a last-ditch effort on the part of the child to retain control. Seeing the fun of throwing tantrums slipping away because it is now a planned chore, the child is likely to attempt to sneak a few by the parent on an unplanned basis so that he can emphasize that he has not completely given in to the parent's control. You might want to try pointing out that he has "only one tantrum a day in him," and then make sure that your child has his scheduled tantrum early each day. It is unlikely that he will want to have an additional tantrum, so you're less likely to run into difficulty than you would be by permitting him to have an unplanned tantrum first, and then trying to elicit the scheduled tantrum. Many children, because they still *think* like the children that they are, will believe that they have the strength for only one tantrum strictly on the basis of your claim to that effect. Additionally, should your child begin an unplanned tantrum, take out the tape recorder and begin recording the event, playing it back as soon as the tantrum ends. Then, be sure to tell him that he is still responsible for his scheduled tantrum later on.

Question:

"It seems to me that a tantrum occurs only when the child loses control of himself, so how can you suggest in PST that a child be held responsible for his behavior when he can't really control it?"

Answer:

If the child can't control his behavior, then who can? It should be clear to the parent of any child who engages in tantrum behavior that the child does so *only* when he is frustrated or angry. When he can't have or get what he wants, he behaves as if he has no control. In reality, this is a ploy to convince the parent that the child can regain his control only when he *does* have what he wants. If you allow yourself to believe that the child has actually lost control of himself, then you would never expect him to behave properly when he is unhappy. It is no coincidence that tantrums don't occur when a child is perfectly content.

Tantrum Control Check List

Use this form to help ensure that you are utilizing each of the correct steps in eliminating your child's tantrum behavior. Be consistent, and familiarize yourself with the directions as given in the PST chapter.

1. Do not display anger.
2 Do not surrender "control" to the child.
3. The child must have a tantrum every day.
4. You determine when and where the tantrum will occur.
5. Each tantrum must be tape-recorded.
6 Each tantrum must be "better" than the last.
7. The child must listen to every recording.
8. Punishment occurs if the tantrum isn't "better."
9. The child must explain why his tantrums aren't improving.
10. Remain firm if the child asks to stop the tantrums.
11. Observe carefully. The child should now hate tantrums.
12. Cancel this exercise only after being certain that the child finds tantrums to be thoroughly unpleasant.

Chapter Four

Sibling Conflicts: There's No Room in the Ring for You

Do you sometimes feel that Cain and Abel are residing in your household? If you have a multiple-child family, your household has likely seen fighting, teasing, name-calling, arguing, envying, and tattling. PST can help you to reduce these annoying and disrupting occurrences.

Current research in the area of sibling relationships reveals that adult brothers and sisters who have the closest relationships come from families where the parents had minimal involvement in the children's conflicts. When a parent becomes involved in such conflicts, the children will probably develop jealousy and anger toward each other. Once you take sides as to who is right and who is wrong, you have become too involved. Stay out of your children's fights, except in those instances in which their behavior could result in someone getting hurt or in something being destroyed.

Children Can Fight All by Themselves

You must project an attitude that lets the children know that you are not disturbed by their problems. The children must learn from listening to you and from watching you that your attitude is "When you fight, it's your problem, not mine! I don't want to hear about it." If the children know that you will listen to their complaints about each other, they will keep approaching you. They must learn from experience that their parents will *never* listen to such problems and that they must resolve these difficulties by themselves. When a husband and wife argue, should the child be allowed to intervene? Of course not; it is an adult problem. When your kids fight, *they are having the problem,* not you.

Their noise may be a bother to you and their fighting may be an annoyance, but the argument is their business.

There is another important advantage to allowing your children to solve their conflicts by themselves. Children must learn "conflict resolution skills." Such abilities are learned through experience, just as other behavior is learned. If children are allowed to experience conflict and to deal with it, they will be prepared for all of the conflicts and arguments that they will face as they grow up. If a parent intervenes in his or her children's fights, the children may not have an opportunity to learn how to solve these problems on their own. Some studies have revealed also that if children are not allowed to resolve their conflicts themselves, some of the unresolved issues may carry into adulthood and have a permanent negative effect on the relationship between siblings.

In the following example, the parent is reacting in a manner that will be detrimental to the relationship between the two children.

Phil: Daddy, Stan punched me on my arm, and it's black and blue.

Parent: Stan, come over here immediately.

Stan: He started it. He threw my radio on the floor, and I'm gonna get him for that.

Parent: I don't care what he did, you have no right to hit someone smaller than yourself. I've told you that a million times.

Stan: I hate him, and I don't want him near my things.

Parent: How can you say that you hate your brother? You really don't mean that. You are *never* to hit him again. In fact, you will not be allowed to watch television tonight because you hit your younger brother.

During this conversation, Phil is watching and smiling. Stan walks away, feeling angry. Now, let's look at another way to deal with this same situation.

Phil: Daddy, Stan punched me on my arm, and it's black and blue.

Parent: Stan, come over here immediately. I am not going to tolerate physical fighting in the house. You are both punished, so I want each of you to go to your own rooms and stay in bed for thirty minutes. Do not touch anything in your rooms. I will call you out when the time is over.

Stan: That's not fair. Phil started it; he threw my radio down.

Parent: I am not concerned about who started. It takes two people to have a fight, so you are both punished.

Phil: He punched me, and you're sending me to my room. That's stupid and mean.

Parent: If you want to feel that it's stupid and mean, that's okay, but you will be in your room for half an hour. Go to your room now. The discussion is closed.

In this case, both children walk off to their rooms and stay there for the next half-hour. In the first example, the parent tried to play the role of a district attorney in determining who might be at fault so that a judgment could be made. But, as a parent, you know quite well that you can never figure out who started a fight between your children. Furthermore, if a younger child starts up with an older sibling and gets hit, the younger child must learn, "I'd better not start up with someone bigger and stronger than I, because I might get hurt." In the second example, the parent does not intervene, but, instead, lets the children know that they are jointly responsible for any fights and that both of them will be held accountable. Regardless of the stories provided by the children, the parent must stick to the PST philosophy: "It takes two to have a fight, and who started it is unimportant. Both of you are to be punished."

There are several PST techniques that have been very effective in reducing fights between brothers and sisters. At the same time, these techniques help to enhance the relationship between siblings. Pick the one technique, or combination of techniques, that could best be adapted to your family and circumstances.

Everyone Gets Punished
In the latter example, both children involved in the fight were punished. In such cases, you can let the children know that they

are responsible for whatever happened and that you will not take sides. Appropriate punishment would be "time out." Time out means that the children are sent to separate areas isolated from the rest of the house (e.g., bedroom). Thirty minutes is probably enough time for most kids to cool off. During this restricted time, the children should not be allowed to look at any books or be involved with anything entertaining. When the time is up, the children can be called out of their rooms. If they do not fight, they can go about their regular activities. If they do fight, they must go back to their rooms for another half-hour. You must *never* get involved in the fight or disagreement.

Everyone Loses Money

If your children are receiving allowances, arrange to deduct a portion of their allowances whenever there is a fight or a loud argument that lasts for more than 30 seconds. The amount that you deduct should be based on the size of the allowance. For example, if the child has the opportunity to earn an allowance of $5 dollars each week, you might decide to deduct 25 cents every time there is a major conflict. Sometimes, you may want to use the deduction of allowance money *and* punishment in the room, concurrently. For some children, this is even more effective.

The Children Must Solve the Problem

Sometimes, there will be an argument over a petty thing, such as what movie to watch on cable television. Years ago, children argued about what TV program to watch, but when families started having several televisions in a household, these arguments ended. Nowadays, these same arguments are occurring as in the past, but with cable television. An effective technique is to tell the children that they must come up with a solution to the problem. In the example of cable television, the children might be told that they are going to be sent to a room with a paper and pencil, and that they must work out a plan or schedule as to how they are going to use the cable television. Until such a plan and schedule can be worked out by all of them, no child in the household will be allowed to watch any television, cable or otherwise. If they do not come up with a plan, they will not watch television. Even if it takes them two years to work out a peaceful schedule or solution, they will not touch any television in the house until there is a resolution to the problem. Forcing the children to work out the problem puts them in a position to think, to plan, and to reason. All of the children in the household involved in the dispute should be held jointly responsible. As the parent, you should not get involved in the problem, nor should you listen to arguments about how one child is monopolizing the problem solving. Do not discuss the issue again until the children have come to you with a plan for resolving the problem.

Everyone Is Held Responsible

Sometimes, it is hard to tell which child in a household was mischievous. For example, imagine that you've gone into the kitchen and found an unwashed knife and fork in the sink. It is your children's responsibility to clean their own utensils. When you ask your two children which one did this, they both say, "I don't know." You should not have to become a detective and investigate or check for fingerprints on the utensils. Just tell your children, "I am not a detective, but I know that whoever left this here knows that he did it. There will be no television, nor will there be any going-out-to-play for either of you until this knife and fork are cleaned. Also, you will not be allowed to get any food, drinks, or snacks from the kitchen until you have cleaned up what you have already used. Now it's your decision. Somehow, you need to get those utensils cleaned up or you will both be restricted from the privileges that I've mentioned." At this point, you might leave the room, and stand firmly by the limits that you've set if the children do not clean up. By holding both the children jointly responsible, you can stay out of the problem and let the children deal with it. If the children become stubborn and refuse, they will have to miss some privileges until they decide to do what you have asked of them.

It's Your Problem, Not Mine

Ignoring fights between brothers and sisters can also help to reduce the problem. Most children who fight do so to gain their parents' attention. Many parents tell us that when they leave the house for a while, the children don't fight, but that as soon as they come home, the fighting starts again. This makes it quite clear that the fighting is designed to gain parental attention. Keeping the children's goal in mind, you must be certain to withhold the attention that they desire *when they seek your attention inappropriately.* If you want to discourage the children from fighting, be sure that you do not reward the fighting behavior. However, when you do ignore a behavior such as fighting, be prepared for it to get worse at first. This phenomenon is well documented in psychology. When you ignore a behavior in an effort to eliminate it, the behavior that you are ignoring will usually become more intense (that is, worse) at first. This is because the children want to see if they can involve you in the fighting so that they can win your attention as they are accustomed to doing. When you ignore them completely, they will become frustrated because they are not getting attention. Logically, then, they will have to fight louder and more aggressively to try to get you involved. If you break down and start yelling or screaming at them, your children will learn that they now have to fight with a lot of noise in order to gain your attention. So, by breaking down and paying attention after you've already started to ignore them, you may make the problem much worse. It is very important to remember that when you start to ignore a behavior, you must carry it all the way. If you do not, then you run the risk of ending up with more problems than you had originally. Be consistent.

Teamwork

The children should see that you look at them as a team. It is advisable to assign each of the children in the household an occasional chore or task, letting each decide how it will be accomplished. For example, you might say, "Tonight you have to take the garbage out and put it in front of the house for the garbage pickup in the morning. All three of you have to work on it together. I don't care how you decide to do it, but it has to be done." If the children do not do it, you should establish a consequence (e.g., some privilege, such as television, to be denied until the assignment has been completed). Don't try to help them pick who will do which part of the task. Instead, let them work it out themselves. If they cannot come to a consensus on how the task should be divided, they will all have to face the consequences of their irresponsibility.

Positive Approaches

As with all other PST approaches, appropriate behavior must be recognized. When your children do follow through with the assigned task, let them know how much you appreciate it and how well they work together. When an evening has passed by and the children have played together cooperatively, take a positive approach by saying something, such as "It's incredible how well you all got along while you were playing checkers. I am going to let you all stay up a half-hour later tonight. You should be very proud of yourselves." When you do praise a child, remember the emotional tone of your voice is extremely important. The children must see that you're really pleased and excited about their achievement. If you make such a statement in a monotone voice, its effectiveness will be limited.

Question:

"Whenever we go out in public, my two sons keep fighting, punching each other, and arguing. I'm sick of it, and I don't even feel like going out with them any more. What can I do?"

Answer:

Brothers fighting in public places is not an unusual situation. It happens in most families in which there are two or more boys, but the key thing to consider is how you react when it happens. If the children see that it is annoying and upsetting you, they will probably keep up the pattern. It is important for you to assert yourself, telling them how you want them to behave, but never allowing them to see you become upset. Since you know that this is a problem with your children, set up an advance plan with them. For example, when all of you leave your house to go to the shopping center, tell the boys that you expect them to get along well and to avoid getting into any fights while shopping. Warn them that if you see a fight or argument occur, a particular privilege will be forfeited or an amount of their allowance will be deducted. You may also want to tell them that for each fight or argument that takes place, they will spend 30 minutes in their rooms with no privileges when you return home. If the children see that they cannot upset you and that such behavior will result in major inconveniences to them, you should see a reduction in the fighting within a few weeks.

Question:

"When I leave my children with the babysitter, they are always getting into fights and arguments, and the babysitter gets upset and calls me. Is there anything that I can do?"

Answer:

Again, it is helpful to have rules formulated in advance so that the children will understand not only what is expected of them but what consequences will be experienced if they do not follow the guidelines. You may even want to write down the rules for them so that there can be no misunderstanding. Let them know that for each time they fight, the babysitter will put a mark on a piece of paper. There will be a specific consequence the next day for each fight. Whatever punishment that you choose to use is fine, as long as the children do not get away with breaking the rules that you have set.

Question:

"My kids always seem so competitive. My older son is jealous of his sister, who does very well in gymnastics and who is always getting awards. Her picture appears in the newspaper, and everyone makes a fuss about how great she is. Is there any way that I can lessen my son's feelings of jealousy?"

Answer:

There's no way that you can change the reactions from people outside the family. However, you can try to do some things to minimize the effects of your daughter's "stardom" on your son. First, be sure that your son receives recognition for anything good that he does, whether it be a crayon drawing from school or a certificate for good attendance. Try to make your daughter's success a family success. If your son tries to congratulate your daughter or if he tells her that she did a good job, praise him for the mature and polite way in which he is acting. As a family, celebrate your daughter's achievement with statements, such as "We are all very happy that you did so well," or "We will all celebrate with you and go out for dinner tonight." By using "we" instead of "I," your son will be included in each of the statements that you make. Recently, we saw a family of nine children. One of the children recorded a song and started to earn money singing. The other children in the family did not react with jealousy, but became supportive of the new singing star in their family. The parents got all of the children involved. The older children helped to select the clothes their brother would wear when performing. Several of the children helped to select the three songs that he would sing in an upcoming performance. The older brothers got involved with working the tape machines and with making sure that the music and everything else was ready for the shows. It became a family project. Everyone worked on it and when there was a success, everyone involved was praised for his hard work, not just the child who was singing. You might also want to find something at which your son can succeed, so that he can feel good about his own abilities, regardless of what you daughter does.

Question:

"I let my fifteen-year-old daughter babysit with our ten-year-old son. They fight and argue so often that it has reached the point where I want to hire an outside babysitter. Is there anything that I can do before giving up and finding a sitter?"

Answer:

It is always good to pay the older child a reasonable amount for babysitting so that she will see that the service she is performing is valuable; however, like any other job, there must be some responsibilities. The house should be in the condition in which you want it to be when you return home. Your expectation should be made clear to the older child, with her payment contingent on her doing the job properly. Explain that if you come home and the house is a mess and there has been fighting, you will punish both of them just as you would have if you had been at home. This is necessary so that they will see there will be major inconveniences for failing to cooperate with each other.

Chapter Five

Word Power: The Magic of Knowing What to Say

Shakespeare may have been correct when he said "A rose by any other name would smell as sweet," but the same does not hold true for successful communication with children. Dealing with children and adolescents involves much more than mere semantics, and yet the proper choice of words can be of tremendous help in achieving whatever goals have been set for the interaction. Parents who hope to communicate successfully on a continuing basis with their children must understand that communication is more than just speaking (or, as many children might say, "more than just giving orders"). Parents must meet several criteria when communicating, and surprisingly for most, a fair amount of practice is necessary to become a skilled communicator. PST is based on understanding how and why people behave as they do, and thus communication is an integral part of the entire process of interacting with others, especially with children. It is not an overstatement to say "No behavioral change can be made in children without some form of communication from the parents."

Communication Has a Meaning All Its Own

The word *communication* is not used lightly in PST; speaking, yelling, hitting, punishing, rewarding, ignoring, and acting are all means by which communication may be achieved. However, real communication involves much more than any or all of the above. Communication is the imparting or exchanging of thoughts, messages, ideas, and wishes. When you communicate with your children, you transmit some form of information to them. The idea behind the communication is, of course, to induce some sort of change in the child. For the purposes of this discussion, it is unimportant what particular change is sought, because the goal is always the same: the alteration of behavior. Imagine, for example, that you are explaining to your child that he must walk the dog; the intention here is clearly one in which the child acts upon your wishes. If you were telling your child that an "F" is an unsatisfactory grade in math, the result should be an improvement in his study habits and effort in school. On a more subtle level, a discussion with your child about what things were like "when I was your age" is intended to foster greater understanding and knowledge of certain things on the child's part. Clearly, then, *communication* and *change* co-exist, with the former serving to make the latter possible.

Listening and Hearing:
There *Is* a Difference

Many children "listen" to their parents. The problem, unfortunately, is that very few of them "hear" what their parents are saying. To get a better idea of what that means, think for a moment about music; perhaps you listen to popular songs on the radio, but do you really "hear" the meaning behind the lyrics? Successful communication enables the listener to do more than listen; it offers him the opportunity to hear, as well. Phrasing things in such a way as to get your message across, even against resistance, inevitably will serve to increase your effectiveness as a communicator. When you want to communicate with your child, make certain that you say things clearly, directly, and firmly, so that you minimize the chances of mere "listening" on the other end. Don't hesitate to check on the success of your efforts: Ask your child, whenever possible, what he understands about what you've said.

Parent: Robin, the dog just went on the living room rug again.
Child: Oh, sorry, I'll go clean it up when I'm off the phone.
Parent: No, that's not good enough. You'll clean it up, now.
Child: Mom, what's the big deal? Would you just leave me alone about the stupid dog?
Parent: I won't ask you again, Robin. If the mess isn't taken care of within ten minutes, you won't use the phone for a week.

Child: I don't understand. Why are you acting like this is such a major problem?

Parent: The problem isn't the dog, the problem is your refusal to accept responsibility. You were supposed to have walked him this morning, but you didn't bother. The mess downstairs is your fault, and you will learn to account for your own laziness.

Child: Okay, okay, I get the message.

Parent: What message did you get?

Child: If I'm going to ignore the things that I'm supposed to do, then I'm going to pay a price for it.

Parent: What else?

Child: Correcting my mistakes comes before other things, like the telephone.

Parent: Good. I think that I can trust that we won't have to go through this again next week.

Children develop an extraordinary level of skill in "selective apperception" as they get older, choosing to hear only what they want to hear. Note in the preceding example, the child initially refused to recognize the actual source of her mother's displeasure. Although it was obvious to her that the telephone was less important than the mess awaiting her attention in the living room, this child attempted to ignore the situation to the greatest extent that she thought might be acceptable to her mother. The *pretense* of cooperation ("I'll clean it up when I'm off the phone") did not address the actual problem (her demonstrated lack of responsibility). The subtle claims of innocence ("What's the big deal? Why is this such a major problem?"), however, failed to dissuade her mother from addressing the issue both clearly and directly. The mother correctly abstained from a display of anger, even when prompted to do so by the child ("Would you just leave me alone about the stupid dog?") and thus retained her control over the situation. The mother's explanation of consequences ("You will not use the phone for a week") was stated unequivocally, leaving the child in a position of relative helplessness; any response other than the desired one would have resulted in the administration of the punishment. By leaving her daughter without alternatives, the mother virtually was guaranteed success in prompting the immediate behavior that she sought, but something else occurred on an even more important level. By stating firmly that she was dissatisfied by the way in which her daughter failed to handle responsibility, the mother was able to *communicate* something vital: that similar incidents in the future would result unhappily. At this point, the child was able to perceive that only appropriate behavior now *and* later would suffice, and she indicated to her mother that she understood what was expected of her. By asking her daughter for a reiteration of what had been communicated, the mother accomplished two things: She satisfied herself that her daughter understood the communication, and she also helped to implant that communication permanently in her child's repertory of responses by having her say it aloud.

Goal-Oriented Communication

As we've seen already, people communicate because they are attempting (at least theoretically) to alter someone's behavior, thoughts, perceptions. Although such communication seems to have a goal, we reserve the term *goal-oriented* to describe that form of communication in which some end result is not merely desired, but spelled out clearly. Goal-oriented communication is very helpful in the discussion of important issues and is especially effective with children who frequently have difficulty determining the precise goal behind a parent's comments. When communicating something of importance to your child, make sure that there is no doubt on his part as to what you really mean or want.

Parent: Doug, this report card tells me that you're having some pretty big problems in school. We're going to find out what needs to be done to correct those problems, and then we're going to take care of them.
Child: Aren't you going to ground me?
Parent: Did you get these grades because you didn't try?
Child: No! You know that I studied every night.
Parent: Then, what's going on?
Child: I don't know. I just freeze up on tests. I know the stuff, but I just can't think clearly when I know that I have only a certain amount of time to work.

Parent: Then what we need to do is to work on getting you over your test anxiety.

Child: All right!

In the preceding example, even with the father's attempt to utilize goal-oriented communication in the opening of his discussion with his son, the child nevertheless had to struggle in order to appreciate exactly what his father was trying to accomplish. The son's initial reaction was to suspect that his father sought to punish him, but as the goal-oriented communication proceeded, he understood what was expected of him. Note that the father's concern about staying *on goal* ("Then, what's going on?") paid off; the child was able to focus on exactly what it was that his father needed to determine (that he suffers from test anxiety). The phrasing of the father's comments served to communicate to the son that the former was quite serious about the report card; but yet he reached the goal that he had established without anger and without loss of control. The son made a valiant attempt at establishing control boundaries ("Aren't you going to ground me?"), but the father deftly sidestepped the issue by implying that although he had the power to inflict punishment, he chose not to use it ("Did you get those grades because you didn't try?"). A goal was established early in the discussion, the limits were tested, and, after reaffirmation of the goal, an agreement to work on a solution was reached. Remember: Goal-oriented communication is especially effective when the goals might otherwise be ambiguous to the child, as well as when the issue in question is important enough so that no time can be wasted in getting to the point.

Turning It Around:
Communicating Through Questions

One of the more effective styles of communicating with a child is one in which the parent asks questions which guide the child toward a resolution to the problem at hand. Consider, for example, use of the "I wonder" prefix. A more direct question may work, but "I wonder" questions often come across as less intimidating, as well as less authoritarian.

Parent: Sarah, I think that it was very mean of you to pull the dog's tail like that.

Child: I'm just playing with him. He likes it.

Parent: No, he doesn't like it. That's why he yelped when you did it.

Child: So?

Parent: How would you like it if somebody did that to you?

Child: I don't have a tail, Mommy.

Notice that in the example here, the child "wins" the discussion, not by showing her mother a disinterest in the dog's welfare but by revealing a clear lack of concern for the mother's opinion. The mother set herself up for failure by neglecting to note in advance that her child wouldn't alter her behavior simply on the basis of the mother's lack of approval. Had she taken the time to consider the situation, perhaps she would have decided that her child could arrive at the proper conclusion herself, if given the foundation on which to work.

Parent: Sarah, I noticed that you were pulling the dog's tail.

Child: I'm just playing with him. He likes it.

Parent: Oh, then I wonder why he yelped when you did it.

Child: I don't know.

Parent: What does it mean when you yell 'ow'?

Child: It means that something hurts.

Parent: Then, I wonder what it means when the dog yelps.

Child: Oh. I guess it means that something hurts. I'd better not pull his tail anymore.

The I vs. You Phenomenon

In communicating feelings and opinions to a child, parents are often well advised to steer clear of the "you" statements that most of us are prone to make, and instead utilize the "I" statements which are typically far more effective. For example, the statement "You did a poor job of cleaning up your room" can be rephrased as "I would like it if you would do a better job of cleaning up your room." Although the message being communicated to the child is fundamentally the same, the latter approach is more likely to meet with success. Whenever a parent starts a communication with "you," the child is put on the spot. Now, although there will be times when that effect is exactly what you want, the majority of the attempts you make at communicating with your child might go further with "I" statements. Taking another look—"I feel disappointed about your not passing math" is quite different from "You disappointed me by not passing math." In the latter, the child is apt to feel a sense of guilt in that he's let his parent down needlessly, whereas the former remark sounds more like the parent is commiserating instead of judging. "You" followed by anything negative will nearly always sound judgmental, and since such statements are likely to make the child feel guilty, they will serve no purpose other than to ventilate the hostility that you're feeling about your child's inability to satisfy your wishes or standards.

Parent: You've made me so angry that I can't stand it! Now, go to your room!
Child: Okay, you don't have to yell at me.
Parent: You are so rude! How dare you talk to me the way that you did before?

This parent clearly seeks to instill a sense of guilt and remorse in the child. As a result, both the parent and the child are miserable, and the child has learned little or nothing, except of course that the parent is much better at using emotion as a weapon than he is at using control. Consider what happens when the parent uses "I" statements.

Parent: I feel very angry about what you've done. Now, go to your room.
Child: Okay, I'm going, but I don't know what you're so upset about.
Parent: I do not like to be addressed rudely, and I certainly will not tolerate such behavior from you.

Here, of course, the parent is taking responsibility for her own feelings, while the child is assigned (appropriately) the responsibility for only his own behavior. Additionally, in an exchange such as this one, the child is likely to learn that such behavior will not be tolerated in the future, either, and thus is apt to change his behavior accordingly. By becoming comfortable with "I" vs. "you" statements, you can put the emphasis in communication just where it belongs.

Manifest vs. Latent Content

In any communication, the actual meaning of what is being transmitted exists on two separate levels which do not always coincide. The *manifest* content refers to what appears on the surface (that is, whatever it seems is being said). The *latent* content is what is underneath, and this is not always easy to discern, because the latent content of any communication is often very subtle. Surprisingly, though, children often pick up the latent content of communications with amazing skill, sometimes to their own dismay.

Parent: Oh, Jeff, how nice. You've brought all of your grades up to B's.
Child: Yeah. It wasn't fun studying every night after dinner, but I guess that hard work can pay off.
Parent: Oh, yes. And you should see what hard work has done for your cousin. Did you know that he just won the science fair for the third year in a row?

Of course, the child in this example isn't likely to feel very positive at all about the hard work that he's done. Although the manifest content in his mother's communication to him seems fine, the latent content came across all too clearly. By mentioning the accomplishments of a better student, his mother has succeeded in removing all vestiges of approval, making him feel inadequate by comparison. Note that her comments *sounded* supportive and warm, even to the extent that she seemed to be sharing good news about relatives. But the latent content was able to shine through, and she might as well have said, "Oh, very nice, but you're still not up to your cousin's standards, so don't expect me to be proud of you." Let's see whether you can spot the latent content in the following example.

Parent: Oh, Miriam, my son's got a part in the school play. Tell her what you're going to be, Nicky.

Child: I'm going to be a small shrub.

Parent: That's right. Very good, Nicky. But my daughter Sharon is going to be Cleopatra. Wait until you see the costume that she's going to wear. She's got all of the good lines, and she's got all of these kids playing the roles of her slaves, and . . . .

Advanced Communication Skills

There are many different ways of saying the same thing, and by now you've discovered that some ways work better than others. On the far end of the communications spectrum, there are a number of techniques that can have a dramatic effect on your communication with your child, but these require a bit more practice and appreciation than many of the others. Before reading further, take careful note of the fact that these techniques may seem, at first, to be overly manipulative—they may seem to be unfair in that they take advantage of plays-on-words and can seem very much like game playing. However, these techniques are anything *but* a game. In fact, they are no more manipulative than anything else that you are likely to say or do with a child when communicating; the real difference is that they take advantage of your cognitive abilities as an adult and as a parent. Consider, for example, the idea of the "disappearing choice" technique (known to psychologists as a "double-bind"). In a disappearing choice, the parent places the child in a position where he or she is virtually trapped into agreeing or going along with whatever is being said. In a disappearing choice, you present the child with a set of alternatives which offers the illusion of a choice; either alternative ultimately leads to the same result.

Example:

"Are you going to take a bath before you go to bed, or put your pajamas on after your bath?"

As the child searches for the lesser of the evils, he will, in either case, end up taking a bath. Note that disappearing choices, often effective with adults, are especially useful with children, the vast majority of whom strive for control. Skillful use of this technique creates a sense of control within the child, as the illusion of a choice involves, by definition, at least some degree of control.

In the same vein, the disappearing choice can be made to be even more subtle. For example, by using the phrase "did you notice," there appears to be a choice where none really exists. Let's see whether you can spot the disappearing choice in the following example.

Example:
"Did you notice how proud you felt when you got that 'A' on your report card?"

Agreement by the child (i.e., "Yes, I noticed how proud I felt") means that the parent has made his point, but negation does not mean that the point has failed. Because the question was phrased as a disappearing choice, the child who attempts to reject the point will instead be forced to say, "No, I didn't notice how proud I felt," which is significantly different from "No, I didn't feel proud" (the latter being almost impossible to state in response to the phrasing of the question). By leading the child to wonder whether he simply didn't realize how proud he actually felt, he thereby acknowledges that he must have felt proud. The disappearing choice technique can be utilized whenever you have a child who is inclined to argue or to disagree. Although we have already stated that arguing with a child simply creates a host of new problems, this technique can help to eliminate the child's tendency to argue with you. By phrasing things in such a way as to help the child to understand that arguing with his parent is wrong (and useless), you can greatly diminish the child's tendency to do so.

Parent: Okay, everybody grab a broom, and let's get that garage cleaned out!
Child: I don't want to clean the garage.

Parent: Richard, are you going to carry things out of the garage before you start to sweep, or go to play at Jerry's after you've put everything back?

The disappearing choice technique helps the child to grow accustomed to doing what he's told to do by his parents, without the illusion of being able to make his own decisions (e.g., "I'm not going to walk the dog," or "I'm not going to study every night"). As you become comfortable with advanced communication techniques such as this one, you can remind yourself that when you are doing whatever is in your child's best interests, you never need to feel guilty. Instead, by helping your child to understand that he must follow parental directions, you can diminish the intra-family problems that might otherwise develop, and thus devote more of your time to communicating positive and pleasant things to your child.

Question:
   "When I try to communicate with my twelve-year-old daughter, I always think that I've gotten through to her because she acknowledges what I've said. I might ask her to do some chores around the house, and she's very pleasant and agreeable. She promises to do everything that I've asked, but the problem is that she never follows through. It's not as if she's refusing, it's just that she never gets around to them."

Answer:
   You are clearly the object of your daughter's manipulation, and the problem stems from your inability to communicate the real message to her. It's not so much the particular tasks that you are trying to communicate as it is the importance of your daughter doing what she's been asked to do. The actual material to be communicated would be: "I hope that you will have finished chores X, Y, and Z before dinner, because you promised to do so and I expect you to follow through." However, your daughter may need to hear: "I hope that you will have finished chores X, Y, and Z before dinner, so that you can watch television tonight instead of sitting in your room." A child such as yours might benefit from use of the disappearing choice technique ("Are you

going to do your chores before you watch TV, or call Kathi on the phone after you've finished your chores?"). By the same token, goal-oriented communication could work wonders.

Question:

"When you 'communicate through questions', how can you be sure that the child will respond the right way?"

Answer:

A good rule of thumb when dealing with children is that you can never be sure of anything. However, children will typically react to the questions as you would expect them to do, providing of course that you've phrased things properly. If, for example, your child were looking a bit sad, the direct question "Is something wrong?" is likely to get you nowhere. By the same token, an attempt at using the "I wonder" prefix would also be fruitless if you were to say, "I wonder if you're going to tell me what's wrong." Instead, the phrase "I wonder if something's wrong" is far more likely to succeed. Note that communicating through questions involves more than merely placing the words "I wonder" before the same old questions that you're accustomed to asking. What you must strive for is familiarity with the sorts of questions that lead the child into wanting to answer. "I wonder if something's wrong" is the kind of phrase to which any child will feel inclined to respond, because it is non-threatening and non-intrusive; the "district attorney" approach that most parents use is simply not going to work.

Question:

"I'm almost frightened by your discussion of manifest vs. latent content in communications. Am I correct in believing now that everything I say is likely to be misinterpreted by my child as meaning something completely different?"

Answer:

The problem may be that it is being interpreted *correctly*, which is not to say that it is being heard as you meant to say it. The things that you are really thinking when you speak may well come across subtly in your comments, and in that sense, your words are not being misinterpreted at all, but are heard realistically instead. The only time that you are likely to run into difficulty of the nature to which you are referring is when you say things that you don't really mean. At that time, you may not be careful enough to phrase everything just right, and through either your wording or your intonation, you may reveal more about your actual thoughts, feelings, and opinions than you would like. Perhaps you should focus on dealing with your real feelings when you speak with your child, rather than on concentrating on ways in which to obscure those feelings.

Question:
"Does the disappearing choice technique really work, or will my child just shrug off my attempts to corral him into acting appropriately?"

Answer:
The disappearing choice technique works because the tendency of any person (especially a child) confronted with what *seems* to be a choice is to choose the most advantageous position offered. Most children "freeze" for a moment when given a disappearing choice while they search for the best possible response. The illogic of what has been stated to the child is often lost, as another central tendency among people is to assume that confusion is the result of their own misunderstanding rather than the result of an outside problem. As such, children will often pause, and then jump at what seems like the lesser of the evils, failing to realize that they were never really offered a choice at all.

Chapter Six

Habit Busters:
Setting Your Child Free

All children develop habits as they grow, and it would be impossible for them to do otherwise. Through the very actions involved in day-to-day life, habits are created. Whenever we do something often enough, it becomes "relatively automatic," and when that automatic behavior becomes consistent, it is known as a habit. The word *habit* does not imply anything positive or negative in itself because any particular habit may be either helpful or harmful. When you get into the car, putting on your seat belt may be a habit for you, as could be a check of your home's front door (to be sure that it is locked) each night before you go to bed. On the other hand, lighting a cigarette after you've poured the morning coffee may also be a habit, albeit a harmful one. Like an adult, a child may have numerous habits which serve his best interests each day, but clearly these are not the habits in which we are interested; this chapter will focus on habits which must be changed or eliminated to protect the child's well-being.

Why Habits Feel Good
Children and adults share a genuine liking for familiar people, objects, ideas, and behaviors. Whatever is predictable is often soothing and imparts a sense of security to the child. A child who holds onto a security blanket is exhibiting signs of a habit, as the clutching of the blanket is an automatic and consistent behavior. Anyone can understand readily why a security blanket is soothing to a child, as are other habits according to the purpose that they serve. It is a rare habit that is not reinforcing to the child in one way or another. Habits often form because a particular behavior occurs repetitively, but the initial appearance of the behavior was due, in all probability, to its own rewarding nature.

For example, thumb sucking occurs initially because it is pleasant to the child, and specifically because it feels like a positive behavior; it is self-reinforcing. In other words, the behavior is its own reward and thus will remain likely to continue indefinitely. With that in mind, then, perhaps you've figured out why no one stops a habit easily.

Why Habits Are Difficult to Break

Helping a child to break a habit means that you must alter the way in which he responds to a situation that is already familiar to him. A child evidencing a negative habit (one which you feel that you must help him to terminate) is being reinforced each time that he engages in the behavior. The difficulty is that you must stop a behavior that is rewarding, and therein lies the contradiction—such an endeavor is often difficult because the child has to give up something that he doesn't *want* to give up. For you, eating sweets may be a habit, and as such, you can appreciate how difficult it is to discontinue the behavior. Eating sweets is pleasant and *because* it is pleasant, the motivation to stop will be weakened. After all, why would anyone stop doing anything that is enjoyable? There is only one answer: Failing to alter the behavior has to carry with it the probability of something unpleasant occurring. If your physician told you that you had to stop eating sweets (and lose weight) or risk undergoing coronary bypass surgery, you might be motivated to eliminate your habit. Similarly, if your employer told you that the company's tough new no-smoking policy meant that you'd be terminated if you continued to smoke at work, you might well decide to break the habit. As far as the elimination of habits goes, thoughts and behavior must both be considered.

The "Competing States" Theory

The basic logic here is that two thoughts that "compete" with each other cannot be held simultaneously, nor can a thought and a competing behavior. Known to psychologists as "cognitive dissonance," the competing states concept means that you cannot, for example, enjoy smoking cigarettes while believing that they will cause you to develop lung cancer. Because that thought and that behavior compete with each other, one of the two must change. Either you must stop smoking (while maintaining the thought) or you must change the thought (while maintaining the behavior). Thus, cigarette smokers typically believe that they will not develop cancer. Instead, such a thought is dismissed with rationalizations (i.e., "I never smoke all the way down to the filter, so I'm okay," or "You have to smoke for at least twenty years to get cancer, and I've still got five years to go before I have to stop"). For those individuals who cannot change the thought, the behavior must be altered (i.e., smoking is eliminated altogether). Keeping the competing states theory in mind, let's take a look at how this applies to children's habits.

Thumb Sucking Is Unfair to the Other Fingers

One of the most frustrating habits that you may face with your child is that of thumb sucking. There is considerable evidence to indicate that the fetus may engage in that behavior while in the womb, so it is thus a natural behavior that becomes a habit for many children upon birth. Reasoning with a thumb-sucking child is usually of little or no value, and, once again, you may want to pose this question to yourself: Why would a child stop doing something that he finds to be pleasant? The only possible response there can be is that *the alternative is worse.*

Parent: Jessica, I've told you before, you have to stop sucking your thumb.
Child: Mmmmmmmmmmm.
Parent: If you keep doing that, you're going to have to wear braces, just like Renee.
Child: Nuh-uh. Mmmmmmmmmmm.
Parent: Take that thumb out of your mouth this instant. Did you hear me, young lady?
Child: Mmmmmmmmmmm.

No child is going to stop sucking her thumb simply because you've issued a warning about the long-term consequences of pressure on the upper teeth. The child is far more likely to be interested in the rewarding nature of the behavior itself, so eliminating the habit will involve using the competing states technique.

Parent: Jessica, I've told you before, you have to stop sucking your thumb.
Child: Mmmmmmmmmm.
Parent: If you keep doing that, you're going to keep on being unfair to your other fingers.
Child: Huh?
Parent: You have ten fingers. How can you suck your thumb, and just ignore the other nine fingers? That's not fair.
Child: Mmmmmmmmmm.
Parent: From now on, I expect you to be fair. That means that all fingers get equal treatment. You have to suck all of your fingers for the same amount of time, and you can't play favorites with rooms anymore, either. If you're going to suck your fingers in your bedroom, then you have to suck them in all of the other rooms in the house, too. That means that every day you are going to suck all of your fingers, and you're going to do so in every room in the house. No matter how long it takes you, I expect to see you doing it every day.

In this case, the parent is setting the child up for a competing states dilemma (the thought that thumb sucking is pleasurable is now competing with a behavior that is not pleasurable at all). Is the pleasure of thumb sucking worth the work that now must be put into it? In all likelihood, the child will decide that it is not, and the habit will begin to erode. Reinforcing the child for the appropriate behavior on an unpredictable basis (to avoid a stop-start pattern of reward seeking) would increase the intensity with which the habit breaks, thereby teaching the child that the correct behavior pays off, while the incorrect behavior carries with it the problem of decreased pleasure.

Nail Biting Is "Eating Oneself Alive"
The problems inherent in helping a child to break the habit of nail biting are quite similar to those in thumb sucking, especially in that the child is "getting something" out of the behavior. However, nail biting (unlike thumb sucking, which occurs in a great many average children) is often associated with insecurity, fearfulness, withdrawal, and even anger. Although most people never really stop and think about what's involved in nail biting, it

is actually a process in which the child bites off small pieces of his own body (now you know *why* you never wanted to think much about it). What is more important, however, is that thumb sucking and nail biting differ in another crucial way. The former tends to stop spontaneously as the child gets older (and becomes less reliant on such "safe-feeling" behaviors), while the latter may continue throughout adulthood. Pointing out to a child the psychological reasons for nail biting is pointless, so a more subtle approach is needed for success.

Parent: I'm sure glad that I won't have to worry about you biting your nails much longer.

Child: Huh?

Parent: Well, lots of adults know that kids just seem to stop biting their nails about the time of their tenth birthday, and yours is coming up next month.

Child: Oh, yeah, I guess so.

Parent: All of your friends are going to be surprised when you stop biting your nails, but you'll know that it's because you're now ten years old.

Child: Wow, yeah, that's right. I'm getting pretty big now, huh?

The parent in the example here induced a competing states dilemma that will, in all likelihood, work quite effectively. The child is now faced with giving up either the behavior (nail biting) or the recognition of getting older (if the nail biting continues, he won't fit the profile of a 10-year-old as illustrated by his mother). Since the child's desire to appear sophisticated is probably stronger than the urge to bite his nails, the behavior can be expected to change. Note that in a case such as this one, the child's habit was broken without any *direct* pressure by the parent. Instead, a competing states dilemma was created, thereby prompting the child to change his own behavior willingly.

Fat Kids Only *Look* Jolly

Food is a necessity of life, but *eating* may seem like the real necessity to many children. It is not the food that a child consumes which turns out to be the reinforcer, but rather the behavior involved in consuming it. As the old French proverb goes, *Faut il manger pour vivre, ou vivre pour manger?* (Do we eat to live, or live to eat?) The overweight child is often a vivid example of self-reinforcement; feeling that there is no other way in which he can make himself feel good, such a child turns to food. Food is warm, nurturing, and satisfying; it is all of the things that *people* should be. Believing that there are no other individuals from whom he can receive such positive feelings, the overweight child typically utilizes food as a substitute. As such, food appears to work quite well: It is available, there for the taking, and undemanding in return. A lonely or unhappy child can make himself seem to feel better (even though only momentarily) by stuffing himself with food, so it is not the particular substances that he chooses to consume that matter. What is important to such a child is that he can reach out and satisfy what he perceives as his own needs and can do so whenever he would like to experience the same sensation again.

Childhood Obesity: The Vicious Circle

A vicious circle is a situation in which one problem causes another, which in turn makes the first problem worse, which then makes the additional problem even worse, and so on down the line. Any child who is significantly overweight probably has a good working knowledge of how the vicious-circle phenomenon works, because he has been a victim of it as long as he's been overweight. Fat children often have difficulty making and keeping friends, primarily because they're "different," and nothing is more effective as a friendship barrier among children than diversity. A fat child cannot play sports, effectively isolating him from one of the primary areas of socialization among children. Fat children are usually seen as very unattractive by their peers, and this in turn determines the extent to which others will seek them out as friends. Other children nearly always attribute the fat child's obesity to a lack of interest in looking "normal" and assume that he is more interested in food than in anything else. Unfortunately, such a perception is not always completely false. Because a fat child has probably turned to food as a substitute for human emotion or availability, or simply as a security device (an older version of the security blanket—it's difficult to feel scared when you're eating a "Milky Way" bar), he's probably emotionally starved to begin with. Being unable to develop relationships with peers because of his obesity adds to the problem. As those relationships fail to develop, the fat child is likely to turn increasingly toward food for relief, and as he makes himself even heavier, he causes the situation to grow even worse. Before long, the overweight child is in the midst of a classic chicken-or-the-egg dilemma: Is he lonely because he's fat, or is he fat because he's lonely? As chocolate cakes replace friends, the isolation deepens, and the delayed rate at which emotional development occurs may carry forth throughout a lifetime.

Have Some More Dessert, Honey

Strangely enough, an amazing number of parents seem to be either oblivious to or unconcerned with the fact that they have an obese child in the house. Because it is not uncommon for parents to associate the depth of a child's love with the amount of food that he consumes at dinner ("Your mother worked hard to prepare this roast...show her how much you care...that's right, have a fourth helping"), they may actually serve to make a bad situation even worse. The first step in helping an obese child is to stop all attempts to encourage him to eat any more than is necessary to sustain life. The next step is to use the basic principles of PST to change his behavior, as well as his thinking.

PST: Helping Your Child to Take Charge of His Mouth

The techniques that you need to master in order to help your child to lose weight are not difficult to understand. To begin with, most fat children eat impulsively—they eat without really thinking about their behavior. A TV commercial or even the mere mention of food is enough to trigger impulsive eating. The best way to help your child control such bingeing is by teaching him to "log" what he consumes, and here's how to do that.

Give your child a memo pad, a pen, and a calorie guide booklet, and instruct him to carry these things with him everywhere that he goes. Anything that he eats or drinks during the day (with the exception of water) must be entered into the log. Using a separate page for each day, every entry must list the exact time, the item to be consumed, and the number of calories attributed to the item. At the end of the day, the child is to total his caloric intake and write that value at the bottom of the page. However, there is one important point that must be observed when using this system: Whatever is to be eaten must be entered at least *15 minutes before it is consumed*. That is to say, if the child is watching television and he gets a craving for a slice of pie, he must enter that into his log, along with the number of calories in the pie and with the time of day. Then he must wait a full 15 minutes before he can eat what he's chosen. The logic here is that many children no longer want what they chose after 15 minutes and will not go through with eating the food. Additionally, your child may decide that if he can wait 15 minutes, he can wait 30, and if he can wait 30, perhaps he can wait 60, and if he can wait 60, perhaps he doesn't have to eat what he entered into the log at all. Children take great pleasure in crossing out entries that they've already made, knowing as they do it that they have "saved" that many calories. The act of eliminating an entry that has already been made is one of control, and the overweight child typically seeks control constantly. Overeating is a form of control in itself because it's as if the child is saying, "Maybe people can ignore me, and maybe I feel different and left out, and maybe I can't do anything about that, but I sure can decide what I'm going to eat and how I'm going to look, and *nobody* can stop me." By substituting the control necessary to avoid overeating, the child essentially compensates for the control that he would otherwise experience in eating too much. As he becomes thinner and more attractive, the child's behavior is further reinforced by the increasingly positive reaction that others will have to him. Being able to buy new clothes and to engage in physical behaviors that were previously impossible will also serve as reinforcers for losing weight.

Since such reinforcement is crucial here, there is something else that you can do as a parent, and that is to set goals so easy to reach that the child is rewarded frequently for the appropriate behavior. For example, if a child had to lose 30 pounds, you might set each 5-pound increment as an intermediate goal, rewarding the child with something that he wants very much each time he loses another 5 pounds. The desire to reach the point at which the next reward will occur is often so great that the behavior will occur intensely. Imagine this: If someone offered you a million dollars for the loss of 5 pounds, you would take that weight off in record time. It is simple to find rewards that mean as much to a child as that money might mean to you. Therefore, you can reinforce the behavior effectively with relatively little or no difficulty and help to ensure your child's physical and emotional health by doing so.

On another level, you can help by providing a different sort of reinforcement for your child's weight loss. In a procedure known as "charting," you can have the child weigh in each week at the same time and enter the numbers onto a chart like the one you'll find at the end of this chapter. By drawing lines to connect the weights that are determined each week, you can easily form a graph which will show just how successfully the weight loss regimen is proceeding. Assuming that the child is losing weight adequately, the chart is tremendously rewarding; watching the graph slope downward helps most overweight children feel better about themselves. Should the graph indicate that the child is not losing weight, then it serves a different purpose — it will become almost impossible for the child to deny to himself that he has failed to take any degree of control in this behavior, and as such, the chart is likely to cause a competing states dilemma to occur. In this case, the child will experience conflict between the thought "I am in control" and the behavior (failure to exhibit control by losing weight).

Question:

"My son is eight years old, and he still sucks his thumb. The problem is, he always seems to do it when I'm not around. I tried telling him that he had to be fair to his other fingers, but now he just waits until I can't see him before he starts sucking his thumb. What am I supposed to do?"

Answer:

You must tell your son that a person who acts fairly doesn't do so only when he can be seen by others. Instead, he acts fairly as much of the time as possible. Explain that you expect him to play by the rules that were set (every finger in every room of the house) and that when you catch him cheating on the rules, he will lose privileges just as he would for any other violation of household policy. You might want to tell your son that since sucking on one finger is so much fun, he might want to spend even more of his time enjoying the others. Point out that you will understand if he wants to give up watching television and other endeavors so that he can devote more time to his fingers.

Question:

"What's so bad about having habits? You say that everyone has them, so why do they have to be changed? I think it might be better to allow my child to have habits just like everyone else."

Answer:

There's nothing wrong with habits in general, and that's a point that was made early in this chapter. Certain types of habits are negative in that they are harmful, have the potential to become harmful, or could interfere with a child's day-to-day life at some point. Thumb sucking, for example, can cause future orthodontic problems. The habit of overeating can lead to significant emotional problems for any child who becomes obese. These habits really need to be changed, and as a caring parent, you might want to do whatever you can to help your child overcome them. On the other hand, a habit such as finger tapping is unlikely to become a significant problem and thus might just as well be left alone.

Question:

"If an overweight child is likely to be fat because there is an emotional basis to the overeating, why does PST involve dealing with the behavior? Shouldn't the child be dealt with on a psychological level instead?"

Answer:

PST does not involve ignoring emotional difficulties in children, but rather centers on removing maladaptive behaviors that cause problems in the child's life. A fat child needs to lose weight, and PST techniques can help him to achieve that goal. By doing so, the child may make strides in the emotional areas that previously were satisfied only with food, and as such, can benefit from use of the strategies put forth in PST. Discretion is always necessary, however, and any child who is showing signs of depression or anxiety that might be associated with obesity should, of course, be evaluated professionally.

Question:

"I promised my daughter a new wardrobe if she were to lose forty pounds, and now I'm wondering if I did the wrong thing. Wouldn't that be bribing her to lose weight? I think that she has to want to do it on her own."

Answer:

All human behavior takes place because it serves some purpose, however subtle that purpose may appear to be. Your daughter, at the present time, may have little motivation of her own to lose that weight, and yet she could probably benefit tremendously from doing so. Offering her new clothes as an incentive is not wrong, because you are rewarding appropriate behavior and therefore increasing the likelihood that such behavior will persist. Not only will the clothes be exciting to her, but they actually will lead to other secondary rewards (e.g., increased attention from peers). The clothes may also turn out to be a self-regulating reward: If she starts to gain weight again, the new clothes will no longer fit and the inability to wear them will serve as a punishment of sorts.

Sample Weight Chart

Use this chart as a model for one that you can make to help your child to keep track of his/her weight. Be sure to familiarize yourself with the directions as given in the PST chapter.

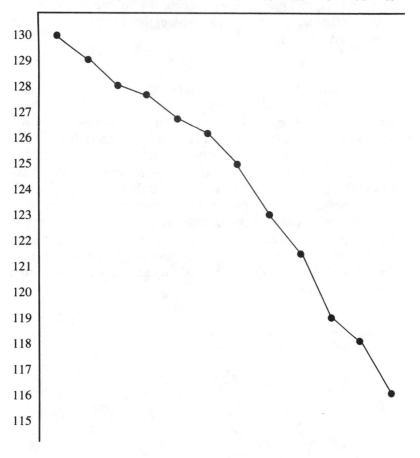

Chapter Seven

Fear Fading: The Antidote to Being Scared

At one time or another, every child will experience fear. The world is full of a variety of fear-provoking situations, and so it is natural to expect that children will react to them. As an adult, it may often be difficult for you to understand or to relate to your child's fears, simply because they are so far removed from the things that may frighten you. If a 10-year-old child were to tell you that he can't sleep because the monster from the movie that you just let him watch is going to come through the window and attack him, you can see the irrationality behind his thinking and his behavior. Unfortunately, what makes the fear quite difficult to resolve is that the child cannot understand why his thinking is irrational. Thinking differently from an adult, the child's fears seem to make sense to him, and he is therefore reluctant to let them go. At the same time, he may find it incomprehensible that you can't understand why he is afraid. The child who is afraid to go into a dark room may find that his parents can empathize because they are fearful of walking down dark alleys. In the same vein, the child who is afraid of a visit to the doctor's office may find that his mother can fully appreciate his sense of fright because she feels similarly about going to the dentist. But what about all of the childhood fears that have few, if any, counterparts in the adult world? It is precisely such fears that are the most intimidating to children. They may worry that no one understands just how they feel, and they may well be right.

Most Fears Are Irrational

With the exception of relatively few fears (e.g., sharks, fire), most fears have a generally irrational foundation. That is to say, either the object or the situation (often referred to as the "stimulus") is simply one which poses no real risk (e.g., fear of school) or is one that poses a risk so remote that it is not worth considering (e.g., fear of cats). Unfortunately, neither of these situations is any easier for a non-empathic parent to understand than is the other.

Parent: Okay, grab your books and your lunch and let's go, or you'll be late for school.

Child: I'm not going.

Parent: Don't start that again. I told you yesterday, you're going to school.

Child: I'm scared! I'm not going, and you can't make me.

Parent: I'm going to count to five, and if you're not in the car, I'm going to pick you up and carry you outside.

Child: No! Leave me alone! I want to stay home!

Parent: Did you hear me? I said, 'Get going!'

Child: Nnnnooooo. I'm afraid!

Parent: I told you before, there's nothing to be afraid of. Now stop acting like a baby, and get in the car.

In the example here, notice the parent's lack of empathy for the child's feelings. Because the parent associates a sense of safety with the school environment, she cannot relate to the reality of the child's fear. Instead, the situation is handled with strong-arm tactics that serve to do little more than reassure the parent of her own ability to intimidate. What the parent has failed to understand here is that the child's fear is very real to the child. When dealing with a legitimate fear, the parent who hopes to be successful will have to do more than disregard the child's feelings in a vain attempt to bully the child out of being frightened. Failure to do so is likely to make the situation worse, because the child will realize that he now has two things about which to be frightened: the fear stimulus itself, plus a parent who won't make an effort to understand. Using the basic principles of PST, such a scenario can be avoided. Look at what happens when we rewrite the example.

Parent: Okay, grab your books and your lunch and let's go, or you'll be late for school.

Child: I'm not going.

Parent: But I told you yesterday, you can't just stay home from school.

Child: I'm scared! I'm not going, and you can't make me!

Parent: What are you so scared about? Is someone picking on you? Do you have a test today? What's so scary about school?

Child: I don't know. It's just everything. As soon as I get there, I start feeling scared and kind of sick to my stomach.

Parent: How about if I take you inside, and walk you to your classroom?

Child: Nnnnooooo. I'm afraid!

Parent: Okay, I don't understand yet what you're so scared about, but we're going to work together on this, and I'm going to expect you to try hard. Now, here's what we need to do first . . . .

Now, the parent is making an effort to understand, and the child is likely to respond to that effort. Remember: The child's fear doesn't have to be realistic in order to be real. In fact, *phobias* are intense fears that are, by definition, unrealistic.

Phobias Are More Than Just Fears

A phobia is a unique kind of fear that meets three criteria:

1. It is irrational; there is no logical basis for the fear.
2. It is intense and is not something that a child can be "talked out of."
3. It is longstanding and is likely to interfere with the child's day-to-day life; he may go out of his way to avoid the phobic stimulus.

A child who has a phobia of dogs, for example, would not feel merely uncomfortable if there were a dog in the room. On the contrary, he might become hysterical and would look frantically for a way to escape. Such a child might find himself checking with friends before visiting at a home where he had never been before to be certain that he wouldn't encounter a dog upon arriving. Seeing one in the street, he might run in the opposite direction, thereby "taking himself out of the situation." Efforts aimed at calming such a child when he's confronted with a dog would be destined to fail; a phobia is too intense to dissipate quickly.

Fear Fading

There are several different techniques which can be utilized in dealing with children's fears and phobias. Each is effective in its own right, especially when employed in a situation which lends itself well to the use of that particular technique. The first of these strategies is called *fear fading* (known to psychologists as "systematic desensitization").

In fear fading, you must expose the child gradually to whatever it is that frightens him. The logic here is that no matter how frightened a child may be of something, he can certainly say the name of the fear stimulus. Of course, if he can say the name, then he can visualize it. If he can visualize it, then he can look at a picture of it. If he can look at a picture, then he can look at the stimulus itself from a great enough distance. Setting up a fear-fading program first involves creating a *fear intensity list* (known to psychologists as an "anxiety hierarchy"). Before reading further, at the end of this chapter there is a blank form labeled Fear Intensity List, as well as a matching sample for you to study.

The Fear Intensity List

A fear intensity list is nothing more than a collection of situations relating to the fear stimulus, rank-ordered from least to most frightening. If, for example, you had a child who had developed a phobia of dogs, the first entry on your fear intensity list might be "thinking about the word *dog.*" The second entry might be "saying the word *dog* out loud." The following entries might include "imagining what a dog looks like" and "looking at a picture of a dog."

After you've made up the fear intensity list, you'll have a series of perhaps dozens of individual steps, each one getting closer and closer to contact with the fear stimulus (in this case, playing with a dog). Over a period of days, or even weeks, you can bring the child down the list gradually, step by step, watching carefully to be certain that each step is being mastered before the next one is undertaken. Have the child relax thoroughly before beginning each session, perhaps by sitting or lying in his favorite spot in the house. Talk about light and fun things for a while, and then begin with the least frightening item (from the top of the list). When the child can deal effectively with that item (that is, when there is no evidence of any fear), you can move to the next most frightening item. Continue to do so slowly, stopping at any point where the child begins to look or to seem anxious. When you reach a point where the child is becoming frightened, back up to the safe item that you just completed. For example, if the child had no difficulty imagining what a dog looks like, but became frightened upon looking at the picture of a dog, you would go back and once again have him conjure up just the mental image of a dog. You might have to stay with that item for some time, but if you do, the child eventually will be ready to move to one item further down the list.

Because any child undergoing fear fading actually prepares for each item by mastering the item before, you're unlikely to run into any intense reactions of fear. Any given item on the list is only marginally more frightening than the previous item, so there's no reason for the child to panic. As you proceed down the fear intensity list, the child gradually will master being able to watch video tapes of dogs and will be able to describe what it would be like to touch a dog. Eventually, he will be able to visit a pet store where he can see dogs safely restrained, and finally, he will be able to permit dogs to come into contact with him. Buying a puppy is often a wonderful way to help fade a fear of dogs; the puppy's growth is so gradual that fear fading actually occurs as the dog slowly gets bigger.

Your Child Can Help to Set Things Up

Some parents prefer to enlist the child's help in setting up the fear intensity list. If the child is old enough to handle the task, present him with a set of twenty-five index cards and ask that he write on each one (or as many as he can) a frightening sort of situation involving the fear stimulus. Have him sort the cards into a set (from least to most frightening), instructing him that the last item is to be so frightening that he "can't even stand to imagine for very long what it would be like." When the child returns the set of cards to you, you can add, delete, or modify the items, but you already have a good beginning. By entering the items correctly on the PST form, your fear intensity list is ready to go.

Fear Fading in Action

As you read through the details of the following example, you might want to ask yourself how you would have handled this problem if it had occurred to your child.

Gary was a 10-year-old boy who had developed a severe phobia about school. It seemed to increase in intensity rapidly, and his mother brought him to the office just days after he began refusing to go back to school. A fear intensity list was created and Gary went through fear fading. When he reached the point on the hierarchy where he had to enter the school building, he was told that "entering" and "staying" were two different things and that he could walk in and walk out in seconds if that's what he wanted to do. Instructed in PST, his mother had the following interaction with him.

Parent: You're still scared about going back to school, aren't you?

Child: Yeah. I know that I'm not gonna be able to stay. I'm gonna wanna leave as soon as I get there.

Parent: Okay. Just walk in, and then walk out. How long will that take you?

Child: A few seconds, I guess.

Parent: Right. And no matter how scared you get, you can stand it for two seconds, can't you?

Child: I guess so. I guess I can take anything for two seconds.

Gary spent the predicted two seconds at school the next day. But because he wasn't being pressured to stay there, he was able to relax somewhat. The next day, his mother asked that he wait for half a minute before leaving, and he was able to do so without anxiety. He voluntarily stayed almost an hour the day after that, and was back in his classroom for the full day less than a week after his two-second visit.

Because fear fading can work in such a relatively short period of time, it is an ideal technique for dealing with childhood fears. Consider the following example in which an 11-year-old girl's phobia about bathrooms was eliminated (pardon the pun). Lisa had developed such an overwhelming fear of bathrooms that it had completely disrupted her daily life. Without being able to enter a bathroom, she had, of course, to find an alternate site, and she chose the center of the living room carpet. This had been going on for months before her parents finally brought her to the office, and they were desperate by that time. It was explained to them that the problem could be solved within a two-week period if they were to follow some very simple principles. They were then instructed in PST.

Instead of yelling and punishing their daughter, as they had been doing, they now approached her with understanding, because they realized that as awful as the situation seemed to them, it was actually worse for Lisa. A fear intensity list was established, and Lisa quickly reached the point where a toilet no longer caused her any anxiety. Rather than have her confront the bathroom itself at that point, however, the fear fading was taken a step further. Lisa's parents were told to cover the entire living room rug with newspaper and to put a portable potty directly over the spot where Lisa had been relieving herself. Lisa was told that she could use the potty (which no longer frightened her), and although she didn't realize it, the newspaper created boundaries around her. Each day, her parents were told to remove a sheet of the newspaper from around the perimeter of the room, thereby shrinking the boundaries. At the same time, a line of newspaper was made to extend from the potty to the bathroom. As the area of the living room that was still covered with paper was reduced to just a few feet, the potty was very slowly moved toward the bathroom. Lisa, in using the potty, was slowly fading her fear of the bathroom because she was gradually getting closer and closer to it. At the end of the two-week period, the potty actually was placed in the doorway to the bathroom, and Lisa quickly generalized her behavior, switching from the portable to the permanent toilet. This was accomplished without punishing Lisa, without upsetting her parents further, and without the need for extended intervention and time. One other technique, counter-conditioning, often can be as effective as fear fading.

Counter-Conditioning

Counter-conditioning is a technique that works on the simple principle that opposing thoughts and behaviors cannot exist simultaneously. For example, a child who is afraid of the dark cannot enjoy a movie and feel frightened by the dark at the same time. By choosing situations in which the new behavior is more powerful than the one that you are trying to eliminate, counter-conditioning can prove to be highly effective. In treating a fear of dentists, for example, you might try pairing a visit to the dentist with something that the child likes a great deal. Having him listen through headphones to a record that you know he enjoys while the dentist works would cause a conflict. Which emotion is stronger—his fear of the dentist or the pleasure derived from a favorite record? The more powerful of the two will tend to override the other, so that if you've paired things properly, the fear response should diminish.

How to Make Counter-Conditioning More Effective

Counter-conditioning can be used with more than just one pairing at a time; the stimulus causing the fear can be matched with several different competing responses simultaneously to maximize the chances of eliminating the fear. For example, a school-phobic child whose favorite pastimes are working on a computer and playing football might be able to compensate for his fear of going to school if he knew that he'd be given some time to work on the classroom terminal during the course of the day, and if he knew that tryouts for the school football team were being held. When counter-conditioning a fear or phobia, attempt to pair the fear-provoking stimulus with another stimulus that is so powerfully positive that it will overwhelm the child's tendency toward fear.

Question:
   "Wouldn't it be dangerous to use the fear-fading technique for certain kinds of fears? I wouldn't want my child to be able to

climb up on the roof for excitement. I think that he ought to be afraid to go up there."

Answer:
Fear serves an important purpose for children; it prevents them from doing many dangerous things. Children should be afraid to cross a crowded highway, to swim in rough water, to play with fire, or to get into cars with strangers. A certain level of fear is healthy as it is a good ounce of prevention. With PST, however, we are referring to those fears that are irrational in nature—fears that have no real basis for existing. You wouldn't want your child to be so frightened of a visit to the doctor's office that he wouldn't go when he's feeling ill, or for him to be so frightened of flying that the family couldn't go on vacation. Fear fading is a technique that can be utilized with children who have irrational fears interfering with their day-to-day lives and who could benefit from having those fears eliminated.

Question:
"My wife says that my son has a phobia about being in crowds, because he flatly refuses to go to football or baseball games and insisted on staying home when some of the kids in his school were putting on a play. It seems that whenever there are a lot of people around, he can't handle it. But I say it's not a phobia because he went to a rock concert last week and had a great time. Who's right?"

Answer:
You are correct in stating that your son is not experiencing a phobic reaction to crowds. A true phobia is so intense that a child would go to great lengths to avoid whatever it is that is frightening him. A child who can go to a concert and enjoy himself is probably not panicked by crowds of people. The reasons he may have had for not attending the other events you mention might range from a simple lack of interest to a desire to avoid particular children that he expected to see at those places. You might want to test your theory by taking your son to crowded areas, such as shopping malls, in an effort to determine whether it's really large groups of people that concern him or something else entirely.

Question:

"I tried to set up a fear intensity list to help my daughter get over her fear of traveling long distances from our house, but I had trouble coming up with more than four steps. Is that enough to work with, or am I doing something wrong?"

Answer:

You're not doing anything wrong per se, but the list must be far longer in order to be effective. The idea behind a fear intensity list is that fear fading occurs gradually, and to use only four steps is not gradual enough. Each step should be so slightly more fear-provoking than the step before that the child hardly notices the difference (and therefore can handle the step). The fear-fading procedure will not work if you advance from one step to another too rapidly. If you find that you cannot develop a longer list, ask your daughter to help you by using the index cards, as described in this chapter, or ask your family and friends to help by thinking of individual steps that will take your daughter farther and farther away from home.

Question:

"The one thing that I don't understand about fears is, where do they come from? Why do children develop fears or phobias?"

Answer:

People, including children, are susceptible to what is known in psychology as a "paired association." What this means is that one thing (an object, person, situation) can become associated with another, just as you might associate the word *mother* with feelings of warmth and security. Behavioral specialists use the term "stimulus-response" to describe what happens. When a child is exposed to something that frightens him, he associates that emotion with the source of the fear. A vicious, snarling dog that lunges at a child may be enough to form a powerful association in that child's mind: Afterward, whenever he sees a dog, he may recall the terror he experienced in that first incident. The dog serves as the stimulus and fear becomes the response. To know how simple the stimulus-response process really is, imagine that you hear a long, drawn-out screech of car brakes. What is the next thing that you expect to hear? Well, it doesn't matter whether or not the sound of crunching metal actually occurs, because what's important is that you *expected* to hear it; the stimulus was the sound of screeching brakes and the response was the expectation of a car crash. The two have a powerful association, and the same process can occur in the formation of fears. There are some fears within children that seem to have a natural foundation (i.e., the fear of heights), but most fears are instilled through experience.

Sample Fear Intensity List

This is designed to provide you with a clear example of the way in which the items need to be structured for a fear-fading procedure. Please note that each item is only slightly more fear-provoking than the item preceding it.

1. Thinking about the word *dog*.
2. Saying the word *dog* aloud.
3. Imagining a dog.
4. Looking at a picture of a dog.
5. Watching a videotape of a dog.
6. Imagining going to a pet store.
7. Driving over to a pet store.
8. Looking thru the store's window.
9. Entering the store.
10. Walking over to a dog's cage.
11. Standing next to the cage.
12. Touching the dog with a finger.
13. Petting the dog with a hand.
14. Letting the dog out of the cage.
15. Putting a collar and leash on the dog.
16. Walking the dog on its leash.
17. Giving the dog a biscuit.
18. Petting the dog with both hands.
19. Letting the dog lick your face.
20. Rolling around and playing with the dog.

Fear Intensity List

Use this form to create a list of increasingly fear-provoking situations to be used in a fear-fading procedure. Be certain that each item is only slightly more fear-provoking than the item preceding it. Proceed slowly and follow all directions as given in the PST chapter.

1. _____   11. _____

2. _____   12. _____

3. _____   13. _____

4. _____   14. _____

5. _____   15. _____

6. _____   16. _____

7. _____   17. _____

8. _____   18. _____

9. _____   19. _____

10. _____   20. _____

Chapter Eight

The Schoolhouse Syndrome: It Doesn't Have to Happen to You

If you learn that your child is having difficulties at school, you may be a victim of the "Schoolhouse Syndrome," wherein you feel helpless because you are not at school all day to make sure that he behaves, does his work, and follows school rules. But you are *not* helpless! There are techniques that you can use. However, before you assume that your child has the power to change his behavior, work habits, and attitudes about school, you must rule out certain possible causes of school problems. Let's look at some of these possible factors prior to presenting the strategies for improving the school performance of your child.

It's Not Always Motivation

Be sure that your child's eyes are functioning properly. A screening exam using an eye chart is not sufficient to detect a wide variety of vision-related problems. Your child should be examined regularly by an optometrist or by an ophthalmologist. Certain types of visual difficulties, such as muscle balance problems, can cause a child to appear hyperactive, when, in fact, he is exhibiting tension and stress because of the visual problem.

Before you can require your child to follow directions, you must make sure that he can hear properly. Check with your child's school to determine if audiometric screening was done and, if so, find out whether your child passed. If not, ask your pediatrician to give you a referral for a thorough test of your child's hearing. Most school screenings test only for hearing in the area of air conduction and not of bone conduction. Again, consultation with your pediatrician to determine the need for further evaluation is advised.

Always let your pediatrician know about any problem that your child is experiencing and ask if there is any possibility of an organic basis to these problems (e.g., improper blood sugar levels, neurological difficulties).

A child also could have a learning disability or below-average intelligence which would prevent him from performing adequately at school. Ask your child's teacher if it is possible that such a problem exists. School teachers and counselors are good at identifying children who may have such problems; however, a parent should ask questions to make sure that this possibility has been eliminated. If the teacher or counselor suspects that there is a learning disability, the child needs to be tested by a school psychologist or a psychologist in private practice to determine whether difficulties of this nature are a factor in the child's work.

You Can Help Your Child

If your child does not have any of these problems and is free of other disabilities, you can help to back up the school's efforts by motivating your child to improve his school performance.

Let's look at an example. Nine-year-old Jimmy is constantly getting out of his seat, talking, and refusing to do his work at school. His father has a plan. As you read the following paragraph, ask yourself whether this plan will result in an improvement in Jimmy's behavior.

The Plan

Parent: Jimmy, if you improve your behavior in school and do not get any bad-conduct marks on the report card that you will be getting in seven weeks, I will give you twenty dollars.

Child: Wow! Yeah, I'll try!

Parent: Good. I'm expecting all satisfactory grades in conduct. Now, let's go, Jimmy. It's time for the football game.

It's unlikely that the father's plan will result in improved school behavior for a number of different reasons. To begin with, seven weeks is too long a period of time for a child to wait for a reward. Secondly, the $20 will have little meaning to Jimmy because he really doesn't need the money; his parents give him toys, presents, and activities (such as the football game) all of the time. If someone gave you everything that you wanted and paid all of your bills, would you still be motivated to put in 40 hours a week on your job? Most people would quit! Finally, a child cannot eliminate a host of poor behavior patterns all at one time. Expecting a child to progress from a variety of misbehaviors to almost all good behaviors is an unrealistic goal.

Corporal Punishment Misses the Target

By now, you must be wondering "What can I do?" How about spanking your child every time that he misbehaves at school? If you use corporal punishment frequently, you may see an improvement for a short while, but the poor behavior will probably return. Also, corporal punishment is over too quickly and usually is not painful enough (unless you are a child abuser) to alter the child's behavior. It is too easy and too fast.

Consequences

Here is what you can do. You can back up the school in a planned program to help your child improve. We suggest that your child learn that there will be consequences for his actions. Just because he is alive and breathing does not entitle him to privileges such as television, playing with friends, going to fun places on the weekend, or eating ice cream or dessert. Your child must learn that there is a direct connection between his behavior and the privileges that he enjoys.

A Way to Help Your Child

If your child has been having some problems with school behavior or motivation, it is essential that you know of his school performance on a daily basis. Rewards or punishments are most effective if they occur right after the behavior is exhibited. Thus, rewarding or punishing a child for school performance should be done on a daily basis when you are working on reducing problems. In order to do this, you must ask your child's teacher(s) to fill out a daily progress report form. Several different types of forms can be used, depending upon your child's school schedule and organization. At the end of this chapter, there is a form labeled Daily Report Form 1.

How to Use the Progress Reports

Form 1 is appropriate for a child who is with one teacher for most of the day. The following is an example of the way in which a parent might present this program to the child.

"I have spoken with your teacher and she has agreed to check this sheet for us every day. This is so that I can know how you're doing in school. You are going to be responsible for bringing this sheet home every day. First, let's look at each of the things on which the teacher will rate you. The first item on this sheet is *Amount of work completed:*

☐ All   ☐ Most   ☐ Little   ☐ None

"If your teacher checks *All* or *Most* for *Amount of work completed,* this will be considered to be good and acceptable. However, if your teacher checks *Little* or *None,* this will be considered to be bad. *Amount of work completed* means how hard you tried to finish the work that your teacher gave you in class during the day.

"The second item on this sheet asks the teacher to let me know about the *Quality of classwork.* To have good quality classwork, your papers should be neat and well organized; you should have followed the teacher's instructions for the assignment; and you should show that you really tried your best to do it. If the teacher checks *Superior* or *Good,* I will consider that to be okay. If the teacher checks *Poor,* I will consider that to be bad.

"For the third item, your teacher is going to check *Behavior.* If the teacher checks *Excellent* or *Fair,* I will consider that to be acceptable. However, if your teacher checks *Poor,* I will consider that to be bad.

"For the fourth item, your teacher will let me know about the quality of your homework. If the teacher checks *Good,* that will be acceptable, since you did your homework and did it well. If the teacher checks *Poor* or *Not submitted,* I will consider that to be bad. *N.A.* means 'does not apply.' This means that there may not have been homework or that there was perhaps some other reason why the teacher is not concerned about homework on that day.

"For the fifth item, the teacher will indicate with a checkmark whether or not you have homework to do tonight. I expect you to have all the necessary books and materials at home to do it, or if you did it in school or on the bus, bring the finished assignment home so that I can look it over.

"The teacher will sign the slip in ink everyday. Then, when you bring it home, I will sign it so that you can return it to the teacher the next day so she will know that I saw it. If, on number three, the teacher checks that your behavior was poor, I have asked her to list on the back of the slip exactly what it is that you did that was not acceptable.

"I spoke with your teacher and she realizes that you either will be punished or rewarded, based upon the indications on the sheet. *You must bring the sheet home everyday.* I will not accept any excuses, regardless of what the excuse might be. Even if you tell me, 'The teacher was sick and threw up on my paper,' you will be punished if you do not bring the sheet home. If you tell me that the school was on fire and that all of the children stood across the street watching the fire department put the fire out, you will be punished unless I've heard on the news that there was really a fire. *I will not accept any excuses.* If an emergency does occur, and your teacher leaves early and you cannot get the sheet, you must bring home a note from some adult at the school telling me that the teacher left early and explaining what occurred. You can get a note from the principal's office, the secretary, the custodian, the substitute, or any other adult at the school. If you do not bring home such a note, you will be punished.

"Any day that you have one of the 'bad' items checked on your sheet, you will spend three hours in your bedroom with no privileges. 'No privileges' means that you will not touch any toy, any game, any radio, any stereo, or any books. You can walk around the room without touching anything, but basically you will be sitting and looking at the walls most of the time. If you fall asleep, then *the time that you are sleeping is not counted towards the punishment time.* You can leave the room only to go directly to the bathroom a reasonable number of times, and you must go directly back to your room. I will leave some water in your room in case you get thirsty. If you touch any toy or game in your room, I will take it away from you and you will never get it back. I will probably donate it to a charity so that some less fortunate children who do not have many toys will have an opportunity to play with your toy.

"If you do very poorly and have two 'bad' items checked on your sheet, you will be restricted to your room from the time that you come home until it's time to go to school the next morning. You will stay in your room with no privileges, and the only thing that you will be allowed to do is your homework. Your brother will take out the things from the room that he needs, and no one will come in and out of your room. After you finish your homework, slip it under the door for me to check. I will not stand over you, and no one will come in to disturb you. As I said before, you are not to touch anything in your room except the items that you need to do your homework.

"If you do get punished, remember that it was your decision. You have the opportunity to complete your work in school, to do it as neatly as you can, to follow school rules, and to behave well. If you do not, you must face the consequences of your behavior. It is not my decision as to whether or not you get punished; it is entirely up to you. You will decide whether or not you want to follow the school requirements. If you do everything that you are supposed to do in school, nothing will happen. If you have a whole week in which you receive no punishment, I will let you pick a special activity on the weekend, such as a movie, pizza, bowling, or whatever you would like to do, to celebrate having had an incredible week."

Your Child's Reaction

Do not be concerned about your child's reaction when you present the above program. It is not unusual for a child to go into a tantrum and let you know that there is no way that he is going to follow these procedures. Basically, the child does not have a choice, so don't worry about it. If he doesn't bring the sheet home, he is automatically punished for the entire day and evening, and will have no privileges nor come out of his room (except for trips to the bathroom) until the next day. *Most children will be resistant to such structure at first.* After improvement occurs, the child will feel happy and proud to bring home a good sheet.

Please follow these procedures carefully. Do not feel sorry should the child have to miss any special event. If the child is scheduled to go to football practice or karate class, but is restricted to the room with no privileges for the entire day and evening, he should not go to any of these special classes. The only exception should be something that is education-related (such as a tutoring class). Again, as a parent, you must learn not to experience guilt because the child is feeling miserable as a result of missing an activity or because he is sitting in his room for so many hours. *You must realize that it is better to have the child feel some misery now than for both of you to go through these school problems for years to come.*

Most children will not show an immediate improvement. Sometimes, the child hopes that if he does not show that this program is working, you will stop using it. You must guard against falling into this trap. Let the child know that he has no choice. Either he conforms with school requirements, or he will be very uncomfortable when he comes home.

About the worst thing that can happen is for a child to be in school all day, not being cooperative and not completing work, and then come home and watch TV, go out to play, and have a good time. This teaches the child that he does not have to do anything that is required of him and that he can still have access to all of his privileges. Such a situation is very destructive, since the child learns that he can do whatever he wants to do.

Secondary School Kids: Form 2
For a child who has several teachers during the day, or who is in middle, junior, or senior high school, Form 2 would be appropriate. The rules should be set in a fashion similar to those for Form 1. When you use Form 2, you must fill in the left column indicating the teachers' names. On this sheet, the teacher is checking to let you know if the child submitted his homework, if his behavior was satisfactory or unsatisfactory, and if his effort was satisfactory or unsatisfactory. The sheet also allows the teacher to indicate whether the child has homework to do for that evening, as well as if there are any upcoming tests for which to study. With this information, you can monitor your child to make

sure that he is being prepared properly for upcoming school assignments and exams.

Since the average child in secondary school has five or six teachers during the day, and each teacher is checking three categories that you will monitor (homework turned in, behavior, and effort), the average child will have about fifteen to eighteen boxes checked by teachers. It would be appropriate to let the child know that for any negative rating in these boxes, there will be 3 hours of punishment (restriction to his room with no privileges). If the child has an extremely unsatisfactory sheet and there are not enough hours in the day for that restriction, the child should be told that he will have to make up the additional hours on the weekend.

As with Form 1, the same rules must apply regarding bringing home the sheet. The child can be told that for each teacher who does not sign the sheet, he will spend 3 hours in his room without privileges. *No excuses will be accepted.* As in other behavior management procedures, the parents should not lecture, yell, question, or get into any long discussion. Either the child meets the goals or he doesn't.

Praise and Reinforcement

Please remember the importance of praising a child and giving positive feedback. If the child has a good report, show your approval so that he will realize that good things happen when behavior is appropriate and negative things occur when inappropriate behavior is exhibited.

As discussed with other issues, some children do better for a while, but then suddenly revert to their old ways of behaving. This is often the child's last attempt to get you to give up the approach. The child would rather not have consequences to face when he misbehaves. Don't give up! Continue to use the approach for the next few weeks until the child shows improvement again.

When There Is Improvement

After the child has had a few good weeks, you can start with a weekly report system using the same sheet. The title should be changed to Weekly Progress Report. Then start monitoring the child's performance each Friday. If the child continues to do well, the weekly progress report could be used for a few months. If there is a regression, you might have to return to the daily progress report. Soon, all the report forms can be phased out, and you can check with the teachers every few weeks to make sure that things are going well.

No Success
If you try this approach and there is no success, ask yourself the following questions:

- Was the report form checked every day?
- Did you praise the child verbally for successful days?
- Was there consistency in that the child always received the reward or punishment that he was told he would receive?
- Did the reward or punishment occur on a daily basis?
- Did you avoid screaming at, yelling at, and lecturing the child?

Your answer to each of these questions should be "yes" if you expect this approach to be effective. If you have used the approach properly for a month and a half and a serious school problem remains, you may need to consult with the school's guidance counselor regarding the need for special services, such as psychological testing, counseling, and tutoring.

Helping Your Child to Succeed in School
"What can I do to help my child succeed in school?" is a question that you have probably asked yourself many times. The first step toward helping your child with school performance is to examine your own attitude. Your expectations must be realistic. A child should not be expected to do more than he is actually capable of doing. He should be praised and recognized for any improvement or achievement. For example, if he gets a "B" in math, you shouldn't react by saying, "Why didn't you get an 'A?'" First, accept his achievement, and then work toward improvement. Obviously, brothers and sisters should never be compared for school achievement. Each child in the family is an

individual with different abilities, and should be recognized for his or her own accomplishments.

Sometimes, tutoring by a qualified professional is needed when a child is having difficulty in a particular subject. It is one thing to help your child with homework, but a completely different ball game when you actually have to teach him specific skills. If you have to do this, many of your emotions will probably interfere with your really being able to help. At that point, a tutor may well be a viable solution.

If you are actually going to try to help your child with homework or school assignments, you must try to do it unemotionally. Very often, a child will say that he forgot or that he doesn't remember what you just went over with him so that he can elicit an emotional reaction from you. Do not allow yourself to respond.

The Home-School Relationship

To be really helpful to your child, it is necessary to have a good exchange of information between the home and the school. You must know, as a parent, what is going on in school in order to be helpful. Also, if a child knows that you are carefully monitoring his school progress, he will be more likely to comply with school requirements.

Teachers can help by giving advance notice of tests so that parents can monitor their child's study period. For example, you should have the child's spelling words at home. Since most children get weekly spelling tests, you might ask the child to bring home his spelling book so that you can copy the words for the next few spelling units. Then, you will know what to review with the child each week. By the middle of the week, you should give the child a test on the words and have him practice, usually by writing several times each of the words that he has not yet mastered.

The child must perceive that the parent will back up the school's efforts. If a parent says negative things about the teacher or the school in front of the child, the child may take this as permission to do whatever he wants to do at school, knowing that his parents are more supportive of him than of the school's procedures and of the teacher's judgment. If you do have problems with something being done by the teacher or by the school, be sure to handle this on an adult level. Have a conference with the teacher, call the principal or guidance counselor, or write to the superintendent's office, but *never discuss your negative feelings with the child, since he will then feel that you will back him up instead of the teacher.* This gives him a "ticket" to do whatever he wants at school. It is important to have periodic teacher/parent conferences. Report cards usually come out every nine weeks, but that is too long a period for you to wait for feedback on a child who is having school problems.

Getting Feedback from the School

One simple but effective way of getting interim feedback about your child's progress is to send a letter to your child's teacher(s), asking him or her to indicate to you the child's progress. Enclose a stamped, self-addressed, return envelope. A sample copy of such a letter is included at the end of this chapter.

Be sure to monitor the child's progress carefully. If you feel that your child is being instructed on a reading level that is below his standardized test scores (and below what you think he is capable of doing), ask the teacher to show you the data that helped to determine the level on which the child was placed. If you are still not satisfied, ask the teacher to give the child the test for the next highest reading level to determine whether the child is actually ready for it and to rule out the possibility that he is being taught on too low a level.

Getting Ready for Tests

A simple way of helping children to prepare for tests in subjects such as science and social studies is to use a cassette tape recorder. Since many parents have busy schedules and time is often a problem, using a tape recorder can be extremely helpful.

You can review the chapter that the child must study, and on tape dictate to the child the key facts and vocabulary words that he may need to know for an upcoming test. At the end of a chapter, there are usually questions that you can ask on the tape. Leave enough blank time on the tape for the child to answer before he hears you give the answer. Since the information that the child must study is on tape, you can play the tape in the car, in the bathroom, or anywhere else when you have a few minutes for the child to practice. The child can listen to the tape several times until he has learned the information. Using the tape recorder is a supplement to the learning of concepts and to the thorough reading of the chapter that occurs in school and as part of homework assignments.

When you make such a tape recording for study, be sure to talk slowly and to leave time for the child's response. For example, you might repeat key phrases several times. "The Pope was the head of the Roman Catholic Church during the Middle Ages. Who was the head of the Roman Catholic Church during the Middle Ages?" (ten seconds of silence) Answer: "The Pope. The Pope was the head of the Roman Catholic Church during the Middle Ages."

There are many techniques that can be used to help your child to survive in school; however, remember to make sure to keep communication going so that you will know what is going on. Often, a lot of time slips by, and a child can fail or have difficulty. When this happens, it may be too late to save him from failure for that entire quarter or semester. Stay on top of things!

Question:

"My daughter always forgets to bring her spelling book home on the day that I tell her to do so. Because of this, I cannot go over the words with her and she often gets low grades on her tests. What can I do?"

Answer:

When you tell your child to bring the book home, specify what consequence will occur if she forgets. For example, you might say, "It is very important that you bring your spelling book home from school today. If you forget to bring it home, you will spend two hours in your room with no privileges and you will not be allowed to use the television, to go out to play, or to use your radio. If you forget to bring your book home, you will not have any special privileges tonight. Now, it's up to you to decide whether you'd like to do all of these things and have fun or, if you prefer, to forget your book and miss out on things that you like to do." At this point, the child either remembers to bring the book home or she doesn't. After experiencing the unpleasant consequences of forgetting, she is more likely to become consistent in bringing it home when asked. To be fair, remember to let her know beforehand what to expect if she is forgetful.

Question:
"Why should I have to do so much work to help my child with his homework? Shouldn't the teacher be helping him to develop all of these skills?"

Answer:
Although the teacher is responsible for instructing your child and making sure that he is being taught the skills that are commensurate with his grade level, the teacher cannot do everything. If the child is working at a slower pace, is inattentive, or has missed some skills, extra work at home is probably called for. It is definitely the parent's responsibility to support the school program and to do whatever is necessary to reinforce children's skills at home. Most children who perform well at school have parents who are very supportive of their program, who check their children's homework every night, and who help their children to learn a skill if they see a weakness as a result of reviewing the homework or tests that are brought home. Although such a system can be a burden to a parent, it is something that is necessary, and it comes with the responsibility of parenting. Although a parent shouldn't be expected to be a teacher as well as a parent, he or she is expected to reinforce and to support the school's efforts. This also helps the child to see that the parent values education and is willing to be inconvenienced at times, because education and school are quite important.

Question:
"I have been using the daily progress charts that you talk about. A few weeks have passed, and my third-grade son is still bringing home bad reports. We see no improvement. The teacher tells me that he is capable of doing all of his work and that he has no real learning problem. The system doesn't seem to be working, so what can I do?"

Answer:

Perhaps the punishment that you have selected is not as strong as it should be. Assuming that you have followed our directions and the child still is not improving, possibly a more severe punishment is needed. Sometimes you have to confront a child who is performing poorly despite having good abilities to let him know that school is his number one responsibility and that if he does not deal with that responsibility, his life will be miserable.

We have experienced situations where we have had to ask a parent to strip a child's entire bedroom. This means taking out everything except school supplies and clothing. The mattress is left on the floor and all of the furniture, toys, and television are stored at a friend or neighbor's house. It is important to remove the things from the home so the child realizes that the parent is not playing a game. Since the child's toys, sports equipment, and other possessions have been packed in boxes, the child will know that he had better comply with the school requirements or he is really going to suffer. The child can be told that for each week in which he has not missed submitting any assignments or homework and has not misbehaved in school he will get back one box or one item that was taken from the room. Each time that you learn that he has not submitted an assignment or has misbehaved, one item or one box of toys will be donated to charity. Thus, what he has lost for his inappropriate actions will never be returned. This may seem harsh, but for some stubborn children it is needed so that the child will see that "the party is over." Always remember that a punishment has to be seen as unpleasant by the child if it is going to be effective.

Question:

"My child was suspended from school three days for fighting. Is there anything special that I should do?"

Answer:

Make sure when your child is home during the suspension that he is restricted to his bedroom with no privileges. In the event that you cannot leave him home because of your work schedule, you may have to take him to work with you and have him isolated in a particular room or corner. Since the child is supposed to have his lunch at school, he should not have lunch while he has been suspended. He is expected to be at school at lunch time, and he is not there because he violated school rules. Therefore, he will skip his lunch and have his breakfast and dinner at home as usual. During the entire 72 hours that he has been suspended, he will be restricted to his room. Even if there is an important event or activity in which the child is supposed to be involved, he should not be able to participate during the suspension time. If a child is suspended and can stay home and watch television, have snacks, and enjoy himself, no learning experience will occur. Very often a suspension doesn't work because the child ends up being reinforced when removed from school. Since many children who get into such trouble don't like school in the first place, they are quite pleased when they can miss school for a day and stay at home and watch television. You must make sure that when your child is suspended, his life at home is miserable while he is missing out on a lot of activities. Seventy-two hours in a room with no privileges may sound drastic, but the child must learn from the suspension experience so that you will not have more serious problems in the future. Again, if the child did something that was very inappropriate, don't feel too bad about his temporary misery; he must learn from the experience.

Form 1

Daily Report

Use this form to obtain a daily record of your child's classroom work and behavior. It is intended for children who have one teacher during the course of the day. Be certain that you follow all directions as given in the PST chapter.

Student _____   Date _____

1. Amount of work completed:
   ☐ All   ☐ Most   ☐ Little   ☐ None

2. Quality of classwork:
   ☐ Superior   ☐ Good   ☐ Poor

3. Behavior:
   ☐ Excellent   ☐ Fair   ☐ Poor

4. Homework was:
   ☐ Good   ☐ Poor   ☐ Not submitted   ☐ N.A.

5. Tonight there is:
   ☐ Homework   ☐ No Homework

_____   _____
Teacher (sign in ink)   Parent

To the teacher: If number 3 is poor, please list the specific misbehavior(s) on the back of this sheet.

Date ———

Student ———

Form 2
Secondary School
Daily Progress Report

Teacher & Subject Teacher: Please initial to indicate that you have rated this form.	Homework turned in: Yes or No	Behavior S-Satisfactory U-Unsatisfactory	Effort S-Satisfactory U-Unsatisfactory	Homework tonight? Yes or No	Indicate if there is a test this week student must study for.

Sample Teacher Feedback Letter

Use this letter to help ensure that you are receiving the feedback that you need from your child's teacher. Be sure to enclose a stamped, self-addressed envelope. Familiarize yourself with the directions as given in the PST chapter.

10598 S.W. Third Court
Happy City, FL 33333

Dear _____,

    My son, Herman, is a student in your class. I would be grateful if you could provide me with some feedback regarding his performance so that I will be aware of how he is doing, and so that I can help out with any problems that may be occurring.

    Please check the items below, and return this letter to me in the enclosed stamped, self-addressed envelope.

    Thank you for your help.

Sincerely,

Robin Bird
Mother

1. Homework   ☐ Good   ☐ Poor
                         ☐ Many assignments missing

2. Behavior   ☐ Good   ☐ Poor

3. Effort   ☐ Good   ☐ Poor

4. Please indicate how the child has performed on classroom testing during the last month.

5. Please note anything that would be helpful for me to know about my child.

Chapter Nine

The Marriage Team: There's Safety in Numbers

In a two-parent family, children must perceive that both of their parents are united in their efforts to raise them. It is impossible to expect two different adults always to agree on procedures and techniques for child rearing; however, parents must be mature enough to reach some common agreement as to their philosophies of behavior management. Without such agreement, a family is likely to have children who are confused and anxious, and who may be likely to exhibit behavioral or emotional problems.

How to Lose Your Child's Respect

Imagine that Mrs. Smith has received a telephone call from Billy's teacher, who tells her that Billy has not submitted three homework assignments during the past week. Mrs. Smith becomes perturbed, goes to the telephone, and calls her husband. She tells her husband, "Billy has not been doing his homework in school, and I want you to punish him." Then, Mrs. Smith proceeds to put Billy on the telephone and to turn the whole responsibility of Billy's punishment over to the father. Mrs. Smith has now lost the respect of her son because he sees that his mother is not strong enough to deal with problems concerning him. Since Mrs. Smith has to use her husband as the disciplinarian, she teaches her son that "I, your mother, am not capable of dealing with the problems that you present. I must get someone else to deal with those problems." Every time that Mrs. Smith asks her husband to intervene and to do the punishing, Billy's respect for his mother will decrease.

An extreme example of this occurred with a family that we had seen who had a bright, sociable, and emotionally well-rounded young child. One morning, the mother set her video tape recorder to record a soap opera. The boy changed the setting on the VCR machine to record one of his cartoon programs. When the mother came home and put on the video tape recorder, she saw "Bugs Bunny" instead of her favorite soap opera. She responded to this by yelling and screaming at her son, by throwing a chair against the wall, and by telling him that his father would punish him. The father was a traveling salesman who, at the time, was at a sales meeting 125 miles away and was scheduled to be there for two nights. The mother called the father on the telephone and insisted that he drive back home, punish the child, and then drive back in the middle of the night to be ready for his business meeting the next morning. Unfortunately, the father succumbed to the mother's request and drove two and a half hours to come home and punish his son. Just days later, the mother called our office for a therapy appointment, stating, "My son does not respect me." This mother had difficulty realizing that her son could never respect her as long as she relied on another person to intervene in problems that occurred between them. Additionally, the mother's screaming and yelling further served to eliminate any remaining respect that her son might have had for her. A child will not respect a parent who screams, yells, and relies on someone else to solve family problems.

Teamwork

No matter which parent is with a child when a situation occurs, that parent should deal with the problem himself or herself. It is totally acceptable, of course, for a parent to say, "Your teacher called me today to let me know that you haven't been doing your homework. When your mother comes home, she and I will speak about the problem. After dinner, we will both tell you what the consequences of your irresponsibility will be." Such a strategy would be perceived by the child as a "united front," since the parents clearly are working together. This is quite different from the sort of situation in which one parent shifts responsibility over to the other parent.

Marital Problems Affect Kids

Obviously, problems within a marriage will also have a negative impact on a child. If parents are having significant marital problems, they should consider getting counseling in order to resolve the difficulties. Since a child's mood, thinking, concentration, and emotions will be greatly affected by the parents' difficulties, such problems must be resolved. With this in mind, let's take a brief look at the marital relationship, as well as some of the factors that either can enhance that relationship or can place a strain on it.

When Love No Longer Seems to Exist in the Marriage

Romance and affection must be shown by each spouse to the other. Affection does *not* mean sex. Affection means the verbal and physical expression of care for one another. Complaints from a spouse, such as "My husband doesn't bring me a birthday card," or "He doesn't bring home flowers anymore," can be indicators of some level of dissatisfaction in the marriage. Unfortunately, the husband might assume, "She knows that I love her, so I don't have to remember those things." Each spouse should ask himself or herself, "When is the last time that I told my spouse, 'I love you?'" If the answer is "three years ago," then romance may be fading from the marriage. They might want to consider a candlelight dinner, a sexy negligee, or a romantic night out dancing as ways of signaling that romantic feelings remain within the relationship. Children do notice the subtleties in their parents' relationship with one another and they often respond negatively to a lack of affection.

The leading complaint voiced by women whom we have seen in marriage counseling is the feeling of a lack of romance within the marriage. When people get married, they often have the misconception that marriage is all romance and pleasure; but marriage, of course, is more than that. Marriage involves a great deal of hard work, and romance has a tendency to dissipate as time passes by. When you hold such a romanticized perception of marriage and the romance begins to disappear, things begin to fall apart. Although marriage cannot be all romance, some romance must be part of the relationship if the marriage is to be a good one and is to survive.

Lack of Common Interest

You've heard the saying "opposites attract," but is it true? Actually, opposites attract only in one place: divorce court. Unless a couple has something in common, along with some joint activities to keep them going, problems can be expected. Couples should make every attempt to engage in activities, such as joining a community center or a health club.

Lack of Specificity in Arguing

Being specific means sticking to the problem at hand and not bringing in problems from the past. Arguments should be kept short, and if the argument cannot be resolved in 15 or 20 minutes, then what is called for is a communication postponement. A postponement means that since the problem is not being resolved today, a specific time must be arranged (such as the next morning) when the situation can again be examined. Postponing the argument is superior to walking away angrily, without coming to a conclusion. When an argument is postponed, it must be resolved later and not just shoved under the carpet.

During an argument, couples must stick to the present. There is no need to bring up the past. They must stay with the present and with the specific gripe, and they should not bring into the argument information that is at all irrelevant. Talking about something similar that happened two years ago or bringing their mother-in-laws into the discussion is destructive.

Problems with Child Management
Will Affect the Marriage, Too

Techniques suggested in this book, if used by both parents, may help to improve the marriage by reducing the disagreements regarding child management strategies. A couple needs to come to a consensus about the child-rearing techniques that they want to use.

Problems with In-Laws Can Also Affect a Marriage

In-law problems are among the top three leading causes of divorce. When you marry, you do not marry just the individual, but in a very real sense, you also marry the family. Couples appear to function better when they live separately from in-laws.

Living very close to in-laws can make it too easy for one spouse to run back to the parents for help in solving marital problems. For example, too many young couples constantly ask their parents for money. Later, the couple may feel resentful when the in-laws or parents tell them what to do. You cannot ask for one hand to be *washed* without the other hand being *controlled*. It is important for a couple to try to make it, as best as possible, on their own. Admittedly, this may be difficult, but by taking money from in-laws, problems of control, of dominance, and of interference are likely to occur.

When possible, try to arrange for both sides of the family to get together, especially on holidays and special events. You may find that this will encourage both sets of in-laws to like each other, and it could make it easier for you to get along with your spouse. Try to spend equal time with both sets of parents.

Problems Revolving Around Money Tend to Affect a Marriage

A couple planning a household budget and deciding how to handle savings and investment accounts can help to prevent serious financial problems.

Although some of the preceding suggestions seem to be outside the topic of this book, they are important because the emotional tone of the marriage will be reflected in the children's adjustment. Also, parents must realize that they are constantly modeling behavior for their children. Children will learn a lot about relationships by watching their parents interact. When a child sees cooperation and sensible resolutions to conflict between his parents, he will learn how to resolve such problems more effectively as a result of the modeling. When a child sees two parents get into heated arguments, fight for days, and never resolve the problems, the child may never learn, by observation, how to deal with conflict.

Look seriously at your marriage and ask yourself if the marriage relationship is helping or hurting your parenting abilities (along with your child's adjustment). If your answer is that the relationship is hurting the children, it is strongly suggested that you seek marriage counseling or other appropriate intervention to reduce or to eliminate the problem.

Single Divorced Parents

Divorce does not necessarily have a traumatic effect on children if the two parents who are divorced act like mature adults. If one of the parents has a low tolerance for frustration, is very angry and vindictive, or has personal emotional difficulties, then the divorce is likely to have a more significant impact on the child.

When we run group counseling sessions for children who come from families in which there has been a divorce, we ask the children to list the single biggest problem that they have as a result of their parents' divorce. The problem that the children most frequently identify is the tendency of one parent to talk negatively about the other parent. Children are also disturbed when one parent uses them as spies to get information about what the other parent is doing.

The single parent must not be intimidated when the child compares him or her to the other parent. It is common for a child who is upset to make a statement, such as "I'd rather go live with my father. He doesn't make me do all of these things. You are so mean." The best reaction that the single parent can exhibit is *no* reaction at all. If the child realizes that he can make you upset with such statements, it is likely that the child will utilize such comparisons whenever he feels angry toward one of his parents.

In an ideal situation, the divorced parents should try to coordinate their efforts. For example, the non-custodial parent should be given copies of the child's report card, of his test grades, and of any other important information pertaining to that child. When punishment is needed, it should be coordinated between the two households. If a child has to be restricted to the house with no privileges for a weekend, the parent who has the child that weekend should follow through. Of course, this does not always happen, and then it must be up to the parent who has custody to implement whatever procedures are necessary for the child.

All of the parenting techniques discussed in this book can be used in a one-parent or two-parent family. When there is a two-parent household, it is essential that both parents try to utilize the same approach and philosophy in dealing with their children, in order for such techniques to be effective. When two married adults cannot coordinate their efforts as needed, problems with their children may result.

Question:

"My husband refuses to go along with PST techniques. He says, 'A good beating is all that Victor needs.' What can I do?"

Answer:

Although it is best when both spouses can coordinate their efforts in raising a child, this is sometimes difficult to achieve. How can you expect to help a child to learn appropriate behavior if, as adults, you cannot agree on some common goals? When a couple cannot sit down and come to a consensus on child-rearing methods, there are obviously problems in the marital relationship. You might consider working on this difficulty before being concerned about the child's behavior. Perhaps you and your husband actually need to sit down and have a discussion about how you want to raise your child. If it is truly impossible to reach such an agreement, and other options (such as marriage counseling) are not acceptable to one or both of you, then you may have to try parenting by yourself. Children, like adults, can discriminate as to how they should behave when with different people. For example, the way that you behave at a friend's New Year's Eve party is probably quite different from the way in which you would behave while at work in an office. Your child can do the same thing. He can learn what types of behavior are acceptable to you, and what behaviors are acceptable to his father. Your child will learn that when you tell him to do something, he'd better do it the first time or there will be an unpleasant consequence. He may also learn that when his father tells him to do something and he doesn't comply, his father will yell and become upset. Thus, the child may respond differently to each of you. Because neither spouse is using similar techniques, the child will have an opportunity to observe one adult who reacts to him in an uncontrolled manner and another who reacts to him in a calm, assertive, and stable manner. It is better for the child to observe one model of stability than to have none that he can observe. But again, you should consider marriage counseling, because a couple needs to be able to work out solutions to common problems.

Question:

"I am divorced. My daughter has overnight visits with her father on alternate weekends. When she comes back to my house, her behavior is terrible. It takes about two days to get her back into the routine at home. I don't know what I should do. I try to act understanding when she returns, but this doesn't help her."

Answer:

When she returns to your house, immediately start using the parenting techniques upon which you would normally rely. As stated in the preceding answer, children can discriminate between requirements in different environments. If your daughter knows that you will always enforce the rules that you have set, she will be less likely to take several days to bounce back after returning from her father's house. Do not pay attention to any statements that she may make about how much nicer her father is to her than you are or to any other comparisons. Stick to the issues at hand, and when she brings her father into the picture to distract you, tune it out, making believe that you didn't hear her. If she sees that she can upset you when she says that her father is better than you are, she will continue trying to get this reaction from you.

Question:

"I am divorced, and my son comes to visit me on weekends. His teacher gives him weekly reports that indicate the amount of work he has completed and that describe his behavior during the week. I do not feel that it is fair for me to punish him, since I have him only forty-eight hours each week. How would you suggest that I deal with this?"

Answer:

Your son must know that *both* of his parents are concerned with his performance at school and that each of you will be involved. Perhaps you and your ex-spouse can talk and agree to split up the punishment. Usually, when there is one household, a child who has had a very bad week at school would spend the entire weekend in his bedroom without privileges. You could have the child confined to a room at your house from Friday night through Saturday night and then spend some time with him on Sunday. To compensate for the additional punishment time needed, his mother could restrict him from television for the rest of the week until he brings home a better report. Thus, the child will see that both parents are involved in monitoring his school performance and that both of you care about it.

Question:

"My husband keeps insisting that he works too hard and is too tired to worry about 'little things' with the kids. He says that I should be the disciplinarian, since the little time that he has with them should be for fun things. Is his argument valid?"

Answer:

No, it is not a valid argument. A parent must take the good along with the bad, since both come with the territory. If you become the disciplinarian, the children may learn to avoid you at certain times and may go to their father to get a more favorable reply. You will have to insist that he become involved with punishment as well as with rewards. The children must perceive both parents as a united front, joined in their efforts to help to teach the child which behaviors are appropriate and which are not acceptable.

Chapter Ten

Runaway Emotions: They're Just a State of Mind

Many parents allow themselves to fall into the trap of believing that they have little or no control over their own emotions. Thus, when upsetting events occur, these parents become victims of runaway emotions; irrational and maladaptive feelings take over, and clear, rational thinking temporarily disappears. Unfortunately, such a situation is harmful to children on several different levels—not only is the upset parent unable to help modify his child's behavior properly, but he is incapable of modeling the very sort of behavior that his child should be learning to exhibit. Helping children to deal with their own feelings requires that you, as a parent, first learn how to curb your own runaway emotions. Of course, in order to make changes in the way you react to your children, you must first understand why it is that you think, feel, and behave as you do.

Different People, Different Styles

You have had an entire lifetime in which to develop styles of reacting. You have responded to countless problems in your life, including everything from a flat tire to the death of someone about whom you cared. Perhaps, at some point, it has occurred to you that different people react in different ways to similar situations. One person may accept a flat tire with calm resolve as he changes it, while another mutters obscenities as he waits for the tow truck. The situation is the same, but the styles of reacting are different. Because of these differences in response, the outcome is likely to be different, as well. The person who handles things calmly is likely to get far more accomplished than is the person who becomes upset and surrenders his emotions to the situation at hand. So, when you are facing a hard problem, handle it in the most adaptive way. Fortunately, PST includes (and in fact is based upon) an approach to curbing runaway emotions. With this in mind, let's take a close look at the fundamentals of doing so.

The Three R's

Everything that you do because of your emotional reactions to the things around you (and especially to your children) can be characterized within a simple PST framework which is made up of *R*eality, *R*esponse, and *R*esult.

Reality: Whatever is actually happening. *Reality* cannot be changed.

Response: The way in which you think or behave in *response* to the problem. You can learn to make your *responses* more appropriate.

Result: What occurs after your *response* to *reality*. The *result* (or outcome) can be positive or negative and depends upon how you chose to *respond*.

The first of these, Reality, refers to whatever it is that is actually occurring (e.g., a situation in which your child has refused to clean up his room, has skipped school for several days, or has stolen money). This is the easy part; you cannot change Reality. Whatever has happened already can no longer be altered by anything that you think or do, so in examining the "three R's," the first thing that you must do is to accept the idea that the past cannot be changed. As you sit quietly and read this book, it is likely that the last statement seemed almost as if it could have gone without saying. Yet, when the average person is confronted with a situation that he doesn't like, he typically begins by deciding that something must be done to undo the problem, or similarly, by attempting to deny Reality. Such thinking is wasteful in that it does nothing to address the real problem, but serves instead to elicit emotional responses which make the situation worse.

Parent: I don't believe it! I just *don't* believe it! My son is a thief. Michael, how could you do such a thing?
Child: Dad, I'm sorry. It was only a pack of gum.
Parent: Only a pack of gum? This can't be happening. I take you to the mall, you get thrown out of a store for stealing, and you say 'only' to me.
Child: I won't do it again, I promise.
Parent: That's not good enough. You shouldn't have done it this time. Sure, it's a pack of gum now, but next it'll be hubcaps, and then cars, and pretty soon you'll be mugging old ladies, and knocking over banks . . . .

In this example, note that the Reality of the situation is that the child has stolen a pack of gum. Unfortunately, instead of facing the situation head-on and attempting to resolve it, the parent succumbs to runaway emotions. While any parent would be upset to find that his child has stolen something (and understandably so), nothing is accomplished by experiencing anger, frustration, and despair, especially beyond the scope of the situation as a whole.

Denying Reality is a Poor Response
The denial of Reality ("I just *don't* believe it!") can only make a bad problem more difficult to face, and projections of a worsening mode of behavior(". . . but next it'll be hubcaps. . .") sends the child a dangerous message: "I have absolutely no faith in you, and I expect you to behave even more inappropriately as time goes on." When dealing with your children, and in attempting to curb runaway emotions, don't deny Reality. The last thing that an effective parent would want to do in a problem situation would be to pretend that Reality does not have to be recognized as such. Remember: You are modeling behavior for your children every time that you interact with them, and behaving irrationally sets a poor example, at best.

Results Come from Responses to Reality
In looking further at the "three R's," it is important to take note of the fact that the Result is determined by the way in which you Respond to Reality. In other words, you can't change Reality,

but you can alter the Result by Responding properly. That means that in order to curb runaway emotions and to increase your effectiveness as a parent, you must Respond in the most appropriate manner, thereby taking control of problems and improving the Result.

Parent: Michael, I am genuinely surprised at you. How could you do such a thing?
Child: Dad, I'm sorry. It was only a pack of gum.
Parent: I realize that, Michael, but the principle is the same no matter what it is that you steal.
Child: I won't do it again, I promise.
Parent: Well, I'd like to think that you wouldn't, but I won't be convinced of that until we figure out why you did it this time. . . .

In this latter example, the parent begins by recognizing Reality. His son has stolen something, and that cannot be changed. However, the "three R's" have not gone unnoticed. Because the parent's Response is a rational and adaptive one, the Result automatically becomes a different one, too. In this case, the child is likely to learn from the mistake that he's made. In that sense, something good will come from something bad, but there are advantages to this approach on other levels, as well. This child is being taught that his parent is someone upon whom he can rely; even when he makes mistakes, he will be able to face his parent, discuss the problem, and feel confident that he will be approached with understanding, rather than with condemnation.

Responses Are a Two-Way Street

Throughout, the parent in the preceding example is modeling appropriate behavior by remaining calm and rational, thus demonstrating that people are responsible for their own behavior. As such, the child is receiving an extra message: Just as his parent can be expected to behave rationally in the face of problems, he (the child) is expected to take charge of his own behavior (and avoid stealing in the future). After all, if the parent were to demonstrate a lack of self-control (as in the first example) by arguing about something that has already happened ("this can't be happening . . . that's not good enough . . . I don't believe it"), he would be sending his child the not-so-subtle message that there are times when people just do whatever they feel like doing, whether it's flying off the handle, or stealing, or anything else. Remember: The Result is a reflection of your Response to Reality; if you want a better Result, then you must commit yourself to offering a better Response. Let's take a look at some other examples, so that the "three R's" can be illustrated further.

Parent: Cory, Mrs. Fielding just called me and said that you broke her living room window with your baseball this afternoon.
Child: That old witch! She loves getting kids in trouble.
Parent: Did you break the window?
Child: Yeah, but it was an accident.
Parent: You're entitled to feel any way that you choose about Mrs. Fielding, but I would have expected you to speak with her yourself, and to apologize to her. I am disappointed in the way that you handled this, Cory. Anyone can have an accident, but your refusal to act responsibly afterward is a problem that we need to discuss further.

The Reality of the broken window is an easy one to see, but the Response in this case was one of careful and deliberate restraint. Many parents in situations like this one would offer a Response of anger that would serve to intimidate the child and to make him even less likely to act responsibly in the future. Why would a child volunteer information about a broken window when he knows that the Result will be an infuriated parent? After all, no parent should feel angry simply because his child has done something wrong; children aren't perfect!

Controlling Results Through Responses
As you become more skilled at your Responses, the Results will become more predictable, because they evolve from clear, rational thinking and you have the solution of the problem as your goal. In this example, had the parent reacted with the typical disdain and frustration that might be expected from those not

trained in PST, the Result would have been two uncomfortable people: a frightened, guilt-ridden child and a furious, irrational parent. Reality would have remained the same (a broken window and a somewhat irresponsible child); but from the untrained Response would have come a different (and less productive) Result. Experimenting with the "three R's" will help you to take note of the irrational nature of your own thinking and behavior, and that realization is the first step in changing your style of tackling problems. Continue to remind yourself: I cannot change Reality, but I can change my Responses to it and therefore can change the Results.

Child: Hey, Mom, what's that you've got?
Parent: These are the cigarettes that I just found in your jacket pocket, Judi.
Child: Oh, wow!
Parent: I thought that we had discussed this already, and that you had promised that you were not smoking anymore.
Child: Yeah, well, I tried not to smoke, but you know . . . .
Parent: No, Judi, *you* know what happens now. Twelve-year-old daughters of mine do not smoke cigarettes. You are grounded for a week for smoking and for another week for lying to me. If you feel afterward that you are going to smoke again, I will take you to the doctor or help you in some other way to stop, but that is an option open to you only when you've completed your punishment. Now, go get ready for dinner.

What do you do when your child is engaging in a behavior that is both dangerous and already forbidden by you? The parent in this example handled things with an appropriate Response. Since, once again, Reality couldn't change, the only alternative remaining to this parent was to change her inclination towards a poor Response. As such, the Result was a fine one: The child discovered that her mother could be rational and logical even when confronted with a problem, and, what is more important, the child learned that she is always better off being honest (". . . and you are grounded for another week for lying to me."). This parent sent clear, consistent messages to her child and handled the situation in a way that is almost certain to ensure that it doesn't repeat itself.

Some More of the Three R's

Now, let's take a look at a set of final examples of the "three R's," handled both appropriately and inappropriately.

Child: Dad, I need you to sign my report card.
Parent: Let's take a look. What? An 'F' in science and another one in math? What the hell have you been doing in those classes, Craig?
Child: I don't know. I guess the teachers don't like me.
Parent: Well, that's the biggest load of you-know-what that I've ever heard. You're just lazy.
Child: Maybe I'm not smart enough for school.
Parent: Oh, you're smart enough all right. What you need is a little old-fashioned discipline. When I was your age, if I'd brought home a report card like this one, my father would have . . . .

What is being accomplished here? The answer is "nothing at all." This parent is dumping his anger and frustration on his child. He is ignoring the Reality of the situation, so his inappropriate Response will lead inevitably to a maladaptive Result. The bottom line here is that a child has a bad report card, and, as a result, two things need to be done: The parent must determine why those grades occurred (was it really laziness, or was it inability?), and then he must determine what is to be done about it (if it was laziness, the child must be given less freedom in which to shirk his responsibilities, and perhaps should be punished; if the grades were the result of a real academic or emotional problem, that difficulty must be resolved through whatever means are necessary). Handling the problem as this parent did will accomplish nothing except to produce anger and frustration for both parent and child (the child not only has bad grades, but an angry and irrational parent with whom to contend). Contrast this example to the one below, in which the parent clearly has studied PST's "three R's."

Child: Dad, I need you to sign my report card.

Parent: Let's take a look. Craig, this shows that you earned only 'F's' in science and in math. I'd like to know why.

Child: I don't know. I guess the teachers don't like me.

Parent: Well, that's a ridiculous statement. Can you back it up with facts? I'm going to ask you again what happened, and this time, I'd like you to answer me realistically.

Child: Maybe I'm not smart enough for school.

Parent: Oh, I think that you're smart enough. You have 'A's' and 'B's' in three other subjects. Maybe you're just not studying science and math because you don't like those subjects.

Child: I hate science and math! That's why I leave those books in my locker. They're boring! I don't want to have to take those classes anymore.

Parent: Well, unfortunately, Craig, hating classes in school does not relieve you of the responsibility for passing those classes. You will study science and math for one hour each day when you come home from school, and if your grades don't go up within two weeks, we'll make it *two* hours of study each day. If you need help, let me know, and we'll arrange for a tutor, but failing grades will not be tolerated.

In this case, the parent faces Reality, offers a rational Response, and has a positive and controlled Result already planned. The child is likely to respond with some initial unhappiness simply because of the nature of the situation, but the important point here is that the child will benefit from what is being done. Remember: Your child does not have to be happy all of the time.

In the first example in this set, the parent was angry, and that emotion interfered with his ability to deal adaptively with the problem. Whenever you permit emotion to obscure your better judgment, you do a great disservice to both yourself and your child. Always strive to set the example of rational behavior for your children, because if you fail to do so, you are not in a position to expect better behavior from them. You are not just the parent, but the adult. Behave like one by taking charge of runaway emotions.

Who's in Charge of My Thoughts Today?

The statement "You control your own thoughts" may not be a difficult one for you to accept; after all, if *you* don't control your thoughts, then perhaps you should have the individual who does control them read this book instead of you. It is astounding that so many adults permit themselves to believe that their own thoughts and feelings somehow evade quick control. Instead, thoughts are always within the control of the individual experiencing them; it's not as if thoughts travel aimlessly through the atmosphere, looking for an easy target to zap. If you're thinking it, then you've chosen to think it, whatever it is. If you're angry or frustrated with your child, then you've *chosen* to react that way instead of handling the situation more appropriately. Irrational thoughts and runaway emotions are all the result of poor self-control on your part, so if you expect your children to behave and to respond appropriately, then you must set the right examples for them. A child who watches his mother have an "emotional meltdown" because he misbehaved is not in a position to learn proper modes of behaving. Instead, he's most likely to model his behavior after that of his irrational parent. Before long, in a scenario like this one, there is both an irrational parent and an irrational child, the child being puzzled by the hypocrisy of a parent expecting him to accomplish something that the parent himself is incapable of doing.

The problem with the control of thoughts is that it is very easy (and even satisfying) to allow yourself to believe that you cannot control what you do or think. If you believe that you have no control over your thoughts, then you may feel as if you don't have to accept responsibility for them or for their consequences. Statements such as "I just can't get that girl off my mind" are irrational in nature. You can think about anything that you choose, and no one can decide what you are going to think, except you. Your thoughts are always within your control, and you can stop and start them as you see fit. When your child says, "I can't concentrate on my studying because I keep thinking about next week's trip," you can identify such a statement as irrational—it doesn't make sense, because thoughts are always chosen. Even when you find yourself thinking about something unpleasant, you have *chosen* to do so. Until now, you may have told yourself that you couldn't help it, but that excuse just won't stand up to scrutiny. No one can *make* you think anything.

Feelings Come from Thoughts

Because you have a far greater degree of control over your thoughts than perhaps you've ever realized, the next logical step in handling runaway emotions would be for you to consider the idea that feelings and thoughts go together. In fact, feelings come from thoughts. Since you have control over your own thoughts, you therefore must have control over your feelings, as well.

Whenever you become angry, that feeling is a direct result of particular thoughts (or beliefs) that you are holding. If, for example, you are angry about being stuck in rush hour traffic, the thoughts (behind the feeling of anger) might be "This isn't fair," "Don't these people have anything better to do than to sit around wasting time on the highway?" "Why don't they all just move a little faster, so that we can all get home?" Because there is no way to feel angry in such a situation without holding some set of irrational thoughts, changing the thoughts is virtually guaranteed to change the feeling. It is impossible, for example, to feel happy while believing that you are miserable. If you actually held such a belief, then your feelings would go along with your thoughts. Sincerely believing that you are miserable is the most effective way known to make you feel that way, too. The things that you choose to think will have a direct effect on the way that you feel. If, for example, you were to hold the belief "I can't stand another summer vacation with the kids at home," then you can fully expect to feel as if you're undergoing something that you can't stand. Because you believe that you can't stand it, you will feel as if you can't stand it. Changing the belief will mean changing the feeling. "I'm not looking forward to another vacation with the kids at home" is very different from "I can't stand it." The idea of being unable to stand something means, by definition, that the accompanying feeling will be intolerable. Irrational thoughts, therefore, lead to unpleasant and maladaptive feelings (runaway emotions). As you become more comfortable with the idea that you control your thoughts (and feelings), you will gradually be able to assume greater responsibility for those thoughts and feelings.

Parent: I thought that I told you to be home on time for dinner.

Child: Sorry that I'm a little late, Mom.

Parent: You are a half-hour late. The roast is cold.

Child: I said that I was sorry. The bus broke down, and everyone had to walk the last mile back from school.

Parent: You never think about responsibility. If you cared about me, you wouldn't keep making me angry this way.

Examining the preceding conversation, you can see easily that the parent is angry. However, that anger is a direct result of her irrational thoughts. Look at the last statement: "If you cared about me . . . ." By holding the belief that her son doesn't care about her, this parent will feel as if she is unloved. Despite the fact that such a perception is probably not valid, the feeling will be just as vivid as if it were. On an even more subtle level, consider the statement "The roast is cold." The unspoken thoughts behind that statement are "having a cold roast is a terrible thing . . . this roast is cold, and it's your fault . . . you are responsible for something terrible." By holding thoughts such as these, the parent is likely to become increasingly upset. Her feelings of anger and outrage are the predictable consequence of her irrational beliefs, and if these beliefs were to change, the feelings would change, as well.

Parent: I thought that I told you to be home on time for dinner.

Child: Sorry that I'm a little late, Mom.

Parent: Where have you been?

Child: The bus broke down, and everyone had to walk the last mile back from school.

Parent: Well, the roast is already cold, but I guess there wasn't any way for you to have avoided this.

This time, the parent reacts with rational thoughts that give way, of course, to adaptive feelings. Obviously frustrated that her son couldn't do anything about being late, and clearly disappointed that the dinner that she prepared is now cold, the parent is nevertheless reacting in a logical and healthy manner. When you think rationally, you will have appropriate feelings.

How All of This Affects Your Kids

When you fail to exercise full control over your thoughts, you automatically lose some degree of control over your feelings. Anger, for example, is a feeling that comes typically from the holding of irrational thoughts, and it is perhaps the clearest of the various runaway emotions.

The Thoughts Behind the Feelings

As we've said, the way to feel appropriately is to take charge of your own thoughts, thus putting an end to runaway emotions. The following chart shows a series of unpleasant feelings, accompanied by the irrational thoughts behind them and the suggested substitutions of more adaptive thoughts (to relieve or prevent the listed emotions).

Emotion	*Irrational Thought*	*Rational Substitute*
Frustration	My child is always acting like he's three years younger than he is.	My child isn't mature enough yet to act as I would like. He'll get there.
Disappointment	My son is a failure for not making the team.	My son can't be good at everything.
Guilt	If I had been a better parent, my child wouldn't have been suspended.	No matter how hard I try, my child is going to make some mistakes.
Anger	How dare my daughter refuse to walk the dog that she talked me into buying?	As a child, my daughter has very different ideas than I do. She has to be taught how to act responsibly.

Emotion is Cumulative and Persistent

One of the greatest dangers with runaway emotions is that they tend to persist, and this occurs for several reasons. A basic PST principle holds that the best predictor of future behavior is past behavior. As such, runaway emotions become a habitual way of reacting, and thus continue to occur. Once you've become accustomed to reacting to your child with anger, you will in all probability continue to do so. Furthermore, an emotion like anger will tend to linger after it has been aroused, meaning that once you permit an emotion to run away, you've set the stage for prolonged feelings of that type. Emotion is also cumulative, in that it tends to build up over time. Remember: Feelings come from thoughts, so when you hold a thought similar to "I've had all that I can take," the associated feeling is going to be one of frustration, and even desperation. Such a thought will lead to the sort of feeling that seems to have taken a while to have developed. The moral here is that since feelings come from thoughts, runaway emotions can be curbed through the monitoring of thoughts. Once emotions take on a runaway nature, it is a clear indication that you lack the self-control needed to guide your own thinking.

Teaching Your Children to Curb Runaway Emotions

Part of effective parenting is being able to help your child to learn more effective styles of dealing with his day-to-day world. Once you have assumed a reasonable degree of control over your own thoughts, you may want to help your child to do the same thing. As a model and a teacher, you can be very effective.

Child: Shut up, Darren! Just shut up, and leave me alone.
Parent: Meredith, what's all the commotion about?
Child: Mom, Darren's calling me bad names again. Make him stop.
Parent: Meredith, I'll take care of Darren, but why are you so upset? You're giving your brother a great deal of power over your emotions. All he has to do is to say something that you don't like, and you go to pieces.
Child: I never thought of it like that.
Parent: Sure, you are letting your emotions take over.

Child: How do I stop?

Parent: You have to get used to thinking differently. I'll bet that when you are called a bad name, you think things like "That's not fair. . .how dare he call me that. . .I don't deserve it. . .it's not true that I'm a ***."

Child: Wow, how did you know?

Parent: Because if you didn't think like that, you couldn't feel like you do. Now, try thinking more like this—I feel sorry for the kind of person who has fun by calling other people bad names. I think that you'll be surprised to find that you'll feel much better.

Your child probably will have less difficulty in controlling his own thoughts than you do, partially because he hasn't had decades in which to practice believing that such control is impossible. Again, the better a model you become for your child, the easier it will be for him to make such behavior an integral part of his personality style.

One of the best methods for teaching children to curb runaway emotions is to challenge their irrational thoughts. In this process, you restate and exaggerate irrational beliefs until they seem so clearly maladaptive that even a child can grasp the necessity of changing them. In order to do so, you must be able to spot the aspects of your child's thinking that do not make sense. Take each point, one at a time, and offer the child a more appropriate substitute for the maladaptive belief. Remember: Since feelings come from thoughts, you must help your child to change his thoughts if he is to feel better.

Child: I want another piece of cake.

Parent: I'm sorry, Jeanne, but you can't have a second piece. You know that the doctor said that you have to lose fifteen pounds.

Child: I know, but I need it, just this once. I have to have just one more little piece.

Parent: No, you have to breathe, and you have to sleep, but you don't have to have cake.

Child: Yes, I do! I need one more piece!

Parent: Jeanne, 'need' means something that you can't do

without. If you don't have more cake, nothing will happen to you. You may allow yourself to feel unhappy for a while, but that will be the result of your belief that you are being deprived of something that you need. You don't *need* cake, you merely *want* it.

In a situation such as this one, the child is likely to see the parent as a guide and as a helper, so if you offer a consistent model of rational thinking, your child will begin to respond to the examples that you've set. At times it will be far easier than at others to demonstrate clear, adaptive thinking, but as the parent (and the adult), it is your responsibility to try always to do so. If you abdicate such responsibility, there are two possible outcomes: Either the child will grow up without the benefit of guidance in his thinking and will eventually mirror your runaway emotions, or he will develop some skill in controlling his thoughts as a result of watching all of your mistakes in reacting.

Parent: Where's that pickle jar? There was one pickle left this morning when I went to work, and I want it.
Child: Dad, I ate the last pickle when I came home from school this afternoon.
Parent: How many times do I have to tell you not to eat the last of something? You are the most inconsiderate kid in the world. I was looking forward to that pickle all day.
Child: Dad, I'm really sorry, but remember, we're talking pickles here. Get a grip on yourself.
Parent: I'm sorry. I just had a rotten day, and I guess that I'm taking it out on you. You're right, it was only a pickle.

In reading that last case example, you probably thought to yourself, "Oh, come on now, no parent would really behave that way." But, in fact, that scene actually occurred several years ago between the members of a family that we saw at our office. Fortunately for all concerned, the father was so upset afterward by the extent of his own runaway emotions that he made a concerted effort to change his style of thinking and never again had to face a scene such as that one. His bright 12-year-old son took a great deal of the credit for helping his father to understand the "three R's" thoroughly, a task that the former had managed to accomplish on his own by observing his father's irrational behavior over a period of time. By learning PST, you should be able to avoid having your children learn to think on a more sophisticated level than you've managed to reach yourself. Let's take another look at an example in which a parent helps her child to abandon runaway emotions in favor of rational thinking.

Child: Mom, I just can't stand going back to my math class anymore. My teacher makes me feel miserable.

Parent: Tracy, how does someone else make you 'feel' anything?

Child: Well, it's just that she's so mean.

Parent: It's all right to think that she's not very nice, but she can't have any effect on your feelings. Feelings come from thoughts, and you control your thoughts.

Child: Okay, then my thought is that she's mean.

Parent: But that's not your only thought. In order for you to feel miserable, you have to hold thoughts that lead to that feeling. What if you were to think instead, 'My teacher may act mean, but that's no big problem for me, because at three o'clock every afternoon she becomes someone else's problem?'

Child: How would that help me?

Parent: By thinking differently, you'll feel differently. If you think of your teacher's personality as a major problem in your life, you'll feel miserable. Think of her as a minor problem instead, and you'll feel relieved. Remember, if you can't change reality, you can change your response and thus change the result. It's the three R's.

As a final example in the controlling of runaway emotions, consider the following situation. In this case, a child is complaining about a punishment that his mother has meted out to him for his failure to bring home a daily report from school. Although the child was warned about the consequences of failing to comply, he neglected to act responsibly and now is angry that the punishment actually is coming about. Note that the parent does not get caught up in runaway emotions herself, but instead thinks rationally and actually helps her child to do the same thing.

Child: I don't think that you're being fair! Why do I have to be punished just for forgetting something? Everybody forgets things—even you forget sometimes.

Parent: That's right, everyone does forget things, but this is the third time this week that you've forgotten. You must learn to be responsible, and I wouldn't be doing the right thing as your mother if I didn't help you to learn that lesson.

Child: Well, you're making me feel really bad by punishing me. Is that what you call 'doing the right thing?'

Parent: Brandon, if you were taking care of a little kid and you saw him run into the street in front of cars, what would you do?

Child: I'd run out and pull him in from the street, and I'd tell him that he can't play there anymore.

Parent: And what if he started crying and saying that he wants to play there?

Child: It wouldn't matter. I'd make him do what's right, even if he didn't like it.

Parent: Well, Brandon, that's exactly what I'm doing with you.

Child: Oh. I get it. I still think that you're being unfair, but at least I understand now.

As this parent did, you can help your child to feel better by thinking more appropriately. Memorize the "three R's," practice them, and share them with your children. You may be surprised to find that after a while it will be difficult to remember that you ever thought any differently.

Question:
"You keep stressing the idea that I can control my own thoughts. But I find that when I get upset at my child, I can't control anything. I just get angry and lose control of myself. What am I doing wrong?"

Answer:

Your mistake comes early in the picture when you get upset. Because feelings come from thoughts, the upset feeling that you experience is the result of thoughts that you are holding at the time. You couldn't feel upset without believing that something has happened which not only can cause such a feeling, but which can justify that feeling, as well. Let's assume, for example, that your child has failed to clean up after making something to eat for himself, and you walk in and find the kitchen in disarray. You probably hold thoughts, such as "I can't stand to see the kitchen like this . . . oh no, this can't be happening again . . . this is awful . . .I'll never get any cooperation from this child." If so, your feeling of loss of control comes from your decision to think irrationally—and, yes, each of the thoughts listed above is irrational. Take, for example, "This is awful." A messy kitchen isn't awful. On the contrary, it is merely irritating. *Awful* is getting hit by a bus. If you take the time to practice the "three R's," you can gain a better understanding of where your feelings and thoughts come from, and what you can do about changing them. When you alter the way in which you're thinking, you'll give up the irrational notion of getting upset without being able to do anything about it.

Question:

"My husband tends to blow everything up out of proportion. The slightest problem becomes a big deal to him, and I'm afraid that both of my children are going to end up thinking the same way. Do I have reason to be concerned?"

Answer:

There's a fairly good chance that after watching their father react inappropriately to minor events, year after year, your children will internalize his style to some degree. As we've said before, one of the premises of PST is that parents are always a model for their children, and that goes for negative behavior as well as for those things which are positive. For example, it would seem absurd for a parent to preach about the dangers of smoking and have a cigarette dangling from his mouth. By the same token, your husband is in no position to help your children to control their runaway emotions, because he has chosen not to bother with his own, as of yet. That means that he's doing them a double-disservice: Not only is he failing to set a good example for them, but he's forcing them to live with someone who behaves irrationally and who must be difficult to reason with. Ask your husband to read the PST chapter on controlling runaway emotions and offer to help him practice some of the basic ideas. If all else fails, set a good example for him and hope that both he and the children learn from it.

Question:

"Do feelings always come from thoughts, or can it sometimes be the other way around? I think that I feel frustrated first, and only then think about what it is that's frustrating me."

Answer:

No, the process always occurs in just one direction: thoughts →feelings. What you've hit upon is the idea that your thoughts are so brief and so irrational in nature that the only thing you take notice of is the feeling aroused by your thoughts. In a situation in which you end up with a feeling of frustration, those thoughts must occur first. After all, where else would such a feeling come from, if not from thoughts? When you think about the concept of frustration, it should become clear that it is a feeling of anguish caused by the irrational belief that a lack of success in achieving something is a major problem. Whether the thwarted goal is as significant as a missed promotion, or as incidental as a lack of success in removing a spot from your child's soiled clothing, you must hold maladaptive thoughts about the situation in order to feel frustrated. By working to change those thoughts into clear, rational beliefs, the feelings associated with them will change, and you should find that you notice enough control to be confident about your own ability to avoid negative feelings in the future.

Question:

"I think that I've become quite good at controlling my emotions by utilizing more rational thoughts, but I'm having trouble teaching my seven-year-old daughter to do so."

Answer:

It is entirely possible that your daughter is simply not yet old enough to grasp the ideas behind what you are explaining to her. It may be that she doesn't even understand the difference between rational and irrational beliefs, and it is perfectly natural for a child of this age to have such difficulty. Rather than push her into a style of reacting that is not yet comfortable for her by explaining things formally, why not demonstrate your control over your own thoughts and emotions whenever you can do so? Over time, your daughter will come to see your style of handling things as a good one, and because she will not have had to grow up with maladaptive parental behavior being modeled for her, she will probably adopt your style as her own. There is no reason for a child to experience runaway emotions when her parent has never held up such behavior as an example. The best thing that you can do for your child right now in this area might be to "show her how it's done," and then challenge whatever irrational beliefs she evidences later on when she is cognitively capable of understanding the concepts.

Chapter Eleven

Allowances:
They're More Than Just Money

When a child is old enough to understand that money can be traded in for goods, he is ready for an allowance at home. The timely dispersion of money to a child is a way of giving him the opportunity to learn that with *cash* comes increased *responsibility*. Additionally, an allowance offers the parent new possibilities for teaching the child proper ways of behaving. For most children, an allowance is appropriate by the time they enter kindergarten.

How an Allowance Can Help

There are many ways in which an allowance can help your child. A quick look at some of these factors reveals that an allowance can help him

- to learn the value of money,
- to learn to make decisions and choices,
- to improve his behavior, if necessary,
- to become more responsible.

How can an allowance do all of this? Keep reading—that's what this chapter is all about.

You Won the $40 Million Lottery!
Will You Keep Your Job?

First, you must appreciate the way in which an allowance typically is viewed by the child. To understand the child's perception, think of what would happen if you won a $40 million state lottery. If you are currently employed, would your motivation on your present job change? Obviously, the amount of money that any person has can affect his motivation and his values, as well as his goals. If you give your child money as he needs it, will he really care about whether or not he earns the allowance that you will offer him? Of course not. By setting up an allowance for a child, however, you place him in the position of needing to comply with the expectations that you hold for him so that he can continue receiving the allowance that he wants and needs. If you expect your child to work (by complying) for his allowance, then you must make the allowance large enough so that the child is willing to work for it, and yet you must be sure to keep it from being so large that the child has enough spare cash to be able to afford "goofing off" when he pleases.

Is 50 Cents a Week Enough?
Some parents offer their children an allowance of 50 cents per week if they do their chores. Assuming that the child earns the 50 cents, how much can he actually do with it? Maybe he can buy half of a candy bar at the movies. When deciding how much of an allowance is appropriate for your child, you must think about how much money he needs during a typical week. If a child is involved in many activities and goes places with friends, obviously he has a need for a larger allowance than a child who is less active. The average 10-year-old might do well with an allowance of $5 per week if he fulfills the requirements for earning the entire amount. Thus, for the purposes of this discussion, we'll use $5 as the allowance amount; the actual dollar amount that is most appropriate for your child could be quite different, however.

An Allowance-a-Day May Keep Irresponsibility Away
Contrary to what most parents believe, it is best to give a child an allowance daily, rather than at the end of the week. By doing so, your child will see the fruits of his labor on a regular basis, and this should reinforce his efforts. Using our $5 figure, the child's daily allowance would be 71 cents or, to make it more practical, let's set the amount at 75 cents per day. It is best to give the allowance at bedtime so that all chores will have been completed before the money actually is dispensed.

Easy Come, Easy Go

Although it would be best to tell your child the exact amount of money he will earn for each of the chores that he completes, you would have difficulty keeping up with this kind of an approach. PST involves using a "fine" system in which money is deducted for each predetermined goal that was not reached.

Setting the Goals

The chores (or the specific behavior) that you expect your child to complete will be based on your life style and personal values. If you are a parent who prefers things to be cleaned up each night before bedtime, you may want to make this a requirement for your child in earning his allowance. In order to set the particular goals (that is, to determine what the child must do to earn the 75 cents per day), think about what you expect of your child on a daily basis. If there are weekly chores, such as taking out the garbage, just use follow-directions-the-first-time-told as a goal. This will allow you to have the non-daily chores come under the daily category. Once you have identified the daily goals, make up a chart on a sheet of paper stating exactly what is expected and how much money will be deducted if the child does not comply. Compliance means that you do not have to remind him; he must do the task on his own.

The allowance system should not consist of more than four or five goals. We recall vividly a parent who took our advice about setting up an allowance for her child. Unfortunately, the list of requirements to earn the allowance was three pages long, and, of course, this was too much to expect any child to remember. On a more realistic level, let's look at some typical goals for a 10-year-old child.

If I forget to do this	*I will lose this much each time*
Make my bed before I eat or watch TV or play.	10 cents
Clean my room and put things away before I go to bed.	15 cents

Put any of my things I have left around the house in their proper place before I go to sleep.	5 cents per item
Bring home the right books to do my homework.	20 cents
Follow directions the first time I am told by my mom or dad.	10 cents per direction

Definitions That I Must Understand

1. Making my bed means that no part of the blanket will touch the floor. The pillows will be neatly placed at the center of the front of the bed. The blanket will be neatly placed to cover the mattress.

2. Cleaning my room and putting things away before I go to bed means that my trash can will be emptied into the big garbage can downstairs. My books will be placed back on the bookshelves. All toys, games, and other things will be put away. There will be no garbage or scraps of paper on the floor. If I forget any one of these things, I will lose the whole 15 cents.

3. When I get into bed, one of my parents will look around the house. For each of my things that I have left lying around, I will lose 5 cents. If I were to leave a pair of socks in the kitchen, it would count as two things, which means that there will be 10 cents deducted. The same will go for shoes. My parents will never put these things away for me. They will put them in a box in the hallway closet. I must check that box each day for things of mine and put away whatever is in there, or I will lose the same money tomorrow for leaving these things out again.

4. If I forget to bring home from school a book that I need in order to do my homework, I will lose 20 cents. If my parents find out about this a few days later, they will deduct the money on that day instead. I will try to be honest and tell them

when I have forgotten. If I am honest, they will deduct the money, but they will not yell.

5. When my parents ask me to do something, I will do it the first time that I am told. If I do not follow directions the first time, I will lose 10 cents. Once I have lost the 10 cents, I still will be expected to go ahead and follow the directions. If, at that point, I still don't do what I was told, I will be punished. My parents will, of course, tell me what the punishment is to be.

Be Specific

As you can see, it is very important that you be specific in explaining what you expect from your child. By defining exactly what each rule means and what expectations you have, a lot of confusion can be avoided. We suggest that you write down for your child exactly what you expect of him, just as we have done above. This will prevent you from arguing about what you said originally.

But My Child May Not Want to Do This!

As we discussed in other chapters, don't be concerned with how your child reacts when you implement this system; he has no choice as long as you stick to the program. Remember also that, once again, you are doing what is good for your child, so he doesn't have to like it.

Be One Step Ahead of Mr. Stubborn

A stubborn child may voice an attitude represented by the statement, "I'd rather lose the money than do the chore. Who cares about the money!" Since, as a parent, you need to think ten steps ahead of the child, plan for this possibility. Tell your child that if during any full week (Monday through Sunday night) he fails to earn at least half of his allowance ($2.50 in our example), he will be restricted from some favorite privileges (e.g., using his bicycle, watching TV) until he has had a week in which he did earn at least half of the maximum amount. By doing this, the child will be further inconvenienced if he attempts to avoid his responsibilities. Incidentally, you can avoid disagreements by writing down this rule for the child so that he cannot say, "You never told me that."

The Child Must Use His Own Money

Now that you have the allowance system in place, you must make sure that your child begins to see that he really needs the money. Put him in a position where he has to use his money to buy the things that he wants for himself. Kids' "junk," such as the plastic bugs that are sold in toy vending machines at the supermarket, should always be purchased by the child with his allowance money. When you are shopping with your child and he asks for something that is not on your family's shopping list, you can reply, "You have to buy that with your own money." Most of the things that a child wants, other than school supplies, meals, and clothing, can be purchased with his own money. Of course, if it's something that you want to buy for him, or if it's something special that he deserves, it is always your option to make the purchase.

I'll Gladly Pay You Tuesday for a Hamburger Today

Just as Wimpy in "Popeye" used to say, "I'll gladly pay you Tuesday for a hamburger today," your child will probably give you a similar line. Stick to your plan! Do not allow your child to manipulate you. Remember: *There is no such thing as a manipulative child, but there are parents who allow their children to manipulate them.*

Child: Mommy, I want those chocolate chip cookies. Get them for me!
Parent: No, Patrick. I've already selected the cookies that most of the family asked for. If you really want those cookies, you'll have to pay for them with your own money.
Child: But I have only 15 cents left. I spent the rest of my money playing video games. Please . . . I'll be your best friend if you get the cookies for me.
Parent: If you don't have the money, you'll just have to wait until you save enough to buy them. I am not discussing this with you any further.
Child: Come on, you never get me anything!

In this dialogue, the parent refused to continue discussing the child's desires. The mother let Patrick know clearly that the discussion was closed. At this point, the child could have whined and begged all that he wanted to, but the mother was refusing to answer him or to pay any attention to his continued requests for the cookies.

Once, we worked with a family that had a bright and active 7-year-old. The mother had started an allowance system with him, and one day when she and her son went to a rodeo where the child saw a man selling balloons, he, of course, wanted one. When he asked his mother for a balloon, she reminded him that such "junk" had to be purchased with the money that he had received as his allowance. The boy asked the salesman about the price of a balloon, and in a few seconds, the boy returned to his mother and said, "I'm not spending a whole dollar of my money on that stupid thing!" The mother commented that prior to implementing the allowance system, her son would whine, cry, and beg for as long as an hour in a similar situation. Once he learned that his mother would not give in, and that he had to use his own money for such purchases, he stopped whining. In other words, the child's values changed when he had to use *his money*. He didn't care about using his mother's money to buy "stupid" things, but it was a different story when it came to his own money.

To achieve similar results, you must continually put your child in the position of having to use his own money. If you are involved in a family activity, such as going to the movies, you might pay for the admission but ask the child to pay for his snack, or for extra snacks beyond the first one. As a parent, you might say, "I will buy you one thing at the refreshment stand. It could be a snack, or perhaps a drink. Anything else that you want has to come out of your own money." If the child doesn't have the money, then he should miss out on whatever it is that he wants to buy. Remind yourself that it is okay if this happens, because he needs to learn from experience that money is limited. Once he spends it, it is gone. Again, your child will be learning a new value system from the allowance technique because now he must think about how he wants to spend his money. He will come to realize that once it is gone, he will not be able to buy anything else until he earns more money.

You Can Have What You Want—If You Pay for It

The child should be allowed to use his money in any manner that he wishes, except for things that could be hazardous to his or others' safety or health (e.g., you might restrict him from purchasing gum). Some parents make children save half or part of their money in the bank. It is good to encourage saving, but most children cannot project into the future. Thus, money in the bank does not, to the child, seem as if it is his. Let the child use his money in the manner that he selects, as long as it is spent within the guidelines that you may wish to set up. If he does want to save some of the money, then let him withdraw it when he wants to spend it.

If You Waste It, You Pay for It

Once a child has money, he can learn to be more responsible, and part of that educational process involves assuming responsibility for anything that he wastes or destroys. For example, if Joan leaves her bedroom light on when she leaves for school, her parents could ask her to pay for the wasted electricity. Although it might be only 25 cents, she probably will remember to turn off the light on subsequent occasions. As an adult, you pay for wasted electricity (as your monthly bills continue to rise) if you leave the lights on. In a similar manner, your child is learning, if she is held responsible for what she chooses to waste.

On another level, you may know exactly what we mean when we say that many children have "big eyes." In this example, Laura is in the ice cream store, and her father tells her that she can have a small cone. Instead, Laura insists on having a double-scoop of ice cream.

Parent: Laura, you never finish what you order. I am not going to pay for a large cone and waste money. If you really want the large cone and you think that you can eat it, I'll buy it for you. However, if you don't finish it, you will pay me for whatever is left. The cone costs a dollar twenty. If you finish only half of it, you'll owe me sixty cents. You will pay me for whatever portion of the cone that you don't eat.

Child: Forget it! I'm not gonna pay you anything.

Parent: That's okay, I'll get you the small cone.

Child: No! I don't want anything then!
Parent: Fine, that's your choice, but it's our turn now. Wait
at that table while the rest of the family orders.

Notice that the father does not pay any attention to Laura's
displeasure, nor does he mention the threat that she won't have
any ice cream. He lets her see that he will not be influenced by
her demands or threats, and because Laura ends up without having her ice cream, it is unlikely that she'll behave this way again.

Don't Take Away What They Don't Have

Never take away any money that the child has not as yet
earned. In the preceding example of the ice cream cone, Laura
might have taken her chances in getting a double-scoop cone. If
she had gotten it and then finished only half, she would have
owed her father 60 cents. Laura had no money, because she had
spent all of her allowance. Her parents would have made a mistake if they had said, "We will take the 60 cents out of tonight's
allowance." If you take away from the child money that she has
not yet earned, this could have a negative effect on her motivation for other things, since she would know that she already had
lost the opportunity to earn the money. The PST approach is to
have the child work off the money by doing extra chores. So, if
Laura owes her father 60 cents, she might be assigned the chore
of washing the family's dinner dishes that night, not just her own
dishes as might be the case otherwise. The extra work would be
her way of paying for the wasted ice cream. This way, she still
would have a chance to earn money that evening.

It's Not Right to Bribe a Kid

Many parents react to the allowance program by saying, "I
won't bribe my child in an effort to get him to do what is expected of him." We are not suggesting bribery, for bribery is a
completely different concept. To help you in ascertaining the difference, let's look at an example of what we would consider to
constitute bribery. In this case, a child is touching all of the things
on the shelves in a supermarket.

Parent: Stop touching those things. How many times have I told you not to touch things in stores. I don't know what I'm going to do with you.

Child: I'm sorry.

Parent: If you do not touch another thing on the shelves for the rest of the time that we are in the store, I will buy you a 'Milky Way' bar when we leave.

Child: Okay, but remember, you promised.

This is bribery because the child first had to do something "bad" before the "reward" was offered. Thus, the child in such a situation will learn from experience that if he acts up, his parents will offer him a present so that he will behave in a more acceptable fashion. In this example, of course, the child should have been punished.

The PST approach calls for the parent to set firm guidelines for the child. Then, the child's access to everyday privileges should be made directly contingent upon his meeting predetermined goals. This is *not* bribery; it is reality. We propose that instead of giving your child money as he needs it, you set up an organized allowance program for him. Then, when he gets the money, he will know that he was expected first to fulfill his obligations. Just giving things to a child without requiring him to demonstrate that he has been pulling his own weight is what really could be destructive to him. A child must learn to meet responsibilities before he can expect the privileges that will come afterward. This is the way society's institutions (i.e., schools, the work place) are set up, so by requiring your child to act responsibly now, you are helping to prepare him for what he will be required to face outside of the home.

Question:

"My 12-year-old's allowance is $5 per week, and my 9-year-old can earn three dollars and fifty cents per week. The 9-year-old keeps complaining that it is unfair, and that we don't care about him as much as we do his older brother. Should we raise the younger child's allowance?"

Answer:

It is not necessary always to try to make things equal. However, to be fair, the 9-year-old should understand that he will get a raise when he reaches the age of 10. When he is 12, he, too, will get $5 per week. Future increases not only give a child something to look forward to, but permit him to see that as he gets older, his need for more money will be respected. Don't try to justify your decision to the 9-year-old. If you do, he will see that you are willing to negotiate. One explanation to him about the way in which his allowance will increase as he gets older is enough. Since things cannot always be fair and equal, he will have to accept your method of determining how much each child can earn as an allowance.

Question:

"After I gave my daughter her allowance, I had to punish her (and her brother) for fighting. My daughter took her one dollar bill, tore it into pieces, and shouted, 'I don't need your stinking money, and you can't control me!' I told her that she will not get an allowance anymore, since she has shown no respect for money. Now, I wonder if I really should have done that."

Answer:

Your daughter destroyed the money to "get back" at you for punishing her. Once you give her the money, it becomes hers, and she should be able to do whatever she wants with it. Although she tried to upset you, she actually tore up her own money and therefore no longer had it to spend. Probably, in such a situation, it is more important for you to show her that she cannot get a reaction from you, and that you will just ignore such inappropriate attempts at controlling your emotions. Also, by taking away her allowance permanently, you will find it difficult to set up a behavior management plan because now you frequently will have to rely on punishments other than the deducting of a portion of allowance. Additionally, you will have to start giving her money out of your pocket as she asks for things. Perhaps, at this point, it might be best for you to tell her that since she handled the money so badly, you will cut her allowance in half for the next four weeks.

Question:

"My son has been told repeatedly that he cannot play baseball in front of our house. He did not listen to us, and ended up breaking a large window in our neighbor's home. We had to reimburse the neighbor for the full cost—three hundred and seventy-five dollars. Can we really expect our son to pay us back such a large amount?"

Answer:

Your son must learn to take responsibility for his actions. Therefore, he now owes you $375. Since this could equal a year's allowance, it would be inappropriate to take away his allowance for such a long time. Your son must do work for you as a way of paying you back the $375. We suggest that you do not allow your son to have access to special activities or pleasures until the money is worked off. This means that he will not go to any special places, and will not watch television or have any special treats, such as movies or skating, until you are fully compensated. This could take a few months, and you will have to be prepared to watch him "suffer" while he sticks to the punishment. If he has some valuable possessions (such as a television or stereo in his bedroom), either take them away and hold them as collateral or teach him to resist temptation by avoiding their use even while they remain in his room. Let your son know that you will hold his things (or that he will have no use of them) until he has worked off the money. You can also give him credit toward the money owed for some of his missed activities. For example, since he cannot watch television, credit him $1 every few days for the saved electricity. If the family goes fishing and he must go along rather than be left at home alone, let him sit and observe, and credit him $3 dollars for the tackle and bait that you otherwise would have bought him. These credits can be taken off the $375 that he owes you. He could be assigned chores to help work off the money, such as cleaning the garage, cleaning the bathrooms, washing the family's dishes, folding all of the laundry. He will have a few months without weekend activities since he will be doing whatever chores you choose to assign to him. We anticipate that this experience will teach him something about respecting other people's property. If you were to pay the neighbor, yell at your son, keep him in the house for a few days, and make him apologize, he would not really learn anything. He broke the window, and therefore should be responsible for paying for it.

Question:

"Whenever I go to the supermarket with my daughter, she wants to buy a little toy or special snack, but she always forgets to bring her money. She tells me, 'I'll pay you back in the house if you lend me the money.' What do you think about letting her borrow the money?"

Answer:

It is fine to let her borrow the money if she has enough to cover it at home, and if she pays you back when you return home. If the day goes by and she forgets to pay you, it is time for her to learn that a promise is always to be taken seriously. You could then tell her that for the next two weeks you will not lend her any money if she forgets to bring her money to the store, since she did not keep her word that last time. If you do this, however, remember to stick to what you have told her. If your daughter is to learn anything about the value of a promise, then don't break yours.

Chapter Twelve

How to Praise and to Criticize Your Child

When praise is used appropriately, it can help to build your child's self-confidence and security, to enhance his motivation, and generally to encourage him to feel good about himself. You've heard the term *self-concept* mentioned many times. A child's self-concept (how he feels about himself) is related to the kind of things his parents tell him about himself, as well as to the feedback that he gets from other people in his environment. When a child gets positive feedback about his efforts and his accomplishments, and constructive criticism about his shortcomings, the child's self-concept is enhanced.

Specific Praise

Use specific praise to describe to the child his efforts, his accomplishments, and your feelings. By using specific praise, you can avoid evaluating your child and his personality, and you will not come across as making a judgment about him. When you praise your child, deal with the real events that are happening. Here are some examples that will help you to see the difference between specific praise and critical praise.

Specific Praise	*Critical Praise*
Thank you for cleaning the living room. It has never looked better.	You are a great worker, Sure, your school work is lousy, but you'd make a great janitor!
I like the ashtray that you made—it is fantastic.	Keep busy with your ceramics; at least it keeps you out of trouble.

I like the way that you're practicing the piano. Here's some milk and cookies, so take a break for five minutes.

You're certainly being a good girl for a change.

When you use specific praise, you are telling the child exactly what you like ("You and your brother are playing together so well. I really like to see you behaving like that. I think that we'll go out to McDonald's for a treat tonight."). When you use critical praise, you are making some type of judgment about the child's personality, such as "You are a good boy," and you may be sending the child a mixed message in the process.

How to Criticize Your Child

The type of criticism used by many parents is not helpful to children. To be effective, criticism should tell the child what he has to do in order to improve a behavior. This type of criticism does not attack the child as a person ("You're a bad boy" or "Why do you follow your sister's example and act like a slob?"). Instead, constructive criticism deals with what actually happened; it focuses on specific behavior. Here are some guidelines for using criticism in such a way as to make it helpful:

1. Never attack the child's personality ("You're dumb!").
2. Look at the actual situation or behavior and decide how you would like the child to change that behavior.
3. In your statement to the child, tell him *specifically* what he is doing that is inappropriate.
4. The second part of your statement should tell the child what he needs to do to change or to improve.
5. If necessary, another part of the statement can be added telling the child what consequences will occur if the situation is not improved.

Let's look at an example that will help you to see the difference between effective and ineffective criticism.

On the way home from the supermarket, 12-year-old Joseph turns pale and becomes nervous. He has left his wallet at the store. The parent who uses criticism appropriately might say,

"Let's call the store as soon as we get home, because someone might have found it and turned it in. If not, you'll have to accept the consequence that goes with not taking care of your wallet — you will have neither the money nor the pictures that were in it." A far less effective approach might be to say, "You are so stupid and careless. Why can't you ever be more careful?" Parents who constantly give their children negative feedback and who don't look for appropriate things to praise may contribute to the deflation of their child's self-concept. Give yourself this simple test to make a judgment about the way that you criticize.

Pretend that an observer has followed you around your house all day. He has a chart with a + at the top of one column and a — at the top of the other column. Every time that you give positive feedback to your children, the observer puts a check in the plus column. Whenever you say something negative, the observer puts a check in the negative column. At the end of the day, which column will have the most checks? If there are many more negative than positive checks, you need to change the balance. If there isn't at least a rough equality between the two columns, you may be affecting your child's self-concept negatively.

By praising and criticizing your child in a concrete and specific manner, you will enhance his self-esteem. There are probably thousands of incidents each year for which you could praise your child using the methods that we've just discussed.

When to Praise

It is both helpful and appropriate to praise a child so that you can:

1. Describe to the child his efforts ("Thanks for washing the car. It looks great!").
2. Describe to the child his thoughtfulness ("You shared your candy with Nancy. That was very considerate.").
3. Describe to the child his accomplishments ("I like the drawing that you made. It shows real artistic ability.").
4. Describe to the child how he complied with a rule ("You came home on time, just as you promised.").

5. Describe cooperative behaviors to your child ("The two of you are playing nicely together.").
6. Indicate to the child a positive behavior that you have observed ("You folded your laundry without needing to be asked. That's great!").

Exercises in Praising

For each of the following situations, write down what you would say to *praise* your child (be sure that you use specific praise):

1. Bobby brings home an "A" on his spelling paper.
2. Rachel just said the "9 times" table correctly.
3. Rachel and Bobby have been playing for 20 minutes without fighting.
4. When you put the dinner on the table, Bobby says, "Thank you."
5. Bobby holds the store's door open for you.

Remember, the way that specific praise works: Your responses should *describe* to the child what he did that was appropriate.

Possible Responses to Praise

1. Bobby, you must have worked very hard to get those spelling words right. That is fantastic!
2. Rachel, that's incredible! You learned the hardest table in only two days.
3. Bobby and Rachel, you have been playing together so nicely that I am going to make some popcorn as a special treat for you. Good work!
4. Bobby, good manners! You said 'Thank you' when I put the food down.
5. Thank you for holding the door open for me. That showed good manners.

Criticism

What would you say if you were to employ criticism in the following situations? Remember that you must tell the child what he did that was inappropriate, as well as what will happen as a result.

1. Rachel spills juice on the floor.
2. Bobby leaves the 'Pepsi' bottle open, and the soda loses its fizz.
3. Rachel forgets to bring home her math book as she is required to do.
4. Bobby keeps interrupting you while you are on the telephone.
5. Rachel eats a cookie after you've told her that she cannot have a snack until after dinner.

Possible Responses to Criticism

1. Rachel, you spilled juice on the floor. Get a paper towel and clean that up, right now.
2. Bobby, you left the 'Pepsi' bottle open and the fizz went out, so now it's spoiled. That is a waste of money, so you will not be allowed to have any soft drinks for the next week.
3. Rachel, I told you to bring home your math book and you did not. You will not watch television tonight, and you will not go out to play. If you bring the book home tomorrow, you can again have those privileges.
4. Bobby, you interrupted me while I was on the phone, and it was not urgent that you speak to me. I am deducting twenty cents from today's allowance.
5. Rachel, I told you that you could not have a snack until after dinner, but you ate a cookie. Now, you will not be allowed to have any snacks for twenty-four hours. If you do try to sneak another snack, I will have to take your bicycle away for a week.

Sample Parent Reactions

For each of the following situations, does it seem to you that the parent reacted appropriately? If not, what could be done to improve the reaction?

1.   Steven gets a detention at school for running in the school hallway.

Parent: What's the matter with you? Why can't you follow school rules? Get in your room and stay there all night! If you want to be bad, you can stay in your room.

---

2.   Cheryl is sent to her room without privileges for punishment.

Parent: Don't touch anything in the room while you're punished.
Child: I'll touch whatever I want to (she touches her radio, a doll, a puzzle, and a stuffed animal).
Parent: I told you not to touch anything! If you touch something again, I'll take it away. Don't you dare touch anything!
Child: I don't care if you do take it away!
Parent: Okay, you're finished! Now, give me that damned doll.

---

3.   Shelly gets an "A" on her spelling test.

Parent: Good girl! You are so smart! I knew that you could do this for me!

---

4.   Ronald chews gum in the house. He knows that he is not permitted to do this.

Parent: Get that out of your mouth! What the hell is the matter with you? Why can't you listen?

Comments on Reactions

In Example 1, Steven's father is making statements that would be meaningless to the child. A child can never answer the question, "What is the matter with you?" Asking, "Why can't you follow school rules?" also is useless, since a child would be unlikely to offer a response. Moreover, there isn't any real question about why he *can't* follow school rules; the fact is that he has *chosen* not to do so. Using words such as "bad" means that the child is being labeled, and yet he is not being told directly what it is that he did wrong. The words being used by the father make it appear as if anger is being projected at the child. The father should have strived instead to let the child know what he did that was inappropriate and what the consequence would be. That could have been done without generating anger. An appropriate set of statements might have been, "You are expected to follow school rules. Since you violated those rules by running in the hallway, you will stay in your room until it's time to go to school tomorrow morning."

In Example 2, Cheryl lets her parent know that she can do whatever she wants to do. The parent reacts to this by threatening her and by repeating what was said. Here, the parent is getting angry and the child may get some satisfaction from seeing such a reaction on the parent's part. Since the child originally was told not to touch anything, the parent should have taken it away immediately without having given any further warnings or threats. Repeating a warning or a direction more than once to a child will teach the child that she does not have to listen to what the parent says, simply because it will not be enforced. In this case, when the parent first told the child, "Don't touch anything in the room," the statement should have contained the pending consequence. This way, the child would have known what to expect. The parent should have said, "Don't touch anything in the room while you're punished. If you do, then whatever you touch will be taken away from you permanently." With a specific statement such as this, it would be easier for a parent to enforce the rules that are set.

In Example 3, the parent reacts to the daughter's "A" grade by labeling her as "good" and "smart." The parent says, "I knew that you could do this for me." A more appropriate statement would have been, "You got an 'A' on your spelling test, and that's terrific; you must have worked very hard. You should be very proud of yourself." With such a statement, the parent would be recognizing the child for her achievement and would be letting her know that she should have pride in herself, as opposed to a sense of pride and glory going to the parent. Since the child did the hard work, the child is entitled to feel proud of herself.

In Example 4, the parent again reacts in an angry manner which will not help the child to improve his behavior or to learn from the experience. A better series of statements might have been, "Take the gum out of your mouth and throw it away. Because you bought gum and chewed it in the house, which you are not permitted to do, I will not allow you to take any money out of the house for the next week. Since you are using money to purchase things that you are not permitted to have, you must learn not to do such things." Here, the parent would be offering specific points in telling the child what he did that was inappropriate and what consequences will result from his behavior. It is important to note that this can be done without any anger being involved.

Question:
"How can I possibly be positive and criticize my child at the same time?"

Answer:
Criticism should be helpful to the child. There is no purpose in yelling out harsh words or calling a child names, such as "pig," "slob," or "stupid." If a child were bombarded frequently with such harsh scoldings, he would become demoralized and his self-esteem would sink to a very low level. You want your child to see that you are concerned about him, so that when he makes a mistake and does something wrong, it does not affect how you feel about him as a person. Whether you have to use criticism or punishment, what purpose would be served by showing the child that you are rejecting him or that you see him as an inferior being?

Question:
"How often do I need to praise my child to make sure that he gets enough 'strokes' to continue a positive new behavior?"

Answer:
Since praising a child every minute would be both impractical and artificial, your best bet may be to use praise selectively. When you are trying to encourage your child to establish a new behavior, you would at first praise every display of that new behavior. Later, you may choose to praise it only once every few

times that the new behavior is demonstrated by the child. For example, if you are trying to help your child to improve his manners, then every time that he holds the door open for you when you are walking behind him, recognize this action with "Thank you for holding the door. That was really showing great manners." Every time that he holds the door open for you during the first few days that you are working on reinforcing this behavior, praise him. After a few days, just start saying "thank you" each time that he does it, and do the more lengthy praise every third or fourth time that he holds the door open. If you start praising him randomly (such as the third time that he does it, then the fifth time, then the second time, then the third time), he will not be able to predict when to expect a reaction from you. This type of random praising is the most effective way to strengthen a behavior.

Question:

"I tried the exercise that you gave on praising, but I can't seem to get it just right. I guess that I'm in the habit of being too critical with my kids. What can I do to change?"

Answer:

When you see one of your children displaying a behavior that is worthy of praise, just stop and ask yourself these two questions:

  a. Exactly what is it that my child did that is worthy of praise?
  b. How can I incorporate my answer to "a" into a sentence?

If Jackie takes her dinner dishes to the sink without being asked, you might answer "a" by telling yourself, "Jackie took her dishes to the sink without being asked." To answer "b," you might now make a sentence that would tell Jackie exactly what she did that was "good." For example, you might reply, "Jackie, you took your dishes to the sink, and I did not have to ask you to help out that way. Thank you." Over a period of time, you might be surprised at how easily you will be able to praise your children.

Question:

"What tone of voice should I use when I praise my daughter's behavior? I want to sound just right so that she'll know that the praise is genuine."

Answer:

Your voice *must* express enthusiasm, excitement, and your feeling of being pleased with the child's behavior. Praise in a monotone or unemotional voice is useless. There actually have been research studies that have shown the need for enthusiasm on the part of the adult if praise is to serve as an effective reinforcer of a child's behavior. Your facial expression should also reflect your excitement with the child's appropriate behavior. If the child does not see that you are sincere about your reaction to her behavior, you may as well use a computer to praise her, since without the pleasure and excitement in your voice, the praise will have little or no value at all.

Chapter Thirteen

The Hyperactive Child: You Need Something Special up Your Sleeve

There probably have been at least a few times when you've been convinced that your child, like so many others, is hyperactive. However, diagnosing your child as *hyperactive* is a task that is more difficult than you might imagine. A child who acts out a great deal may not be deserving of that label, and it takes a skilled professional to offer the determination with any degree of accuracy. The diagnosis of an "attention deficit disorder with hyperactivity" should be made by a pediatrician or pediatric neurologist only after an examination and a thorough evaluation and collection of observations on the child's behavior at home and at school. Also, it is not advisable to label a child as hyperactive unless the child has a complete psychological evaluation.

The Psychological Evaluation

This evaluation consists of individually administered tests to measure intelligence, academic achievement, memory, concentration, coordination and perceptual skills, and personality. While administering these tests, the psychologist has several hours to observe the child. These observations, combined with the test data, can help in arriving at a realistic diagnosis that can aid in working with the child. A child should be checked to eliminate the possibility of a vision or a hearing problem which could have an effect on his behavior. All of this should be done before one even thinks of placing a label on a child, and certainly before attempting to treat hyperactivity.

What It All Means

An attention deficit disorder with hyperactivity is often diagnosed when a child's attention span appears to be that of a younger child. Such a child also may have difficulty controlling his impulses (i.e., doing things without thinking about the associated consequences first). He may often be restless, and he probably has had trouble following rules since early childhood. Generally, hyperactivity starts in infancy; it does not just appear magically at the age of 9. Hyperactivity also will occur across many situations, rather than just in school. In other words, if a child truly is hyperactive, he will be likely to evidence this problem at the movies, while watching television, while reading, while playing with friends, or while doing a puzzle. Although the child's activity level may vary depending upon his interest in whatever he is doing, the problem must be visible in more than just one environment.

Professionals Don't All Agree
No definitive conclusion has been reached in the professional community as to what hyperactivity really constitutes. It could be an imbalance in brain chemistry, a dysfunction with the section of the brain that deals with selective attention, or some other neurological problem. It is also important to remember that a person can act "hyper" without actually being hyperactive. A child who is tense, anxious, or who has a "type A" personality may appear to be suffering from this syndrome, although he really is not hyperactive. Thus, it is important that a proper differential diagnosis be made by a qualified professional before you reach conclusions on your own.

The Hyperactive Child
Hyperactive children (more of whom are boys than they are girls) typically are described as children who cannot appreciate the long-term consequences of their behavior and who do not learn very well from experience. They are often disruptive and non-compliant in the classroom and are constantly out of their seats because they are not working on the tasks that have been assigned. As a group, hyperactive children often have problems with handwriting skills; handwriting problems are reported more often in the population of hyperactive children than they are among non-hyperactive children. Hyperactive children tend also to have emotional problems. It is not uncommon for such a child to hear teachers and parents say, "You are out of your seat

... what is the matter with you? ... why can't you sit still?" When negative comments occur perhaps 20 times a day, the child begins seeing himself as different from others and as being a "problem." After this has gone on for years, the child's self-esteem and emotional development almost certainly will have been injured.

Quite often, hyperactive children have problems with sleeping, and they awaken more during the night than does the typical child of the same age. Although research hasn't confirmed this sleeping problem to be related directly to hyperactivity, therapists who work with hyperactive children often have observed sleeping difficulties. Many hyperactive children after sleeping for only a few hours will appear to have a lot of energy and to be free of fatigue.

It has been observed that hyperactive children often can tolerate more pain than can children who are not hyperactive. Also, hyperactive children, as a group, tend to be more prone to colds and to other types of respiratory infections than are their non-hyperactive peers.

Diet
Although there has been a lot of talk about how diet affects children's activity levels, research has not confirmed the relationship between diet and hyperactive behavior. When a parent puts a child on a special diet, the child begins to receive so much parental attention that he starts improving as a result of this increased care. When a parent has to prepare special meals and do special shopping for a child, the child may respond to all of the parent's concern and to all of the invested time rather than to the diet itself. There is nothing wrong with trying a sugar-free, additive-free diet with a child, especially since it represents obviously better nutrition. However, with most hyperactive children, the special diet will probably not be enough to reduce the problem.

Medication
If a child actually is diagnosed as suffering from an attention deficit disorder with hyperactivity, medication may be suggested. It is estimated that over a half-million children in the

United States take medication daily to help to increase their attention span and to reduce their hyperactivity. When medication is prescribed, it is very important for the parents to follow the physician's directions in giving the medication to the child. It is also important to have regular reports from the child's teacher(s) regarding observations of the child's behavior in school. These teacher-reports should be presented to the physician to help in determining the proper dosage of medication. Also, the physician needs to know of any side effects that may be occurring while the child is taking any medication (such as "Ritalin"). When a child is on medication for hyperactivity, teachers and parents should observe the child, taking note of:

1. How well the child responds to rewards and punishments.
2. How the child acts with other children.
3. How the child is performing academically.
4. The child's level of aggression.
5. The child's appetite.
6. Physical complaints such as stomachaches, headaches, tremors of the fingers or other parts of the body, nervous habits such as a twitch or blinking, skin tone problems (e.g., too pale), and changes in weight.

Whether the child is or is not on medication for hyperactivity, the behavior management techniques suggested throughout this book are critical for a child with this problem. The hyperactive child is in need of structure and of consistency in his parents' attempts to deal with his behavior. The use of daily progress report forms that the child brings home from school is quite important. As discussed in Chapter Eight, the child's receipt of everyday privileges in the home environment should be based upon his meeting a reasonable goal that has been set up for his school behavior and work. It is extremely important to reinforce (with praise, extra privileges, special gifts or activities) any small improvement whatsoever.

The Need for Movement
Since many hyperactive children need to engage in a lot of movement, it is unreasonable to expect such a child to sit in a seat for a full hour. Therefore, programs often have to be adjusted so

that a child might be required to do assignments or homework in blocks of 15 or 20 minutes, with a short break or opportunity to move around before continuing the work. A break should consist of activities involving movement, such as going around the classroom to pick up the trash, bringing something to another room, or working on a puzzle.

Unmet Needs in School

Although most schools have special programs for children who are emotionally handicapped or learning disabled, it is rare to find a program that is geared to the unique needs of a hyperactive child. Such a program should consist of more physical education time than is usually allotted for non-hyperactive children, and the other components of such a program should include a well-organized behavior management program, daily reports to parents, and emphasis placed on remediating the student's deficits (e.g., in reading, math).

The Kitchen Timer

Believe it or not, using a kitchen timer can help a child to stay on task when he is doing his homework and schoolwork. It should be explained to the child that you are going to watch to see if he will stay at his seat and do the work that he is given. Whenever the child hears the bell of the timer ring, he or she should look at the parent or teacher for a signal. If the parent or teacher nods his head "yes," it means that the child has been on task since the timer was started. The timer should be set for different time intervals each time it is used. During the first few days that the timer is used, emphasis should be put on short time periods (for example, 3 or 4 minutes), and these periods should be increased as the child demonstrates that he or she can stay on task for longer periods. So, on the first day, you might set the timer for 4 minutes. If the child stays with the task that he is doing, the next period can be 6 minutes, then 7, then 10, then back to 4, then 7, then 12, etc. It is important not to set up a pattern that the child can identify. Keep changing the time intervals. If the child is successful, you may eventually reach 30-minute or longer periods in which he remains committed to his work. However, always throw in some shorter periods (5 minutes, for example) so that the child cannot predict the actual amount of time between the setting of the timer and the ringing of the bell.

Remember, verbal praise is very important. When the child remains on task, make a big deal out of it by praising him. Some parents and teachers find it helpful to give the child a token (such as a poker chip) whenever the child stays on task during the timed period. These poker chips or tokens can later be traded in for special activities or prizes.

Paying Attention

You can help to teach your child how to pay attention. By reading a short story to him and by asking him questions after you have finished reading it, your child can increase his ability to attend to such stimulation. Ask him to remember facts, names, and things that happened in the story. Praise the child each time he gets an answer correct. You can tell him that if he answers three out of four of the questions correctly, he can have a special snack, or stay up later that night.

Read a series of numbers or letters to the child and ask him to repeat them backwards. For example, tell your child, "I am going to read you some letters. After I say the letters, I want you to say them to me backwards." Then say the letters "A, K, X, L," leaving about a second in between each of them. See if the child can say them backwards. If he cannot, try to give him just three letters or numbers, and determine whether he can say those backwards. As the child masters this memory task, increase the length of the string of letters (or numbers) given.

The child who suffers from attention problems should participate in organized activities (e.g., sports) where he is likely to experience success. To develop a positive self-image, the child must have some successful experiences. Since the hyperactive child often has difficulties in school, you must get that child involved in activities outside of the regular school program. Activities which involve movement and coordination and which are also non-competitive are best (e.g., karate, gymnastics).

Above all, remember: Do not try to diagnose your child as hyperactive by yourself. For a proper diagnosis, the child must have a professional evaluation.

Question:
"I have heard that hyperactivity tends to diminish as a child reaches adolescence. Does this mean that my son will not have any long-term problems?"

Answer:
Although a child's attention span may improve as he gets older, the emotional effects of hyperactivity could last a lifetime. The hyperactive child grows up with constant exposure to negative statements, such as "Why can't you sit still?" The constant criticism (combined with low academic and conduct grades) will have an impact on any child's self-esteem. After hearing so many complaints about his behavior, such a child will begin to feel worthless and incompetent. The PST techniques are especially important for a hyperactive child, since statements such as "I forgot my medicine today" will not be accepted as an excuse for maladaptive behavior by others.

Question:
"My pediatrician recommended that my child take Ritalin for his hyperactivity. I am scared to give him this stimulant. Can it really be harmful to my son?"

Answer:
There is no need to be frightened of the medication if your child really needs it. To the best of our knowledge, there are no dangers in using "Ritalin" with school-age children if it is properly monitored by the child's pediatrician or by a pediatric neurologist. The emotional damage that can occur if the child's attention span is not improved could be more harmful than any potential risk from this medication. If this relatively safe medication can prevent such problems, it certainly seems as if it would be worth taking. The dosage that is administered, along with the child's blood, must be monitored regularly by your physician. Medication should be prescribed only after the child is thoroughly evaluated by a psychologist and a physician, and this should include the collection of behavioral observations from the parents and teachers.

Question:
   "My child is hyperactive, and I am thinking of putting him on a diet that is sugar- and additive-free. Will this help him?"

Answer:
   This diet is unlikely to have a major impact on your child's behavior unless he is in the small minority of children with attention deficits who really do have an allergy to these additives. It might be a good idea for you to consider first having a consultation and subsequent testing done by an allergist. Since a diet such as the one that you are thinking of could not hurt a child, there is no risk in trying it. Be sure, however, that you don't go overboard with the diet and forget the importance of the PST techniques in helping your child learn to function the best that he can.

Question:
   "My child fits most of the characteristics that you described for a hyperactive child. Can I now conclude that he is really hyperactive?"

Answer:
   Absolutely not. Do not conclude that a child is or isn't hyperactive based upon our discussion of the common characteristics of a hyperactive child. There are many medical conditions that could also result in "hyper" behavior. These conditions could include problems with blood sugar levels, neurological impairment, and emotional problems that can resemble hyperactivity. If you suspect that your child is hyperactive, consult with your pediatrician, since you want to rule out other organic problems that could be affecting him. Also, the physician should be the one who makes the official diagnosis of "attention deficit disorder with hyperactivity." Be sure that your physician does a thorough exam before medication or other interventions are considered. Unfortunately, some physicians see a child for only a few minutes, and this is not long enough for the proper assessment of a child. We recommend that the child have a complete psychoeducational battery of tests performed by a psychologist. The psychologist will have about four hours in which to observe the child in a testing situation that requires the child to be atten-

tive. The psychologist also should get a detailed history from the parent and should collect behavioral observations from the child's teacher(s). When the testing is completed, the physician should be given a detailed written report. This data may help the doctor to determine whether the child is hyperactive, whether additional medical testing is warranted, and what course of treatment appears to be appropriate.

Chapter Fourteen

Kids and Sex:
Teaching Them "The Right Stuff"

Kids have sexual feelings. You may choose to ignore that truism because it's upsetting for you to consider, but the child's sexual feelings will remain. Parental discomfort with the words *children* and *sex* in the same sentence is understandable, but it is an indication of fear and embarrassment on the part of the parent more than anything else. A child will not benefit in any way from interacting with a parent whose own insecurities prevent him from dealing with "delicate" matters, so responsible action on your part is in your child's best interests.

Starting with the Basics

Sigmund Freud (often referred to as the father of psychology) was the first to suggest that sexual feelings don't appear magically at the onset of adolescence; instead, they're always there, but merely intensify when puberty begins. Although PST involves a rejection of many traditional Freudian ideas, the concept of childhood sexual feelings is maintained. Because children do experience some degree of sexual interest, it is natural for them to seek greater knowledge and understanding of these feelings. As the parent, you are the obvious source for information. The better prepared you become for the questions and the situations that are likely to arise, the more effective a role you can play—and that is what PST is all about.

Returning now to one of the points made above, note that all children are capable of sexual feelings. Therefore, when such feelings become evident in your child, there is no reason to feel concerned. In fact, the appropriate expression of such interest is perhaps a healthy sign. A child who can ask questions without fear or humiliation is obviously responding to what he perceives as a warm, safe, nurturing environment. After all, where did *you* learn to feel modest or even embarrassed by discussions about sex? The answer is simple: You learned to feel that way at home, and the environment in which you were raised was one created by your parents. If you still blush when you hear sexual terms spoken aloud, or find it difficult to say anything of a sexual nature in front of other people (much less within earshot of your children), then those inhibitions are a reflection of the way in which you were taught to view sexuality. There is absolutely no justification for perpetuating such problems within your own child. Instead, as a concerned parent, you should strive to create a household in which your child can feel comfortable asking questions and expressing himself. This chapter will help to prepare you to accomplish that.

Honesty Is the Best Policy

In PST, we recommend answering a child's questions directly and honestly, with the insect-, animal-, and plant-life analogies of times past left behind. When your child wants to know where babies come from, no purpose will be served by telling him about pollination. Unless you are preparing him for a career as a gardener, he doesn't need to know anything at all about how plants reproduce. If he asks about the names for bodily parts, don't condescend with foolish metaphorical terms ("That's your weiner, Evan"), unless you hope to see him working someday for Oscar Mayer. Does it actually seem plausible to you that a child would be more upset by a realistic explanation of where he came from than he would be by thoughts of having been dropped off at the doorstep by a huge, ugly bird that nearly swallowed him whole? An innocent child is displaying an extraordinary sense of confidence in you by asking you questions; to answer him dishonestly is a serious violation of the blind trust that he has placed in you. Many of the "nice" answers that children receive from parents are not only more likely to be upsetting than would be truthful responses, but also are serving to increase the mass confusion about sex that has failed to improve in recent years, despite sex education courses. The number of unwanted teenage pregnancies that occur each year in the United States is evidence of the misconceptions that are held past childhood by so many young people, and failure to answer your child's questions accurately can only contribute to such a lack of knowledge. It is not an overstatement to say that teaching your child about the fundamentals of sexual behavior is a key parental responsibility. When Dr. Lustig taught "Human Sexuality" courses at several colleges in Florida, he was at first surprised by the incredible lack of knowledge held by 18-to-20-year-old students. When your child wants to know something, he can either learn it properly from you, or learn it with complete inaccuracy from other children. It's up to you.

Practice Makes Perfect
No, the above subtitle doesn't refer to sexual activity; it is a statement on the importance of adequate preparation before discussing sexual matters with your child. Although you have a good "working" knowledge of sex (or you wouldn't be a parent), it may be that you are unsure of exactly what to teach your child, or of what ways are best for explaining things. If so, you may want to take the PST Crash Course in Sex Education so that specific topics of the greatest importance do not escape your attention (and subsequent explanation). Before studying this outline, consider the examples below. These are actual case references of children asking questions and expressing beliefs, and they serve to illustrate the naive ways in which children think about sexuality (and the need for adequate education).

Child: Dad, I still want to know what happens when a guy has sex with a girl.
Parent: Keith, we've talked about this a little before. How much do you already know about what happens?
Child: Well, I've been watching cable TV a lot, and it seems like it's always the same. The guy gets on top of the girl and does it for a while, and then he gets off and makes himself a martini.

Child: Mom, Sabrina just got her period, and she explained it all to me today.
Parent: She did? Did you understand everything that she said?

Child: Yeah, there's just one thing that seems stupid. How come girls don't go to the hospital and get stitches so that they don't bleed anymore?

Child: Hey, mom, guess what? I learned how to have oral sex at school today. I figured it all out.
Parent: Oh, my God, you did? What is it?
Child: Oral sex is when a bunch of guys stand around bragging about the different stuff that they've done with girls.

Some Surprises, Perhaps Even for You

Did you know that male babies are capable of achieving erections from birth onward and that they are often born with erections? Such information is important for you to know for two different reasons: Not only will it help you in dealing with your child's sexual development, but it will permit you to teach your child many of the things that he needs to know. What percentage of Americans will contract a venereal disease by the time they are 25 years old? Surprisingly, statistics indicate that nearly 50 percent (yes, that's one out of every two individuals) will be infected. Test your knowledge with this question: What is the one bodily part that can move in direct response to temperature? Answer: the scrotum. If you're still dubious about the need for preparation in teaching your children about sex, take the short quiz (on basic material) listed here. The answers can be found within the PST Crash Course.

1. There is only one sexual organ that doesn't serve both a sexual *and* a reproductive function. What is it?

2. What causes the penis to become erect (physically)?

3. How often do adolescents masturbate?

4. Where is the *endometrium* to be found?

5. What is *fellatio?* What is *cunnilingus?*

6. Which method of birth control provides at least some protection against venereal disease?

7. What are the two functions performed by the ovaries?

8. What is the difference between an embryo and a fetus?

The PST Crash Course in Sex Education

Each of the following sections is a part of the crash course, and each serves a dual purpose: The information presented is helpful in determining what you should explain to your child, and on another level, some of the information may prove to be informative for you. By studying this section, you can prepare yourself by knowing the fundamental bits of knowledge that your child will need to understand. You will have to judge how much to explain to your child, based largely upon the age at which he has shown an interest in learning about sex. In PST, it is advocated that even the youngest children receive realistic answers to their questions, although those answers may have to be watered down enough to permit them to be understood. In any case, the attitudes about sex that children carry into adulthood are set while they are still quite young, and so it is in the child's best interests for you to help him to manage his sexuality in a healthy, adaptive, and natural way.

The Penis

The *penis*, which is typically described as the "male sex organ," actually serves three distinct functions: It is a source of sexual pleasure, an integral part of the reproductive process, and an avenue for the elimination of bodily waste. The main part of the penis is known as the *body*, with the *root* being the bottom (attached) part, the *glans* being the top section, and the *corona* being the raised ridge which separates that glans from the body. The penis is normally relaxed (or flaccid), but can become harder when an *erection* occurs. There are no muscles or bones inside the penis, so erection is the result of blood flowing into the penis and being absorbed by the spongy tissue inside. Although every penis becomes larger when erect, a small penis tends to increase more in size during erection than does a penis which is larger in its relaxed state. Penile growth tends to accelerate at about age twelve and adult males tend to have penises that average about six inches in length. Sometimes, the *foreskin* (a layer of skin covering the glans) is removed in a procedure known as *circumcision,* and research has shown that although this tends to make hygiene easier to maintain, it has little or no effect on sexual pleasure. Males urinate through the penis, although urination cannot take place while the penis is fully erect.

Males also *ejaculate* through the penis, and this process involves the ejection of *semen*.

The Testicles and the Scrotum

Below the penis is a pouch-like structure called the *scrotum*. Inside, there are two *testicles*. The testicles serve two functions: They produce *sperm* cells (more on that later), and they produce the male sex hormone *(testosterone)*, which is a chemical that is important to a male's bodily development and functioning. The testicles are delicate, and thus the scrotum can move up and down, raising the testicles so that they can stay warm (up close to the body) or lowering them so that they can cool off (by being farther away from the body). Sexual stimulation can also cause the scrotum to move up closer to the body. It is perfectly normal for one testicle to be somewhat larger than the other and thus to hang lower in the scrotum.

Sperm and Semen

Sperm are so tiny that you need a microscope to see them. Looking almost like tadpoles, they contain genetic information *(chromosomes)* about the male who ejaculates them, and they are an essential part of the reproductive process. Because they can survive in only a narrow temperature range, the movement of the scrotum helps them to stay at the right temperature. *Semen* refers to the entire liquid that males ejaculate, with sperm being just one of the elements contained in the semen. Remaining elements include acids, bases, water, enzymes, fructose sugar, and other materials. There are about 300 million sperm in each drop of semen.

The Clitoris

Perhaps the most mispronounced word in any adult's sexual vocabulary, the *clitoris* (accent the first syllable) is the only sexual organ that exists purely for pleasure and that doesn't also serve in the reproductive process. It is a small piece of tissue that is located in front of the opening to the vagina. Like the penis, it has a *shaft* (body) and a *glans*, it varies in size from one female to another, and it can become erect when stimulated. The most sexually sensitive part of the female anatomy, the clitoris is covered by a *hood*, much like the foreskin on a penis.

The Mons

Known as the *mons pubis,* this fatty and padded piece of tissue is the most easily noticed part of the female sexual anatomy. Underneath the skin are the pubic bones, and this area becomes covered with hair after puberty.

The Labia

The *labia majora* (or outer lips) come down from the mons and surround the opening to the vagina (see next paragraph). They are often darker in color than is the skin of the thighs, next to which they lie. The *labia minora* (or inner lips) are located inside the outer lips and may even stick out noticeably. They cover the clitoris and vary a great deal in size and shape from one female to another. They sometimes cover the vaginal opening because they are folded over and are very sexually sensitive.

The Vagina

The *vagina* serves three separate functions: It is the organ that accepts the penis during sexual intercourse; it is part of the canal through which a baby is born; and it is the opening through which menstrual blood flow is discharged. In a relaxed state, the vagina is about four inches long and is tilted slightly back. The walls of the vagina function like a balloon, expanding during sexual arousal. Highly elastic, the vagina can accommodate a penis of virtually any size (it can even stretch enough to permit a baby to exit during childbirth). However, the deeper parts of the vagina have very few nerve endings, and thus it is a myth that a longer penis necessarily produces more sexual pleasure (since its full length cannot really be felt inside).

The Uterus

The *uterus* (or womb) looks a bit like a pear and is roughly the size of a fist—about three inches long (but longer after a pregnancy) and is tilted forward. It can move a little inside, but is held in place by a set of six ligaments. The uterus is the place where a *fetus* (developing baby) resides, and it is also the source of menstrual flow. Each month after puberty (when there is no pregnancy), the inner lining of the uterus (or *endometrium*) is shed and replaced.

The Ovaries

The *ovaries* serve a dual purpose: They produce eggs (the female equivalent to sperm) and manufacture the female sex hormones—*estrogen* and *progesterone*. About the size of an almond, each of the two ovaries lie on the sides of the uterus. A female is born with about 400,000 immature eggs, one of which is released each month after puberty.

The Fallopian Tubes

The *fallopian tubes* connect the uterus with the ovaries. Thus, they serve as the place where the egg makes its journey to the uterus, and where it can be fertilized by sperm (if present).

The Breasts

The *breasts* are mainly fatty tissue and milk-producing glands (15 to 20 per breast), and are the main area of attention typically given to a female's physical shape in American society. Breasts vary greatly in size from one female to another, and they are an area of sexual pleasure, despite the fact that they are not considered to be *sex organs*. In the center of each breast is a *nipple,* with pinpoint openings from which milk can come forth. The area surrounding each nipple is know as an *areola,* which is usually of darker color than the surrounding skin. Although most women wish for larger breasts, there is little difference in the number of nerve endings between large and small breasts, so the smaller ones actually may have a larger number of nerve endings per square inch (making them more sensitive to stimulation).

Puberty

Contrary to popular belief, *puberty* is a long process, rather than an exact event or time. At puberty, both males and females go through significant bodily changes on the way to becoming physically and sexually mature. Sex hormone levels increase dramatically, and there is often a growth spurt (a sudden increase in height over a relatively short time). Puberty begins typically between the ages of about ten and thirteen, although there is a great deal of variability.

Menstruation and Other Changes in the Female

After the onset of puberty, the female begins a monthly process known as *menstruation* (typically called her "period"). The inner lining of the uterus is prepared by the body for the implantation of a fertilized egg (pregnancy). Interestingly, females tend to menstruate before they can produce mature eggs, so that they are not yet capable of becoming pregnant for as much as two years after menstruation has begun. In menstruation, the walls thicken and prepare themselves for the egg, but if no pregnancy has occurred, this inner lining is shed, preparing the uterus for the next *cycle* (monthly chain of events). The menstrual fluid is not composed merely of blood, but also of degenerated cells and mucus. On the average, about four tablespoons of menstrual flow are discharged each month, although it often seems like more. This discharge is absorbed by sanitary napkins (worn outside the vagina) or by tampons (worn inside). For many females, the "month" is actually every 28 days, although there is variation.

Many females notice the onset of puberty because of the increase in breast size. Simultaneously, the fatty tissue surrounding the hips and buttocks becomes enlarged, thus rounding out the shape of the body. Girls often go through a growth spurt earlier than do boys, which helps to explain the incredible differences in size and maturation that can be seen among the students in a typical seventh-grade classroom. Puberty also involves a thickening of the vaginal walls, increased blood supply to the clitoris, and a quick increase in the size of the uterus.

Nocturnal Emissions and Other Changes in the Male

As with females, greatly increased hormone levels cause changes in the male to occur rapidly. The first noticeable change is often an enlarging of the testicles and the scrotum, as well as the appearance of pubic hair. The penis lengthens and thickens beginning about one year later, and as hormone levels continue to rise, this growth becomes even more rapid. Males tend to experience erections more often, and usually can begin ejaculating at this time. *Nocturnal emissions* (typically called "wet dreams") may occur; in this process, ejaculation takes place during sleep. However, it sometimes takes several additional years before the semen contains mature sperm. While females notice an increase in their fatty tissue, males see an increase in their muscle mass. There is often a temporary condition in males known as *gynecomastia*, in which the breast tissue enlarges slightly. This normal situation is the result of the presence of small amounts of female sex hormones, which are produced by the male, as well.

As the *larynx* (voice box) increases in size, a male's voice typically begins to become deeper, and this change is also the result of raised hormone levels. Approximately two years after the occurrence of many of these changes, facial hair begins to appear.

Sexual Intercourse

If you're like most parents, you probably don't want to sit down with your child and explain the details of sexual intercourse unless you absolutely have to do so. In PST, we suggest offering such an explanation only when one of the following criteria is met: Either the child has asked about it and is expecting you to supply him with the answers that he seeks, or the child has reached the age of about ten or eleven and has not yet had a talk with you about sex. Unlike other parenting theories, PST does not promote the notion that very young children necessarily should learn about sex; instead, it is suggested that young children be taught about sex *if* an interest has been expressed, because to do otherwise could be problematic in the long run. In the latter case (when an older child has not begun to ask the questions that would provide a convenient lead-in to such a discussion), remember that you are running risks if you choose not to deal with the situation simply because it doesn't seem like a pressing problem. At that point in time, a child probably has heard a great deal about sex from his peers and is likely to hold a vast array of extraordinary misconceptions. Furthermore, if the child has never approached you with questions, it may be that he is afraid to do so. You might want to ask yourself whether you have offered subtle messages over a period of time that have contributed to his reluctance to approach you. Again, it is your role as an effective parent to help to teach your child the things that he needs to know. In explaining sexual intercourse to your child, you may want to emphasize that there are two different reasons that such behavior takes place. First, sexual intercourse is the method by which conception takes place (see p. 174). Secondly, it is a pleasurable act that a male and a female may choose to enjoy together.

Many parents are concerned that once a child understands the workings of sexual activity, he immediately will seek to attempt such behavior on his own, or, at the very least, will do so at an earlier age than he would if he were taught about sex in his late teens. Although such concerns cannot be dismissed as totally invalid, they represent a highly unlikely chain of events and should not prevent you, as a parent, from facing reality with your child. Sexual interest and even some experimentation does occur among children, and many parents are upset about such behavior. As a result, the manner in which such events are handled is problematic. By punishing a child for the expression of sexual interest, the child is learning that such feelings are wrong and that they must be hidden, or curbed altogether. Such a situation is quite likely to lead to the association of sexual feelings with guilt later on and to a lifetime of less-than-satisfying sexuality. In PST, it is advocated that a child be taught that sexual feelings are normal and healthy, but that sexual activity is something that is reserved for older people. By helping the child to understand that it's "okay" to feel an interest in sex and that he is not "bad" for having such feelings or thoughts, the child is able to learn about sex in a healthy fashion, gathering knowledge and developing feelings that will serve him in a well-adjusted adult life. By teaching your child that sexual activity is something for which he must be emotionally prepared, you can aid him in understanding that sex is not something in which he should engage simply because he is physically capable of doing so. Don't hesitate to tell your child that it is always acceptable to say "no" to invitations for sexual activity, and that such activity is not encouraged for 12- or 13-year-old children, no matter what they "feel." One of the most important things that you can teach your child is the difference between "having sex" and "making love." Answer his questions honestly and openly, and your child will learn from you.

Conception

About halfway through her monthly cycle, the average female *ovulates*. An egg is released from the ovary, and it travels through the fallopian tubes on its way to the uterus. It will not complete its trip unless it is fertilized by sperm, because without fertilization, the egg disintegrates in less than 2 days. *Fertilization* is the process by which an egg and a sperm join to produce (eventually) a baby. Sexual intercourse is the method by which the sperm enters the female's vagina, then makes its way up toward the fallopian tubes. Sperm swim at a speed of about 1 inch per hour, and yet they can arrive at the egg within 90 minutes because muscular contractions in the uterus help them along. If the egg joins with a sperm cell, it will reach the uterus after about 5 days and will implant itself in the uterine wall. Such a combination of sperm and egg is called a *zygote*. The zygote then begins to divide, with 1 cell becoming 2, 2 becoming 4, and continuing to grow during the entire period of *gestation* (pregnancy), although it is no longer called a zygote after that cell division has started. For the first 8 weeks, it is known as an *embryo*. From the ninth week onward until birth, it is known as a *fetus*.

In those cases in which two eggs are released from the ovaries at the same time, each one may be fertilized separately by sperm. When this happens, the result is *fraternal* twins, either or both of whom can be male or female. These twins actually have little more in common than do brothers and sisters born at different times (they do not look alike, any more than do other siblings). However, when one egg is fertilized by one sperm and it splits in half, the result is *identical* twins, each one of whom is an exact genetic duplicate of the other (and is always, of course, of the same sex).

Contraception

If there is any one thing that you should teach your child about sex, it is undoubtedly *contraception* that must be discussed. Known more commonly as "birth control," contraception involves taking steps to ensure that pregnancy does not take place.

Whether your child is male or female, PST advocates that you teach him or her that contraception is a mutual responsibility, as carelessness will affect both sexual partners. In giving your child an overview of the different contraceptive devices that are available today, you are helping him to understand that any or all of them are preferable to an unwanted pregnancy. Parents sometimes prefer to avoid discussing contraception, with the idea that since they are talking with a child, they wouldn't want him to believe that birth control devices "legitimize" his right to begin sexual activity. On the contrary, however, failure to inform your child about the need for contraception and the ways in which it works is tantamount to saying that you don't object to the problems that will arise, inevitably, when he does eventually begin sexual activity. The better prepared you make your child through knowledge now, the more likely he will be to act responsibly when the time comes. The following section contains a brief look at each of the major contraceptive techniques currently in use.

The Pill
When a female becomes pregnant, she stops menstruating. The inner lining of the uterus doesn't shed during a pregnancy, because that is where the fetus is developing. The body reacts to pregnancy with greatly elevated levels of estrogen, and that is the key to the way in which the *Pill* works: It raises estrogen and progesterone levels artificially, fooling the body into reacting as if it's pregnant (thereby preventing ovulation). Menstruation still occurs, although the discharge is often greatly reduced. The Pill is the most reliable method of birth control. If it is used properly, the odds of avoiding pregnancy are approximately 99.7 percent. The Pill is the most widely used contraceptive in the United States.

The Intrauterine Device (IUD)
The *IUD* is a small piece of plastic that is inserted into the uterus (through the vagina) by a physician, and which remains there until its removal is desired. The IUD comes in a variety of shapes, and typically has two plastic strings which hang down into the vagina where they can be checked (so that the IUD's placement is ensured). There is no certainty as to how the IUD

works, but most experts believe that it irritates the uterus so that a fertilized egg cannot implant itself. The reliability rate for the IUD is as high as 97 percent.

The Diaphragm

The *diaphragm* is a thin, dome-shaped piece of rubber attached to a flexible metal spring. It is inserted into the vagina and prevents sperm from reaching the uterus. It must be used along with a foam or jelly that is spermicidal (one that kills sperm) in order to be fully effective. The diaphragm must be inserted 2 hours before sexual intercourse, and be left in place for 6 hours afterward (but never longer than 16 hours). If a female is menstruating, the diaphragm may help to catch some of the discharge. If used properly, along with a spermicide, the diaphragm can be effective up to 97 percent of the time; in actual use, however, its reliability is as low as 83 percent.

The Condom

The only realistic method of birth control in which the male assumes full responsibility is the *condom.* Also known as a "prophylactic," this thin sheath fits completely over the penis and prevents sperm from entering the vagina. Made of synthetic latex, or from lamb intestines, the condom *must* be unrolled onto the penis before beginning intercourse. Many males complain that it reduces sensitivity and pleasure, but the condom has one advantage over the other methods of contraception: It is the only birth control device that can help to prevent the spread of venereal disease. The condom is effective 97 percent of the time.

Other Contraceptive Choices

The other methods of birth control are so poor in terms of reliability as to make labeling them "contraceptives" a questionable decision. The *rhythm method,* in which intercourse is avoided near the time of ovulation, is effective as little as 65 percent of the time. The *withdrawal method,* in which the male removes his penis before ejaculating, is effective in only 75 percent of the cases in which it is used. The *douching method,* in which the female attempts to wash out the semen that has already been ejaculated into her vagina, is highly ineffective because it often pushes sperm higher, rather than forcing it out. Using spermicides alone, the effective rate is only about 70 percent, so it is inadvisable to use them without using either a diaphragm or a condom simultaneously. As you teach your child about how contraceptives work, you will help to ensure that he is aware of their usefulness and applicability when he is old enough to begin engaging in sexual activity. Remember: Responsible parenting involves helping your child to do the things that he must do in order to live as happily and as appropriately as possible. Teaching him about the basic aspects of sex and the responsibility associated with it is clearly in his best interests.

Masturbation

Masturbation is an act in which an individual stimulates his own genitals. Virtually everyone who reaches adulthood has masturbated at least a few times, and it is an extremely common phenomenon in children. Contrary to popular opinion, there is nothing wrong with masturbation. It was widely believed, until just several decades ago, that masturbation caused a variety of problems: slowness of growth, weakness, loss of memory, blindness, restlessness, hairy palms, red eyes, paleness, epilepsy, headaches, baldness, pimples, suicidal tendencies, and insanity, to mention just a few of the ills associated with it. So, at this point, it is important to emphasize that masturbation does *not* cause any of these problems, nor is it associated with any others. Instead, it is a normal and even expected human sexual behavior. It has been estimated that as many as 63 percent of all male children have masturbated by the age of 12, and that 33 percent of female children have done so by that age. By the age of 15, the percentages jump to 82 percent for males and to 58 percent for females, and several years later to 92 percent and 72 percent, respectively.

Infants often masturbate, although it is sometimes difficult for parents to accept that such behavior is actually directed toward self-pleasure. Research in the field of human sexuality has shown that orgasms have been observed in children as young as 5 months of age. In fact, signs of sexual arousal (penile erection, vaginal lubrication, and pelvic thrusting) are seen commonly among very young children, so it is important to understand that masturbation is an everyday occurrence, and is not something about which a parent necessarily should become upset. As they get older, children typically discover that masturbation feels good, although by the age of 6, most children also have learned that masturbation is something to be done only in private. Interestingly, the ways in which masturbation is first conceptualized differ for males and females; male children tend to be told about it by their friends, to observe others doing it, or even to read about it, whereas girls tend often to learn about masturbation accidentally, by touching themselves just so.

As they approach the age of 11 or 12, male children tend to discuss masturbation with their peers, although female children still tend to avoid discussing it with others. The attitudes held by males under the age of 12 often differ markedly from those of children past that age. Prior to 12, many males describe such behavior as "gross," and make statements, such as "I would never do that!" (despite what is often a long history of already having done so), while older males often acknowledge such behavior to their closest friends, dropping the pretense that there is something wrong with it. Masturbation is the subject of a great deal of humor among pre-adolescents, but few feel guilty about masturbating; instead, they merely feel embarrassed sometimes.

The reaction that you have as a parent when you discover your child masturbating may have a significant effect on his feelings about sexuality. Research has shown that acceptance in such situations is often the best approach. There is nothing wrong with discussing the situation openly with your child, thereby reassuring him that what he is doing is not unusual or "bad," and that you understand why he has chosen to do so. Sometimes, especially with a younger child, you may need to teach him that masturbation is okay when he is alone, but that it is something that is not to be shared with other children, or performed where others can observe it. Unless masturbation occurs with unusual frequency in a young child, concern on your part is unnecessary.

By the time a child has reached puberty, the frequency of masturbation will probably have increased. Adolescent males masturbate 2 to 3 times per week on the average, while females of the same age masturbate once a week.

In discussing masturbation with your child, emphasize the idea that it is something that most people do at one time or another, but that it is not anything that *must* be done. What should be accomplished is to help your child to free himself of any guilt or humiliation that he may be experiencing as a result of masturbating, and at the same time to help him to understand that nothing is wrong if his friends claim to masturbate and he chooses not to do so. Your attitudes about masturbation and in fact about sex in general are easily transmitted to your child. If you approach the subject with no apparent sense of discomfort, your child will be able to learn to do the same thing.

Orgasm: One of the Four Stages

There are four stages of human sexual response, and both males and females go through these stages during sexual activity. The first, *excitement,* is basically the beginning of sexual arousal. Males experience erection, as well as a thickening and an elevation of the scrotum. Females experience a lubrication of the vagina, a swelling of the clitoris, and a hardening of the nipples. These responses are the result of a process known as *vasocongestion,* in which blood flow to a specific area results in the dilation of blood vessels. Next comes the *plateau* stage, in which both males and females undergo a rapid increase in their blood pressure, heart rate, and breathing. Males experience an increase of up to 50 percent in the size of their testicles and a further increase in the swelling of the glans. Females undergo a thickening of the tissues comprising the outer third of the vagina (the *orgasmic platform),* making the opening smaller, while the clitoris angles farther up into the body, and the breasts and the uterus increase in size. The third stage of sexual response is the *orgasm,* in which there is a further increase in blood pressure and pulse rate for both sexes. Although orgasm is a difficult term on which to find any consensus of description, it is the "height of pleasure during a sexual act." In males, there is ejaculation, which often accompanies orgasm. In females, there is a series of rhythmic muscular contractions of the orgasmic platform, as well as contractions of the muscles in the uterus. While females may have several orgasms in a row, males typically are capable of only one at a time. The final stage, *resolution,* involves a returning of the body to its natural, unaroused state. For males, this involves loss of erection, as well as a lowering of the scrotum and a shrinking of the testicles. Males have a *refractory* period in which they cannot become sexually aroused following orgasm; this period can last anywhere from minutes to hours. Females experience a reduction in the swelling of the breasts, as well as a shrinking of the clitoris (which occurs within just seconds of an orgasm), and a diminishment in the size of the orgasmic platform. Orgasm does not always occur for males or for females, and sex researchers suggest that it should never be considered to be a "goal." Instead, as sex partners relax and enjoy their activity together, orgasm can be a natural and "unplanned" result.

Fellatio and Cunnilingus

The major alternative to sexual intercourse is oral sex. Sometimes referred to as *oral-genital* sex, such activity involves the stimulation of one individual's sex organs by the mouth of another. Although you may find the idea of discussing such a subject with even a 12-year-old child to be unsettling, you might want to remind yourself that such sexual activity often occurs among older children and adolescents *before* such a time as intercourse is first attempted. Because children and adolescents typically see oral sex as less of a significant step in the ladder of sexual conquest, they tend to consider it to be a good "beginning."

Cunnilingus refers to the oral stimulation of a female's clitoris and surrounding area. Surprisingly, the vaginal area has fewer bacteria than does the mouth, and thus cunnilingus does not involve any physical risk to either party (except in cases of venereal disease). Many females find that oral sex helps them to achieve orgasm, and that they enjoy knowing that there is no risk of pregnancy.

Fellatio refers to the oral stimulation of a male's penis. This technique often helps males to achieve erection quickly and involves the same lack of risk just described. Even in those cases in which the female swallows the semen that is ejaculated, there is no cause for concern; pregnancy cannot be induced through ingestion, and semen is actually high in protein content.

Venereal Disease:
A Quick Look at the Most Common Forms

Sexually transmitted diseases occur primarily as a result of carelessness based upon a lack of knowledge. The best weapon with which you can prepare your children for later avoidance of venereal disease (VD) is education. There are many different forms of venereal disease, and all are transmitted through sexual contact. *Gonorrhea,* for example, has been at epidemic proportions for many years. It is second only to the common cold in terms of frequency in this country and is diagnosed through the laboratory analysis of the discharge taken from either a male or female. Males first notice symptoms, such as a thick, colored discharge from the penis, several days or weeks after infection. Urination becomes painful, and many complications can result from failure to obtain treatment. Most males seek treatment promptly because of the level of pain that is being caused by the infection, but 80 percent of all females are *asymptomatic* (have no symptoms). Within 10 weeks, such an infection can cause sterility if left untreated. Gonorrhea can also invade the throat or rectum as the result of oral sex or anal intercourse with an infected individual. *Syphilis,* another major form of venereal disease, is less common than gonorrhea, but is far more serious; it can lead to death. Several weeks after infection, a *chancre* (a lesion with a hard edge) appears at the spot where the disease originally entered the body, and while this is quite noticeable for males (the chancre is often on the penis), it is more difficult for females to see (it often appears on the cervix). The chancre can also appear in or around the mouth, as well as the rectum, and can even enter the body through a cut in the skin (if this spot were touched by a chancre). The disease progresses through a series of stages, and although the symptoms disappear as time goes by, the damage being done to the body actually increases. Syphilis can be transmitted to a developing fetus if the mother has the disease and can lead to paralysis, insanity, and death in its later stages, if left untreated. Blood tests can reveal the presence of syphilis, and like gonorrhea, the disease must be treated with doses of penicillin. One of the other major diseases about which your children need to be taught is *nongonococcal urethritis,* an infection that is caused by a microorganism known as *chlamydia.* Often causing pain during urination, this disease can be as dangerous as gonorrhea, but must be treated with tetracycline because it doesn't respond to penicillin. *Genital herpes,* a disease which has existed for over 2,000 years, is now becoming far more widespread than ever before. This viral infection usually begins with the appearance of clusters of small blisters around the penis or anus in males, and around the vagina, anus, and cervix in females. It takes a few days or weeks for these blisters to begin appearing, and there may be at first an itching or burning sensation during urination. As the blisters appear, they may be accompanied by headaches, fever, swollen glands, and discharge. Over the next 10 days, the pain level may increase, and can last for as long as 6 weeks. When the symptoms finally abate, the individual may go through a period where he doesn't appear to have the disease, but (as with syphilis) the infection is still present and can flare up again. Because there is no cure for herpes, care must be taken to avoid the things that can cause recurrences (such as stress, fatigue, and even sunburn). The risk of infection can be decreased by avoiding contact with any person who has an active case with visible blisters.

Acquired Immune Deficiency Syndrome (AIDS) has received widespread media attention during the past several years and will continue to do so for many years to come. AIDS is at this time incurable, and is a syndrome in which the body's immune system weakens so that it no longer can ward off infection. Contrary to popular opinion, people don't actually die from AIDS itself, but rather from the various diseases and infections which strike the body in its weakened state. Although AIDS originally appeared to be restricted to male homosexuals, it has since begun to affect heterosexual couples, as well. There is still a great deal of research to be done on AIDS, but at the present time, it appears that casual contact is not sufficient to spread the disease. In fact, there are currently no recorded cases of family members developing AIDS even while living over extended periods with an infected relative. Instead, it is transmitted through sexual intercourse (particularly through anal intercourse, where the membranes are thinner than in the vagina), through contact with the semen or the feces of an infected individual, and through blood transfusions. Thus, your child is unlikely to contract AIDS even from a classmate or a friend who might already have been infected. At this time, discretion about sexual partners may be the best weapon against it. As medical research progresses, AIDS will be far better understood and will remain the object of a large-scale search for a cure.

Mere Information Is Not Enough

Teaching your children about sex involves much more than mere explanations of what things are and how they work. Without question, children do need to know all of those things, but PST advocates that you teach your child more than that. Remember that your child is to some degree a "blank slate," and thus you are in a position to determine what appears on that slate. Don't be afraid to teach your children that sex is pleasurable, and that people enjoy sex because of the physical sensations that are involved. But, be certain to explain also that sex is an activity of intense emotion between two people and that it represents an opportunity like no other. Encourage your children to associate sex with warmth, caring, tenderness, love, and passion, rather than solely with lust. Your children will model their outlooks and ideas after yours, so that as they observe you being comfortable with the idea of sex, they will internalize such values and make them their own.

As you were reading through each section of the PST Crash Course in Sex Education, you probably wondered why the sections were not divided into "For Males Only" and "For Females Only" topics. The reason, quite simply, is that PST involves teaching your children the things that they need to know, and children of each sex need to understand the basic functioning of the other. In fact, because children typically are eager to learn whatever they can about sex, you have the golden opportunity to foster a real appreciation in your child for all people in general and not just for the members of one sex. Sex education is a chance for you to teach your child values and principles, rather than mere facts alone. As you prepare for the challenge, remind yourself that there is really no option involved at all; the question is not whether your child will receive sex education, but whether he will receive a realistic and healthy education from you or a frequently absurd and unhealthy training course from the media and from other children or adolescents.

Sex Play with Peers

It is not uncommon for children to engage in exploratory sex play with other children. Although this is often a frightening scenario for parents, it does not necessarily represent a real problem. Children spend most of their time with peers of the same sex because it is not until the onset of adolescence that the average child is interested in the company of the opposite sex. As such, children sometimes express their sexual interest physically with the most accessible partners, and those partners are other children, sometimes of the same sex. If you discover your child experimenting with a friend, there is no reason to panic. What your child is doing is normal in nature and is not justification for extreme concern. Unless the specific behavior is unusual or is occurring with great frequency, your child is engaging in an activity which doesn't seem "bad" to him. Should you react by punishing the child, or by indicating that you think that he has done something "awful," he is likely to associate feelings of guilt with the behavior and sexual activity will begin to take on a negative connotation for him; it becomes something that must be done secretly, because "people who are caught are punished for their misbehavior." Instead, you should sit down with the child and discuss what it is that he has been doing. Explain to him that such behavior is best left for older people, and that in a few years he will be old enough to make decisions about what to do with his body. In the meantime, he can talk to you about what he thinks and feels, and you will answer his questions and explain things in such a way that he never has to feel hesitant about asking you anything. If the behavior is heterosexual, you may want to discuss the risks of pregnancy and such (assuming that the child is approaching adolescence), and if the behavior is homosexual in nature, you may be best off explaining, "Children sometimes play sex games with other boys (or girls) because they know them better and because they're not as scary as members of the opposite sex." You can then go on to say, "When you get older, you will be able to have sex with girls (or boys) because you will want to and because you will be old enough to do so." Don't punish the child or do anything to make him feel as if he has behaved inappropriately, because you do not want him to feel guilty or even to be tempted to challenge your authority by continuing the behavior. Limited sex play with peers is not abnormal and is not anything to which a parent should react too strenuously.

Incest

Incest refers to sexual activity between blood relatives (e.g., father and daughter) or between immediate non-blood relatives (e.g., stepfather and stepdaughter). The most surprising thing about incest is the frequency with which it occurs. Reliable figures are impossible to calculate, because only a tiny fraction of the suspected cases actually are reported. However, any practicing psychologist can tell you that the number of cases is staggering. A major study done in the 1970s revealed that incest occurred in 15 percent of American families, but it is now thought the figure could be far higher than that. Although father-daughter incest has long been thought to be the most common form, many researchers now believe that it is the most commonly *reported* (or prosecuted) form, while brother-sister involvement actually comprises the most frequent form of incest. In most cases of incest, the sexual activity involved never reaches the level of intercourse and consists mainly of "fondling." When an adult is involved, it is a male adult almost exclusively and is typically a father, stepfather, uncle, or cousin.

One of the most damaging aspects of incest is that on those occasions when the child attempts to seek help from another parent or adult in the family, he is rebuffed. Children sometimes fail to realize that something is "wrong" with what is being done to them, and thus later on feel angry in retrospect. Children who do appreciate that such behavior is inappropriate often feel guilty about tolerating it or uncomfortable about revealing the identity of the adult to others. When they do discuss the matter with another parent or adult, the stories that they tell often are not believed. Many wives, for example, refuse to believe that their husbands could be capable of such behavior and thus deny that such sex ever took place.

When incest involving an adult family member is discovered, the entire family may be torn apart. In most states, criminal prosecution takes place, and thus a "Catch-22" occurs. If the child informs others of what has happened, he runs the risk of seeing a family member imprisoned and of facing the accompanying publicity. If he fails to alert others, the sexual behavior may continue. This would be a difficult decision for an adult to make, and it is an incredibly difficult one for a child. If any child whom you know ever alludes to incidences of incest, take him seriously; fabrication of such stories by children is rare.

In cases where incest occurs between brothers and sisters, the research indicates that such behavior is not always as harmful as might be expected. Because siblings often must share bedrooms, incestuous behavior has ample opportunity for occurrence. In such instances, the emotional damage caused by the behavior seems intense primarily in those cases in which it takes place before the age of 9 years.

In PST, it is suggested that children of different sexes not be permitted to share the same bedroom. Even if one child has to sleep in the living room each night, it is preferable to a shared room. Brothers and sisters naturally will have sexual feelings as they grow up, and thus will be forced to deal with all of the emotional demands that are brought about through constant contact with the opposite sex. Because such situations are avoided relatively easily, there is no justification for placing opposite-sex siblings in a bedroom together. For that matter, children of the same sex should be given their own rooms whenever such an opportunity presents itself.

A discussion on incest would be incomplete without a few words on the subject of nudity in the home. During the past decade, it has been suggested that parents can instill a healthy outlook on the human body by encouraging nudity around the house. Nothing could be more preposterous, or more inappropriate; parents have absolutely no business parading around unclothed in front of their children. Your child will not develop pride in his body by watching you in the nude; he will instead experience conflicting sexual feelings and confusion about the nature of what it is that you're doing. Nudity and seductiveness are too closely aligned for a child to be able to discern the difference. Unless you are seeking to create an unhealthy and even risky environment for your children, or are trying to satisfy your own exhibitionistic urges, keep your clothes on. By the time that a child is old enough to display some sense of modesty about his own body, he, too, should be permitted to remain clothed in front of others. There's a world of difference between being modest about one's body and being ashamed of it. Similarly, there is no reason to assume that a natural sense of modesty is anything but appropriate, so keep family nudity to a minimum.

Child Molestation

If this book had been written several years ago, it is unlikely that this subsection would have been included at all. Unfortunately, the recent past has seen an extraordinary number of child molestation cases brought before the public, and therefore it is a subject that more and more people are willing to discuss. Please note that no book on parenting techniques could possibly teach you what needs to be done in the case of child molestation, and so we will not attempt to do so, either. If you suspect for any reason that your child has been molested, arrange immediately for a professional in the mental health field to interview your child and to assess the situation thoroughly. Remember the age-old adage: "Better safe, than sorry."

Pedophilia is the technical term for sexual attraction to children (in most states, a "child" is defined as being 12 years of age, or younger). There are few crimes which are more difficult to accept than child molesting, and even in prison, men convicted of such abuse are at the bottom of the social ladder. The average child molester is a middle-aged male, who knows his victim beforehand. He may be a neighbor, a friend of the family, or even a relative. He probably has poor relationships (social or sexual) with other adults and may feel inferior and inadequate in dealing with them. Enjoying the power that he has over a child, the pedophiliac rarely succeeds in his interactions with adults, preferring instead to lure children into sexual activity. Instead of using brute force, most molesters find ways in which children can be "convinced" to engage in sex. Intercourse is not attempted often, with most activity being limited (as in incest) to fondling.

The number of cases of child molestation is surprisingly high: It has been estimated that as many as one out of every three Americans has been molested at least once during childhood. Because it is often difficult or impossible to know in advance when such a situation is likely to occur, the best thing that you can do as a parent is to watch for signs of molestation, as well as to teach your child that he doesn't have to tolerate such behavior. Explain to your child that there is "good" touching and "bad" touching. "Good" touching is when an adult pats you on the back, or shakes your hand, or makes contact with you in any way that doesn't make you feel uncomfortable or embarrassed. "Bad" touching is when an adult puts his hand in a private place, or makes contact with you in some way that you don't like. When that happens, your child should know that he can say, "Stop, I don't like that. I'm gonna tell a grown-up what you did." By all means, encourage your child to tell you anytime that someone has touched him, and reassure him that he will never be punished, or thought to be a "bad" child because someone else has done that to him. Keep in mind, too, that your child should understand that it's okay for two adults to touch each other in private places if they both want to do so, but that it's different when an adult does that to a child who doesn't want him to touch such places. Never ignore your child's reports of molestation; again, children tend not to make up such stories. Although there are instances of fabrication, comments made about such things should always be explored fully until they can be ruled out conclusively. Do not panic if your child shares such information with you; he needs to see that he has not contributed to the problem, and hysteria on your part will make him feel that he has caused you to become upset. Children who are the victims of molestation often carry tremendous burdens of guilt, so it is crucial that you do not add to the situation by producing any more discomfort for your child.

There are several indicators of molestation, among them a sudden fascination with sex where none previously existed. A child who begins acting out sexual activity with dolls, for example, had to learn such things somewhere. Unusual insecurity in an otherwise confident child is also a sign that perhaps something is wrong; if your autonomous child suddenly (and inexplicably) refuses to leave your side, perhaps you need to wonder why. Sleep and eating disturbances, a dramatic drop in the quality of schoolwork, or any other major change in a normally well-adjusted child should be taken as an indicator of some problem having occurred, although not necessarily one of molestation. Molestation should never be presumed to be the problem, but rather, should be kept in mind as a possibility until it can be ruled out.

Some Final Notes

Children are faced not only with the demands being placed upon their bodies by physical development but by the expectations of society, as well. As children become more precocious sexually, there is more and more potential for emotional problems to occur. Many children today believe that they must be dating by the age of 10, or they risk rejection by their peers. Many children feel guilty about the dreams they have, or about bodily functions (e.g., menstruation, erection) they don't understand. Children need to be taught respect and concern for others, so that their psychological development will coincide with their physical maturation. By establishing an environment where your children can learn what they need to know, you will have served as an effective parent.

Question:

"My husband says that there is something wrong with anyone who believes that children have sexual feelings. He says that he doesn't remember feeling anything like that until he was fifteen."

Answer:

Your husband is revealing more about himself in those statements than he probably intended to reveal. Children do have sexual feelings, which is *not* the same thing as saying that children should be permitted to have sex. On the contrary, PST involves teaching your children that sexual activity is something for which one must be emotionally prepared, and for this reason, it is reserved for older people. The fact that children masturbate and that they find it to be pleasurable enough to continue is proof of their sexual feelings. Children do not need to have such feelings encouraged, but merely accepted as an inevitable part of the development process. By doing so, a child will learn that sexual feelings do not have to be hidden as if they were evil. On another level, your husband's statement about not feeling anything sexual until the age of 15 is simply an example of repression: It is more comfortable for him to remember being "pure of thought" until that age, and so he has buried such memories in his unconscious as if they never existed—but they almost certainly did!

Question:

"My seven-year-old daughter wants to know where babies come from. I'd like to tell her, but there's just no way that I can face her with such facts. I'm afraid that she won't understand, and I'm too embarrassed to be able to talk to her about sex."

Answer:

If you stop and think about it, you'd probably conclude that sex is a normal and expected part of human behavior, and is certainly nothing about which you have to feel embarrassed. In fact, we have a rule of thumb in PST: Never be embarrassed about anything, unless you've done something wrong! The sensation of embarrassment that you are feeling now is a reflection of your opinions about sex and indicate that perhaps you think of it as something "dirty," something which shouldn't be discussed out in the open. You need to work through your own ideas and feelings before you can approach your daughter in a way that will be beneficial to her. She certainly won't get anything positive from watching you struggle through a muted discussion of the facts of life. Re-read the PST Crash Course in Sex Education, and say all of those words out loud until they don't seem embarrassing to you anymore. Memorize the information about the body and the ways in which it works, so that you can speak knowledgeably to your daughter when you're ready. As far as her level of understanding goes, just present the information slowly, and give her time to assimilate it all. It will take several sessions for you to get through even the basics, so don't get frustrated. Feel free to simplify (without distorting) when necessary, and you might be surprised at how much she will learn.

Question:
"Why don't you supply the slang words that people use for bodily parts? It sounds so formal to say 'testicles' instead of 'balls.' What's wrong with using everyday language?"

Answer:
Nothing is wrong with using everyday language. The point you have missed is that when you are teaching your child about sex, you have the opportunity to teach him *properly*. Every child should know the correct words for the parts of his own body. Once that education has taken place, he may choose to use everyday language instead, and that's fine. He will know the difference between the correct terminology and the slang words that the other kids will be using on the streets. The correct words are important to know, because he won't always be a child, and getting him into the habit of utilizing proper terms now is in his best interests. After all, how would you feel if you went for your yearly physical exam, and the nurse handed you a bottle and said, "Here, go piss in this"?

Question:
"My twelve-year-old daughter wants me to put her on the Pill. I'm thinking of refusing, because it would be the same thing as telling her that it's okay with me if she goes out and has sex with every boy in her class. What should I do?"

Answer:
Refusing outright to help her might be the same thing as telling her that you don't mind if she gets pregnant. Your daughter was mature enough to ask for your help in averting a terrible problem. Perhaps she is also mature enough to listen as you explain the seriousness and the ramifications of what she is about to do. If she's receptive to you, and if you say the right things, you may be able to teach her that sex at 12 is a mistake; if not, don't *make* the mistake of believing that the simple lack of birth control pills will prevent the behavior, or you may end up with a pregnant 12-year-old. Wouldn't that be a harsh way of teaching a lesson?

Chapter Fifteen

The Bully and the Wimp: Strategies for Change

In this chapter, we will concentrate on a number of different techniques that you can employ to help

- children who are overly aggressive,

- children who lack an appropriate amount of aggressiveness in their interactions with others,

- children who need to increase their assertiveness.

Aggression

The purpose of aggression is to overpower others, to dominate, and to win. Although that has a negative sound to it, there are many instances in which a child may need to be aggressive in socially acceptable situations (such as in sports). At other times, a child may need to be aggressive in order to survive with his peers—letting other children see that they cannot intimidate him easily. Unfortunately, some children use aggression too often and in the wrong situations, and they will express thoughts and feelings inappropriately, basically engaging in physical and verbal muscle-flexing.

Let's imagine for a moment that Johnny is in a judo match, trying very hard to be aggressive, putting a great deal of energy into his techniques, and eventually overpowering and winning against his opponent. The chances are excellent that he will get praise and applause from the onlookers, simply because people consider this to be an appropriate use of aggression. If, later that same day, another child tells Johnny that he is ugly and stupid, and Johnny reacts by yelling and hurts the child by knocking him to the ground, Johnny may end up getting into trouble for being overly aggressive in a situation that did not call for such a reaction.

Aggression has, as its goal, a victory of sorts over one's opponent, even at the cost of potential harm to him. Whether your child is acting aggressively with a teacher (verbally) or is behaving aggressively with a classmate (physically), the definition remains the same. Obviously, there is not necessarily anything wrong with being aggressive per se; however, a child must learn to discriminate between situations when aggressive behavior is appropriate and those instances in which it is not.

Assertiveness

Assertiveness refers to a willingness to stand up for one's rights and to express one's thoughts, beliefs, and feelings in such a way as to avoid interfering with anyone else's safety or rights. When being assertive, a child is trying to express his thoughts, his feelings, and his perceptions without downgrading or humiliating another person.

Let's look at an example of a child who is acting assertively. Here, Miles must respond to another child's request in an assertive manner.

Frank: Miles, give me your homework page so that I can copy the answers. I didn't have time to do my homework last night, and I'm going to get into trouble.
Miles: I can't give it to you. You know the teacher doesn't allow that, and I'll be in trouble if we get caught.
Frank: You'd better give it to me, or you'll be sorry.
Miles: No, I just told you, I can't.
Frank: That's it—I'm gonna get you after school!
Miles: If you want to fight me, that's your choice, but I'm still not going to give you the paper.
Frank: If you know what's good for you, you'll give it to me right now!
Miles: No way, Frank. Leave me alone.
Frank: Drop dead! I'll get it from Elizabeth.

Here, Miles stuck to his decision not to let his classmate copy the homework, and despite the threats and the aggressive statements that were made by the other child, Miles stood up for what he believed was right. Miles showed the other child that he could not be intimidated. Notice that no *aggressive* statements were made by Miles; he said only things which reflected *assertiveness*.

The Overly Aggressive Child

Often, parents will complain to us that their child is too aggressive and too quick to fight, and when he attempts to deal with a problem that he has encountered, he becomes upset and frustrated. Very often, one of our first questions to such a parent is, "Does either of the parents in the household get upset and 'explode' easily or become aggressive?" Quite often, as you might imagine, the parent will respond, "Yes." It is very important that we look at the influence exerted on the child by the models that he is observing in the house.

One of Dr. Silverman's personal experiences showed him the powerful effect of modeling. "When I adopted my oldest son from El Salvador, he arrived in the United States never having had a pair of shoes before. Typically, when I take off my sneakers, I tend to kick them off my feet without opening the laces. When my son had his first pair of shoes at the age of eight, he began taking his shoes off the same way that I do. He had never experienced having shoes in the orphanage that he came from, so he learned how to take off his shoes just by observing how I did it."

If a child can pick up something so easily from a parent's modeling, just imagine the variety of behaviors that the child can pick up by watching how his parents react to the stresses in their lives. If the child frequently observes a parent who is overly aggressive, there is a good chance that the child will pick up that behavioral pattern. If a parent is modeling behavior that is inappropriate for a child to display, the first place to start must be in reducing the parent's exhibition of such behavior. Thus, if the parent of an overly aggressive child behaves that way himself, the logical starting place in reducing the child's aggressive behavior would be a reduction in the parent's exhibition of aggression. It is unrealistic for us to expect a child to refrain from a behavior that he or she sees modeled in the environment constantly. Of course, the same thing can be said about *positive* behavior; so clearly there is the potential for you to teach your child to behave properly.

Reducing Aggression

One very effective means for helping an aggressive child to reduce the number of occasions in which he is overly aggressive is to reinforce opposing behavior. In other words, whenever you see the child respond appropriately to a situation in which he characteristically would become aggressive, there should be some reward. By this, we mean praise, special privileges, or special treats.

Tony gets upset and loses his temper easily; he frequently gets into fights with other children. One day, Tony sees another child kick his bicycle down. Tony looks at the child and says, "If you come near my bike again, you are going to be 'finished.'" However, this is a great improvement, as Tony previously would have gone over to the child and hit him. This time, because his reaction was so much more appropriate, his parent would be well advised to call him over and say, "I saw what happened when Billy knocked down your bike. You controlled your temper very well, and you told him not to do it again. I'm very proud of you, and you should be very proud of yourself. Because you controlled your temper so well, I'm going to let you stay up a half-hour later tonight to watch television." If Tony's parents were to look for those times when he responds appropriately and then praise him on those occasions, it is likely that Tony would start to learn that his parents will give him a significant amount of attention when he shows that he can deal with conflict in a healthy way. However, if Tony is scolded continually for getting into fights or for being too aggressive, he will learn that he can gain a significant amount of attention from his parents by evidencing such behavior. Thus, to help Tony with the problem, his parents must reduce their reactions to his aggressiveness, and they must play up their satisfaction with his appropriate responses.

Think First

As a parent, you can teach your child to think more carefully before he acts. If a child does react too aggressively in a situation, the child must learn from the experience. Example: In the preceding situation, if Tony had punched and knocked down the other child, the parent could have requested Tony to make a list of three things that he could have done in the situation rather than fight. Until he makes that list, he would not be entitled to any privileges or activities. By repeating this procedure numerous times, Tony would start learning to think carefully about his options and would see that there are ways to deal with conflict other than by getting excited and fighting. Such an approach teaches the child to react in a more socially acceptable manner.

Try to catch the child *not* fighting. For example, if one of your children is acting too aggressively toward his brother or sister, you might try to catch the child at a time when he is not being aggressive. If you catch the child playing well with his siblings for about fifteen minutes, you might emphasize how well they are all getting along and point out how pleasant it makes the household. A special treat might be considered initially so your children see that you really value cooperative behavior.

When your child begins to illustrate solid control over his aggressiveness and smiles when one of his siblings calls him a name, you might reinforce him by saying, "Danny, when Sheila called you a 'fat pig,' you smiled and walked away. You didn't let name calling bother you. You should be very proud of yourself; that was a very mature way to behave."

Thus, we can help children to decrease their aggressiveness by reinforcing their appropriate responses to conflict and to stress. By doing this consistently, you are likely to see a reduction in aggressive behavior in a reasonable amount of time. If you are not consistent and follow through on these principles only once or twice a week, you will probably not see any changes.

Helping Kids to Become More Aggressive and Assertive

Before a child can become more aggressive, he must first become more assertive. The shy or passive child may suffer tremendously as he becomes older, because his peers most probably will take advantage of him. A child who is often teased, hit, picked on, and ridiculed by other children usually sets himself up to be a victim of abuse. There is generally something about the victim's behavior that encourages other children to be abusive towards him. Usually, the victim allows other children to see that he is easily intimidated and cannot handle their teasing, and this, of course, encourages the other children to pick on him more frequently.

To teach your child to be more assertive and aggressive, certain behaviors have to be established. *Voice control* is one of the most important behaviors for an assertive or aggressive child. A shy and passive child often speaks in a very soft voice. Thus, you may need to do exercises with your child to help him to increase the volume of his voice. These exercises can include saying phrases, such as the following, in a loud and demanding tone of voice. Here are some sample phrases that you might choose to practice:

1. *Don't* bug me!
2. *Stop* it!
3. *Don't* bother me!
4. Cut it *out!*
5. Hands off, *now!*
6. Leave me *alone!*
7. Get *out* of here!
8. Mind your *own* business!
9. Get *lost!*
10. Give it back to me, *now!*

You need to help your child learn to put emphasis on the most important part of the statement. For example, when the child says, "Don't bug me," the word *don't* should be said more forcefully than are the rest of the words in the sentence. Thus, your child can learn to put more meaning into the message that he is trying to give to the children who are bothering him.

The shy and passive child must learn to establish eye contact when he is communicating with another person, and you can help your child to practice this. One effective way to practice is to have the parent stay in one position in a room, while the child has to walk from one side to the other (maintaining eye contact all the while). Additionally, you can make the establishing of eye contact a normal part of your everyday conversations. Your child must learn that when he is confronted by another youngster, he needs to look the other child in the eye. As soon as eye contact is broken, it is a signal to the bully that your child is becoming intimidated. Finally, as an alternate method of practicing eye contact, you can suggest that your child use a mirror and look directly at his own eyes while he speaks out loud.

After the child has learned to establish better eye contact, he should practice the combination of eye contact and assertive statements. Now, using another child (or, if you choose to do so, you can play the role of another child), the practice sessions should involve combining all of these skills. The child must look directly into the eyes of his practice partner and verbalize some assertive statements (in as loud a voice as possible). The statements mentioned, such as *"Don't* bug me," should be practiced.

Next, the child must learn how to hold his body. When trying to speak assertively, a child must not fold his arms, put his hands in his pockets, put his hands behind his back, or make any other move that could be seen as self-protective or submissive. The child must keep his hands to the side, stand up straight, and look the other person in the eye. One very effective position is for the child to stand with his feet slightly separated, his hands at his sides, and his eyes focused directly on the person with whom he is practicing.

To Fight or Not to Fight

Sometimes, it may be necessary for your child to become aggressive with a child who is bothering him. The decision whether to fight back physically is something that the child will have to make. It is advisable that a child who has always been a victim learn some basic self-defense techniques. These techniques include the proper way to make a fist, as well as how and where to strike an aggressor. When the child perceives that the antagonist is going to hit him, he is often better off striking first, and then removing himself from the situation. A child occasionally may have to get into a fight in order for the children around him to see that picking on him involves a risk to them. Often, once this reputation has been established, children feel no further need to challenge the individual child. If a child is not perceived by his peers as being assertive or aggressive enough to protect himself when he is being verbally or physically attacked by another child of the same age and size, he is destined to become a victim of some other child's aggression.

Organized Activities That Can Help

There are a variety of activities that can be very therapeutic for the shy and passive child. These activities include karate, judo, and acting lessons. A parent who wants to help a passive child should insist that the child go to these activities, even if the child feels uncomfortable about it. Most children don't like to change, preferring instead to maintain the status quo. At times, you may have to force your child into an activity for his own good. Giving a child an antibiotic when he has an infection is important so that the infection cannot spread further. Forcing a child into karate class when he is very passive and non-assertive is important so that he will not become a passive (and possibly dependent) adult. The medicine, as well as the forced physical activity, is something that is for the child's own good, and whether he likes the medicine or the karate class is insignificant because it is something that really needs to be done.

The Teacher Can Help, Too

A teacher can be very helpful in reinforcing a passive child's efforts to become more assertive. Whenever the teacher observes the child standing up for his own rights and asserting himself, the teacher can help by giving the child feedback. Feedback might include saying something, such as "I saw the other kids take the ball from you, and you handled the situation quite well." The teacher might also send a note home to the parent when such a situation has been observed, so that the parent can reinforce the behavior at home. If the shy and passive child can be paired with more assertive and aggressive children as part of special class projects or activities, the modeling provided by these more assertive children could be very helpful (as long as these children are not taking advantage of the passive child). If you are working on increasing your child's assertiveness and aggressiveness, the teacher always should be told about it. Then if the teacher observes the child standing up for himself or possibly getting involved in a fight, she will be more understanding about what the child is experiencing and attempting to accomplish at the time.

Question:

"Whenever my seven-year-old son goes outside to play, he gets into fights with older children and comes into the house crying. He complains about how mean everyone is to him and how miserable he feels. My son wants me to tell the other children to leave him alone. Do you have any suggestions?"

Answer:

Study your child's behavior carefully. Does he do or say anything to these older children that would make him a target for their aggressive behavior? If your son is acting like a "big shot," challenging them, and even boasting about his power to beat *them* up, you should stay out of it. You might help your son by asking, "Is there anything that you do or say to the other children that might make them angry?" If he does not respond accurately, and if you are aware that he is indeed setting himself up for problems, tell him what behavior you have observed that might result in your son alienating himself from the other children.

You can give your child an opportunity to learn how to resolve conflicts by himself. You might help him by discussing possible solutions to the problem, as well as by encouraging him to generate possible solutions. Perhaps, you can even get him to promise that he will try one of the solutions that you've both discussed.

If you were certain that the older children were being abusive to your son without provocation, then perhaps you might have to say or to do something for your child's own safety. Usually, this is not necessary, since most conflicts of this nature are the result of a younger child acting like a "big wheel" around the older kids and, thus, asking for trouble. When this is the case, he will have to accept the consequences of starting up with older and stronger children.

Question:

"My ten-year-old daughter is too shy. When we go to a restaurant, she refuses to tell the waitress what she wants and always wants me to speak for her. Is there any way that I can get her to speak for herself?"

Answer:

Your daughter obviously is old enough to speak for herself, but she doesn't feel a need to do that; she feels more secure having you do the talking. You must put her in a position where she has to speak for herself. You might suggest to her, "Tell the waitress what you want, because I will no longer speak for you. Now that you're such a big girl, you must speak for yourself." If she tells you that she will not do it, let her know that if she wants to eat, she will have to ask for what she wants or she will not get any food, because you will refuse to order for her. You must put her in a situation where she will have to make this kind of a choice. You need to refuse to do it for her even if she whines, cries, begs, or pleads. You see, whenever you speak for her, you reinforce her shyness, and you lose the opportunity to allow her to learn to stand on her own two feet. Of course, when she does speak up for herself, be sure to reinforce that behavior by telling her how well she handled the situation.

Question:

"Will watching television shows that contain a lot of violent scenes make my child more aggressive?"

Answer:

Not necessarily. Although some studies have shown that increased exposure to models of aggression can result in a child becoming more aggressive, there are many other factors to consider. The most important thing is what the child observes in his real-life environment. As discussed earlier in this chapter, your child will observe how *you* handle situations. If he sees you handle them in a peaceful manner, then he will learn how to deal with conflict in an appropriate manner (as you are modeling for him). If and when he does become overly aggressive, your response is important. If you tolerate his abusive or aggressive actions, he will learn that such inappropriate behavior is considered to be acceptable. However, if dangerous or aggressive actions result in punishment, he will learn that such behavior is not acceptable. It is too easy for us to blame television for our children's behavior. As parents, we must take responsibility for teaching our children what they need to know. Discouraging inappropriate aggression is a good example of the proper assumption of parental responsibility.

Question:
"My husband told my son that he could participate in a judo class, but I think that the competition of one child against another is encouraging too much aggression. I really don't know what is right. What do you think?"

Answer:
This may not be a situation with a right or a wrong answer because many factors are involved. A good judo instructor will select opponents carefully, and he will not allow boos from the crowd. Most instructors are skilled at making the loser feel that the defeat is not important, and that he should go on to develop certain skills. Rather than be concerned about whether or not he should join a judo class, your concern should be in picking a judo program that will help your child to get good and regular exercise, to learn skills, to experience cooperation, and to have respect for others and for his own personal abilities. If the child really wants to participate, don't worry about him becoming overly aggressive. At first, he may attempt to use his new skills on everyone nearby (willing and unwilling), but after a while, he is likely to become much less aggressive. This sport emphasizes when and how to use the learned skills, and the exercise serves as a good means for relaxation and for working-off excess energy. Many children who are overly aggressive become less aggressive when they participate in sports such as judo or karate, because such activities serve as a wholesome outlet for aggressive impulses that might otherwise be expressed much less appropriately.

Chapter Sixteen

Mind and Body: The Great Connection

WARNING: When reading this chapter, *never* attempt to use any of the suggested techniques with your children unless you first have consulted with your child's physician. Often, a complaint from a child that seems to be psychological rather than physical is ignored. Because there really can be a medical condition for which the child needs treatment, you must *always* eliminate the possibility of a medical problem before you assume it to be psychological in origin.

Psychosomatic Problems

A lot of people think that the word *psychosomatic* means that the pain or illness is imaginary and "in the person's mind," but that is not what psychosomatic means. A psychosomatic illness really exists, but it is related directly to the person's emotional state. For example, some types of asthma are influenced by a child's inability to deal with stress; stressful situations can often be the stimulus for an asthmatic attack. The important point here is that the asthmatic attack is real: The child is wheezing and having difficulty breathing, and there is nothing imaginary about the situation. However, it is psychosomatic because the illness is a function of the child's emotional state.

In this chapter, we will look at some common psychosomatic disorders of childhood (e.g., soiling and bed-wetting), as well as examine typical childhood physical complaints (including a discussion of the ways in which you should react). We will explore those physical activities which are good for children.

Mommy, It Hurts So Much

Here is a classic example of how attention from a parent can contribute to a child being overwhelmed with pain.

We saw Albert at our office when he was 11 years old. He was referred to us by his pediatrician, who was concerned about the child's complaints of pain several months following an appendectomy. The child had been hospitalized to determine if this post-operative pain had a physical basis, but no medical problems were revealed.

When we saw Albert and his mother at our office, we first had to determine what "reward" Albert was getting for his complaints about the pain in his abdomen. Albert had three brothers and sisters, and when he had his surgery, he got more attention from his mother (a single parent) than he had ever received from her in his life. Whenever he complained about pain, his mother would ask him many questions, sit with him as he would relax on his bed, call the doctor, and take him out of school for medical appointments. Albert really seemed to thrive on the attention.

Our plan was very simple. We told Albert's mother to tune out her son's complaints. She said that she felt confident in the doctor's assurances that nothing was medically wrong with her son so that she could, at this point, dismiss the complaints. The mother was instructed to ignore Albert's attention-getting strategies as completely as possible. She was not to look at him, show any facial expressions, or discuss his reports of discomfort. Albert was told that if he felt some pain, he could rest for a while, but that no one in the house would pay any special attention to him since the doctors had given him a clean bill of health. The mother did a fine job; she resisted the temptation to give in and to pay attention to the complaints. If the mother had attended to her son's complaints (even 1 out of 5 times), Albert would have learned that there was a chance to get the attention that he was seeking. On another level, we had the mother praise Albert whenever a few hours went by without a complaint ("Albert, you are not complaining about the stomach pains because you know that the doctors said that you are fine. I'm glad that you trust the doctors and don't have to waste all of that time worrying about pain."). Albert was now learning that he would get some attention for *not* complaining about the pain, instead of receiving attention only when things were going badly. In a couple of weeks, the mother told us that all of the complaining had stopped and that things were back to normal.

We want to emphasize again that you would ignore a child's complaints about pain only when you have absolute confidence in your physician's assurance that the child is well. Withdrawing your attention from a child's complaints about pain that has no physical basis can and will reduce the frequency of those complaints.

Bed-wetting (Enuresis)

Nocturnal *enuresis* (bed-wetting at night) is a common problem in children, although it is found far more often in boys than in girls. As with any other mind-body problem, you cannot try to reduce the bed-wetting until the child has been properly examined and tested medically to rule out the possibility of an organic disorder. You should never try to treat the bed-wetting behavior of a 2-year-old since, at that age, it cannot be considered a valid problem. Once a child is 5 or 6 years old, however, bed-wetting should be viewed as a definite problem that requires remediation. If the child continues wetting the bed, you can expect social problems, family problems, and problems with self-concept. Therefore, it is unquestionably worthwhile for you to invest whatever time and effort is needed to end the wetting.

Many procedures have been used in attempts to reduce nocturnal enuresis. These include hypnosis, bell-and-pad systems, bladder conditioning, sleeping and awakening schedules, and medication. The bell-and-pad system is an inexpensive and easy-to-implement program for most parents. Research studies have shown that when the bell-and-pad system is properly used, nocturnal enuresis has been reduced in up to 76 percent of the children who used the device.

We recommend highly a device called "Wet-Stop." Wet-Stop is available by mail from Palco Labs, a company based in Santa Cruz, California. The Wet-Stop kit consists of an ultra-small moisture-sensing device that buzzes when only a slight drop of urine touches it. It comes with "Velcro" patches that can be attached to the child's pajamas or underwear, and instructions (and batteries) are included with the kit.

Often, children who wet the bed go into a deep sleep, and the sense of pressure caused by a full bladder does not result in awakening them. When using Wet-Stop, however, the child cannot help but awaken, because as the first drop of urine touches the sensor, a loud buzzer goes off. Ideally, the child should at that point walk to the bathroom to finish the elimination process there; afterward, the child should change the sheets, if necessary. Gradually, the child will be conditioned to awaken himself whenever he senses the urge to go to the bathroom. As a rule, a child uses the device until he has had a full week of dryness. When a relapse occurs, the device is used again until another week of dryness occurs. Most children show a significant reduction in bed-wetting within four to six weeks.

Hypnotherapy is another technique for approaching the problem of nocturnal enuresis. Contrary to what you may believe, hypnosis is a safe and effective technique when performed by a qualified professional. Unfortunately, there are many "professionals" who claim that they can be effective with children, but who really do not have the proper training in clinical hypnosis. If you decide to have your child undergo hypnotherapy, find a psychologist or a psychiatrist who works primarily with children and who is a member of the American Society of Clinical Hypnosis (the most outstanding professional organization of its type). In our practice, many of the children who have undergone hypnotherapy for nocturnal enuresis have responded in as little as one or two sessions, although the technique is not successful with all children.

Soiling (Encopresis)

Although as many as 1 to 2 percent of primary-school-age children reportedly have problems with bowel control, *encopresis* (continual defecation into the underwear or clothing by preschool and school-age children) is not often discussed. Many parents may avoid discussing it simply because of the offensive nature of the problem, but, of course, that does nothing to lessen its occurrence. Like enuresis, encopresis occurs more frequently in boys than it does in girls.

As stated previously, it is very important to rule out the existence of a medical problem caused by poor diet, and any difficulties with the bowels, colon, or nervous system must be considered before approaching the problem. Sometimes, soiling occurs after incidents of constipation, and in some cases, the physician may have recommended certain laxatives or enemas. Although encopresis is not usually the result of a medical condition, you must rule out that possibility.

The procedures recommended here are directed for use with a child who has been given a clean bill of health by his physician. We are referring specifically to a child who has previously established proper procedures for going to the bathroom, but who has suddenly started defecating in his clothes.

Many factors can contribute to encopresis. Sometimes, a child gets so involved with his play, or is in such a rush to do something else, that going to the bathroom becomes of secondary importance. Occasionally, the problem is just another bad habit, and, of course, there are children who soil as an attention-seeking technique. Whatever the reason, however, something must be done to stop the behavior.

Before implementing any behavior modification approach, we recommend that you label your child's underwear. Giving each piece of underwear a letter *(A, B, C, D, etc.)* will help you to monitor your child's behavior so that you can be sure that he is not hiding or throwing away soiled underwear. With the lettering procedure, it will be easy for you to take an inventory, if that becomes necessary.

Since the PST philosophy is that the parent must always maintain control of his emotions, you must handle this situation calmly. The following routine is suggested:

1. Tell the child that whenever he has a whole day without soiling, there will be a reward (which can be a special privilege or other incentive meaningful to the child).
2. Whenever the child soils his pants:
   a. He should wash his underwear by hand with detergent. Then, he must put the washed underwear (with all of his other laundry) in the washing machine, if available.
   b. While the washing machine is working, he must take a bath or a shower two times. He must dry himself off completely after the first bath or shower. Then, he must take another shower, and dry off again.
   c. The child should put the wet wash in the dryer.

d. He must fold and put away the entire wash load.
e. Then, he must go to his room and sit down alone for 5 or 10 minutes.
f. Next, he should sit on the toilet for 5 or 10 minutes.
g. Repeat "e" and "f", as above, two times more.

It is hoped that all of this inconvenience and practice will motivate the child to maintain better control. During the above procedures, you should not lecture, get upset, or comment on the ugliness of the dirtied underpants. The child will begin to realize that refraining from soiling results in a reward or in some pleasurable event, but that soiling will result in inconvenience to him. Your child must be told that the procedures will occur whenever he soils, so that he will know, in advance, what the consequences will be.

If you do not have initial success with these procedures, try to follow them consistently for at least six weeks before you conclude that they are ineffective in reducing soiling. If a major reduction does not occur, it is suggested that you consult a mental health professional. Encopresis is a serious problem which you must help your child to overcome, since it often leads to intense social difficulties (especially to peer rejection and to ridicule, due to the nature of the situation).

Exercise for Mind and Body

The PST philosophy emphasizes the importance of your child's physical development. Athletic activities are excellent in helping children to become acquainted with their own bodies, to learn cooperation and teamwork, and to attend to rules. They serve also as healthy outlets for channeling aggression and energy that could otherwise be directed into anti-social activities. Athletics, for some children, can provide a means of having successful experiences which are important if a child is to develop a good self-concept. Often, we see children join organized sports and spend 90 percent of their time sitting on the side, or standing and hoping that the ball comes their way. Unfortunately, some organized sports programs for children select the more able-bodied child for various positions and participation, leaving the less skilled child out of most of the action. Ironically, of course, the less skilled child is the one who probably needs the participation and exercise the most.

The Klutz

Children with poor coordination, and those who are not as physically strong as most of their peers, often avoid physical activities. This is ironic, since the only way for the "klutz" to improve his agility or strength is to participate in such programs. Unfortunately, when these children attempt to engage in an athletic activity, they are ridiculed, teased, and rejected. Such experiences result in the klutz going out of his way to avoid athletic endeavors, preferring instead to redirect his interests into activities such as reading, stamp collecting, and other non-physical pursuits.

It is very important for the parent of a poorly coordinated child to insist that the child participate in activities that will help him to become less klutzy. If the parent does not intervene, the child may experience a variety of problems. The most significant difficulty to be faced by such a child is peer rejection. When a child is unable to keep up with his friends by participating in activities common to the age and gender, he may begin playing instead with younger children or with children of the opposite sex as a means of avoiding certain activities. He cannot, for example, stay with his chronological peers when they start throwing a football around because he knows from experience what will happen. Such a child can grow up feeling uncomfortable with his peers, believing that he is somehow "different," and this often results in relationship and social adjustment difficulties.

If your child is the classic klutz, we urge you to arrange for the child to participate in appropriate activities, even if the child does not want to do so. Since it is for his own good, you need to explain to the child that it is just one of the things that he has to do. Of course, we are not suggesting that you force the klutz to join the football team so that he can be ridiculed and traumatized by his peers. We are recommending instead that you help him to become involves in activities such as karate, which can help him to develop better coordination, strength, speed, and confidence. In short, you need to help him get over being a klutz.

Helpful Activities

We have found that certain activities which do not emphasize competition, but which focus instead on the individual child's progress, can be beneficial to most children. Karate and gymnastics are the most obvious of these sports, and we usually recommend karate as the preferred activity because it emphasizes so many important skills and values that children can benefit from learning. Contrary to what you might imagine, karate is not an activity that requires initial physical prowess; instead, it helps a child to develop such a quality as he learns.

Karate: Keeping Aggression Under the Belt

There is much more to karate than its obvious value as a means of self-defense. It can help a child to become more confident, better disciplined, and increasingly aware of his own assets, and it can aid him in developing self-control. Karate is a form of controlled aggression, wherein the child is taught how and when to use his skills and to show respect for the power that is being developed. It also is non-sexist, in that boys and girls are treated equally in the sport. Even a child who is overly aggressive learns more control and becomes less aggressive after participating is this martial art, as karate shows a child how to focus physical and mental energy onto a target area through carefully executed moves (punches, strikes, kicks). Traditional karate emphasizes physical and mental discipline, but without contact. You should avoid any karate school in which real body contact is encouraged.

Although we generally show far more concern about a child's academic development, it is important also to concentrate on his physical development. A child who is physically relaxed and who is feeling good about himself will be able to benefit the most from his studies. There is an inexorable relationship between the mind and the body, so let's help our children to keep their bodies in good shape, along with their minds.

_____

Question:
"I agree that my daughter would benefit greatly from partici-

pating in gymnastics or karate; however, she refuses to go. We've tried both activities and after the first session, she told us that she will not go back and that she wants nothing to do with it. We hate to force her to go. Do you have any suggestions?"

Answer:
As we have said before, sometimes you have to force your child to do something that is for her own good. If she really needs one of these activities for her health or for her development, then you should make her go. If both activities would be beneficial, ask her to select the one that would be the least objectionable to her. Tell her that because she must participate in one of the activities, you are giving her an opportunity to make the selection (before you have to pick one for her). Once an activity has been selected, let her know that she is going to participate for at least six months. She has no choice but to go, since you have determined that it is really in her best interests. You can probably lessen her reluctance somewhat by explaining your reasoning, so that she may see that it is to her advantage to go even if it makes her feel a little uncomfortable.

The dropout rate in these sports is highest in the first few months, because that is when children discover that it is hard work. If she gets through the first few months and starts showing progress (e.g., earning a yellow belt), the reinforcement of this success will encourage her to continue. Regardless of how much she complains and dislikes the activity, take her to the sessions and tune out her protests. If she knows that you will provide an audience for these complaints, you can expect to hear them continuously. Be assertive, and let her know that although you understand that she really does not like this activity, you will not give her a choice about attending because, as a parent, you must decide what is best. Remember, we are discussing a child who really needs the activity for a reason, such as for coordination problems or for aggression. If the participation is mandated by you as a result of your own desire to have a karate star in the family, then the child's objections would be quite valid. In such a case, the child should have more latitude about selecting a sport (competitive or non-competitive) to join.

Question:

"My son is seven years old, and he wets the bed almost every night. We know that he can control himself if he wants to, so we told him that he would be spanked any day that he wets. Your philosophy seems to disagree with punishment for bed-wetting. Should we stop the spanking?"

Answer:

Don't ever spank a child for something over which he has no real control. He is sleeping when he wets, so one cannot expect him to be held responsible for remembering to go to the bathroom. Moreover, the spanking will not really help him to learn to wake himself up and go to the bathroom when his bladder if full. If he were to wet his pants while playing because he was too involved in his play, that would be a different story, because he would have some conscious control. We suggest that you try using the Wet-Stop device discussed earlier in this chapter. Use it just as we have instructed, or read a book, such as the one by Nathan Azrin, Ph.D., *A Parent's Guide to Bedwetting Control,* in order to learn proven procedures for reducing your child's enuresis.

Question:

"Our nine-year-old son soils his pants a few times each week. He just doesn't take the time to come in from playing to go to the bathroom, so we came up with an idea. We want to put the dirty underwear next to his bed and leave it there for a week. We figure that if he gets sick of the smell, and if anyone who comes into his room tells him how horrible it smells, he might be motivated to change his habits. What do you think?"

Answer:

PST does not involve using any technique that is designed to intimidate or to expose a child to ridicule. Again, we want to *teach* a child appropriate behavior without trying to humiliate him. The techniques discussed in this chapter have proven to be effective in a short period of time. With these techniques, the child feels proud of not soiling and is encouraged to keep trying. He will be able to perceive his parents as being concerned and as really wanting to help him, not as people who want to make him feel ashamed and embarrassed. Let your son see that you are not angry with him, but that you want him to learn a new behavior: keeping his pants clean by going to the bathroom when he feels the urge to do so.

Question:

"My daughter over-reacts to a sniffle, a slight pain, such as a sprain, or any physical discomfort. We decided to try a new way to toughen her up. Whenever she complains, we want to put her to bed as if she were sick, so that she cannot play or go out. We are hoping that this inconvenience will discourage her from complaining so much. Do you think that this will work?"

Answer:

The plan has some good points, but she still may be getting too much attention for these complaints. We remain committed to the recommendation that you ignore her complaints completely and switch the conversation to another topic. There is a risk that when you put her to bed, she will feel as if you are acknowledging that she is ill, so you may accidentally feed right into her problem. You will be telling her, "Yes, I agree that you are sick, and that is why I want you to go to bed." Let her know that these complaints are so insignificant that they are not worth spending the time that you would need to respond to them. Eventually, she should learn that her exaggerated complaints are insignificant.

When Trouble Strikes:
Lying, Stealing, Cursing, and More

Parents are understandably dismayed when they learn that their children are involved in any behavior that is illegal or dangerous to themselves or others. Antisocial behavior is, by definition, a particularly negative activity, and it is essential that parents respond promptly and properly to the challenge. The problem is, of course, that few parents feel at all confident about their ability to face or to deal with antisocial behavior. In fact, there are few areas of child rearing that parents dread more than that which involves trying to stop children from doing dangerous, illegal, or inappropriate things that they have chosen quite deliberately to do.

It's Really Not All Your Fault

To begin with, let's dispense with the foolish notion that if your child is involved in any antisocial behavior, it says something awful about you. The same parent who feels, vicariously, that he is a "loser" (himself) when his child strikes out in a Little League game is likely to feel the same way when his child becomes involved in some sort of trouble. "Only a rotten parent could have a child that would do such a thing" is the way such thinking usually proceeds. Fortunately, perhaps for you, such is not the case. There are times when children say, think, and do all sorts of things for which their parents are not (and in fact, could *not* be) responsible. Although a child's behavior certainly reflects to some degree the style in which his parents have raised him, it does not follow that every move he makes is determined by the suitability of his parent. You can set good examples for your children and hope that they will be followed, and you can (and should) avoid setting negative examples because they probably will be imitated with enthusiasm. If you shout obscenities at ther drivers because you are angry with the way they are driving, don't be surprised when your child does the same thing because he doesn't like the way you prepared the hamburgers. Similarly, if your child watches you pocket an extra $10 that a store clerk gave to you by mistake while making change, don't be shocked when he "borrows" someone's bicycle and "forgets" to return it. Of course, there may be instances in which your child acts very differently than experience would dictate or predict, and since these most probably will represent the majority of such instances, feelings of guilt have no place in the response to antisocial behavior.

What Did I Just Hear You Say?

Perhaps the most innocent form of antisocial behavior is the use of obscene language. Four-letter words are a child's claim to sophistication, and the use of such language results from several different sources of influence at once. In this case, imitation is the sincerest form of flattery, and children often repeat obscene words that they have heard their parents (or other children) say out loud. If your child doesn't hear the words, then he can't learn to say them. Think about it; people learn new words through the process of experience. As a very young child, you learned specific words because their very utterance was rewarding in itself. Before you knew the words *ice cream,* you must have had a very difficult time requesting any from your parents. When you learned the words, you could make your wishes known to others. You matched the correct words with the things that you meant to say because the use of any other word(s) never would have been reinforced. If you wanted ice cream, but instead said "doggie," you would have learned quickly that "doggie" was the wrong word to use; the utterance of that particular word would not have gotten you what you wanted. The same thing holds true for obscene language: once a child learns the words, he will continue to use them if he is reinforced in any way.

A Time and a Place for Everything

On another level, obscene language has its proper usage. It is woefully unrealistic to imagine that when you've accidentally hit your thumb with a hammer, you are going to say, "Well, golly gee, that certainly seemed rather painful." Obscene language expresses emotion with greater efficiency and effectiveness than does conventional language. It is precisely for this reason that such words exist in languages in the first place. Unless you are a very unusual parent, your child is going to hear you utter obscenities every once in a while. The important thing is not that he learn *never* to say such things, but rather that he understand that there are very limited times, places, and circumstances when and where such usage is permitted, and that such language is always inappropriate for use by young children.

Finally, the use of obscenities is often a direct result of peer pressure. Children are socialized to believe that the proper use of language is a badge of "nerdism," and that the only way to be "cool" is to speak in the vernacular, sprinkling in as many obscenities as possible. Using such language makes a child feel like a member of "the club," in that he will see himself as being more sophisticated if he uses the sort of language that is typically reserved for older people. As he spends more time with his peers, the developing child often will say and do whatever it takes to be accepted, and if that means obscenities are the order of the day, then he will in all likelihood engage in that behavior. There is often a degree of excitement associated with doing anything antisocial; the child realizes that the behavior would be criticized by adults and there is, therefore, a risk involved in attempting to get away with it. Fortunately, there are techniques to be used in curbing such behavior in your child.

Brace Yourself: Here Come the Bad Words

PST involves the unusual use of humor as a technique for removing the reinforcement from the uttering of inappropriate words. If you don't react with anger to the uttering of obscenities by your child, you will be able to maintain the control that you need to have over the situation. The idea here is that your child needs to be made to feel embarrassed by the inappropriate use of such words, and when this takes place, the reinforcement will be weakened enough to permit the behavior to change. Additionally, you will encourage the occurrence of a phenomenon that psychologists call a "paired association." What is meant by that term is that two things are paired together so consistently that when one occurs, the other is automatically expected. When you hear the long screech of car brakes, for example, you expect to hear that sound followed by the crunch of metal. That expectation is the result of a paired association between the sound of brakes and the likelihood of a collision. By associating obscene language with a feeling of foolishness, your child may become less likely to want to use such language at all.

Parent: Remember, Debbie, tomorrow is Thanksgiving and we have to go to Aunt Gertie's for a turkey dinner.

Child: I don't want to go to her house for fucking Thanksgiving turkey!

Parent: Fucking Thanksgiving turkey? That's strange. Most people are content just to *eat* their Thanksgiving turkey.

Note in the preceding example that the parent was able to maintain control by avoiding anger, as well as by saying something that made her child feel foolish for having used such language in the first place. In PST, we are not suggesting that you act in a humiliating fashion with your child, but rather that there are times and occasions when your child can learn from the absurdity of his own behavior. You are not doing your child a favor by permitting him to continue behaving inappropriately; you must teach him to behave in a reasonable fashion. In a case such as this one, the next course of action might be as follows.

Child: I suppose you think that that was very funny. Hah-hah.

Parent: As a matter of fact, I think that what you said was ridiculous, and I want to remind you that such language is uncalled for in a situation like this one. I speak English, and I'd have understood you perfectly if you had said that you simply didn't want to go.

Child: Why do you have to make such a big deal out of it?

Parent: When you speak inappropriately, you can expect a reaction that you may not like. Additionally, I will never take you seriously when you speak that way. Had you asked politely, we could have discussed the issue. Now, there will be no discussion. Be ready to leave for your aunt's house by four o'clock tomorrow.

In using techniques, such as the one illustrated, your child will probably react at first with surprise. Once he understands what to expect from you, however, he will *have* to alter his behavior or be faced with consistent comments like these from you.

> *Parent:* Kevin, I've invited that new kid, Preston, to dinner tonight. No one else seems to be very friendly to him.
> *Child:* Oh, Mom, that's because he's just a dick.
> *Parent:* That's impossible, Kevin. How would he walk?

Although you may doubt the effectiveness of this technique in curbing the use of obscene language in your children, many parents have reported that their children became so accustomed to being the butt of a witty remark that they end up correcting themselves before their parents even have a chance to respond. Once this begins to occur, you have positive proof of the effects of your campaign to halt the use of inappropriate language.

> *Parent:* I'm glad to see that you are taking your homework more seriously these days.
> *Child:* I hope so. I've been working my ass off. Wait! I know, I know. That would be a neat trick, if I could really do it.

With younger children, you may find that you need to respond a bit more directly. A child who is not yet even pre-adolescent is not subject to the same peer-pressure demands that are typical of older children, so there is less external force compelling him to engage in the behavior. In such cases, the most direct approach has proven to be the most effective.

> *Parent:* Gwen, why don't you come out and let me see how that new blouse looks on you?
> *Child:* It looks like shit, Mom.
> *Parent:* Okay, then you don't have to keep it. You *do* have to write the word 'shit' five thousand times, though. Since you like using that word so much, I know that you'll enjoy writing it each and every one of those times.

We have never seen a child in our offices whose language

couldn't be changed through one technique or another. Remember that when you remove the rewards associated with a behavior, there is no longer any reason for that behavior to continue. Be consistent, be firm, be reasonable, and be realistic. If you set positive examples, the inappropriate use of obscene language by your children should become a thing of the past.

Stealing: It's Anything but Kid Stuff

Stealing and vandalism are antisocial behaviors that are not merely inappropriate, but illegal, as well. Although such behavior can often be described as attention-seeking in nature, it is clear that children must be taught that negative attention is *not* necessarily better than no attention at all. There are many varying explanations for why children steal from others. The simplest, of course, is that someone else has something that the child wants, so the object is taken. Yet, there are two other explanations of importance to consider: A young child may not yet have developed a sense of right and wrong that is sophisticated enough to make such behavior "feel" inappropriate; or on another level, with an older child there is some likelihood that stealing is a way of beating the system, and that the thrill that comes from unpunished stealing is tremendous for such a child. The following example is based largely on an actual case that we worked on in our office.

Parent: But Mitch, how could you have stolen so much?

Child: It was easy, Dad. When the store gets busy, they can't possibly watch all of the people who are in there. So, when no one is looking, you just grab something and get out the door.

Parent: But I give you allowance money every week. Why would you have to steal this stuff?

Child: Dad, it's cool. Everybody does it. It's no big deal, unless you get caught.

The child in this example, a pre-adolescent, clearly holds the view that stealing is a reasonable way of getting what he wants because it seems acceptable to his peers and because the price that he has paid (so far) has not been too great. Once again, a basic PST principle is that behavior which is reinforced is likely to continue to occur, so what needs to be done in a case like this one is to remove the reinforcement. Teach your child that if he steals, the police are only one of the things about which he has to worry. In the following example, please note that we are dealing with a child who sees stealing as an acceptable means of having fun and who is old enough to understand already that such behavior is intolerable.

Parent: Mitch, I simply cannot allow you to continue doing what you've done. I understand that your friends are stealing and that it's very important for you to fit in, but what you're doing is wrong.
Child: So, what? I haven't been caught. The store can afford it.
Parent: Do you have any idea how it feels to have something taken from you?
Child: Yeah, I lost my keys a few weeks ago.
Parent: That's not what I meant, but you're going to understand better in a few days. I am going to take everything that you own, except for a few basic pieces of clothing, and pack it away in boxes. It will remain inaccessible to you for one month. Then, if there's been no further trouble, you can have it back. If this happens again, you'll lose your possessions for three months; and if that isn't enough, the next time everything will be given away to charity. Also, you will need to get a job to pay for what you've taken. You can mow lawns or deliver newspapers, but all of your privileges are revoked until the merchandise has been paid for in full.
Child: That's not fair!
Parent: Neither is stealing. Get the message?

What the parent in this example has done is to send his child the message that stealing is not a game and that the behavior will be met with specific and serious consequences. In a case such as this one, you should structure the response in stages.

The Only Thing to Take Is Lessons
The first time, discuss the reasons why stealing is considered to be inappropriate in a civilized or organized society. Begin by

removing everything that the child owns for a one-month period. Pack these possessions away in boxes and be certain that they are placed securely in a place where the child will have absolutely no access to them. During that time, the child should have nothing more than the clothing that he needs to be able to leave the house for school, and he should be grounded completely, with all privileges revoked—no television, no radio, no telephone, no visitors. Furthermore, all travel outside of the house should be banned, except for whatever freedom of movement is necessary to enable the child to earn enough money to repay the debt that has been created. If the child is too young to be able to do any outside work, such as washing or waxing neighbors' cars, then be certain to assign enough household chores to compensate. Finally, explain that because you want to be sure that he understands the reasons why stealing is wrong, he is to write a series of four compositions on those reasons and is to submit one of these essays to you each week. Make sure that the length of the composition matches the child's age and abilities (e.g., half a page each time for an 8-year-old, three pages each time for a 12-year-old). After a month of such a lifestyle, it is likely your child will understand that the penalties for stealing are greater than he previously understood, and that he will have explored all of the various reasons why such behavior is philosophically unjust.

That Should Do It

If stealing occurs again, the penalty is increased to three months. This time, the compositions can be replaced by the loss of those possessions which are equivalent to what was stolen. If your child removed a video cassette from a store, then make sure that all of his videos are given to a charity and be certain that he understands that they will not be replaced. A three-month period is an eternity in the life of a child, and, thus, stealing should not re-occur unless the child is actually undergoing a serious emotional disturbance. Alternatively, in the event of a third incident, you may choose to have the child lose everything that has been packed away during the previous two periods of punishment. If there are further problems, you may want to consider seeking professional assistance in the form of a psychological evaluation and subsequent psychotherapy.

Vandalism Is Hardly Different

The ways in which acts of vandalism can be approached do not differ radically from the techniques suggested as responses to stealing. It is important for you to note, however, that vandalism is somewhat *more* antisocial in that it occurs not because a child wants to possess something, but rather, purely for the maliciousness with which it is performed. Children rarely engage in acts of vandalism alone, or at least not without some visibility, because the thrills involved typically necessitate the approval of peers. Vandalism may be targeted against someone or something that a child dislikes, but often it is targeted at random. Whether the specific actions are relatively mild (e.g., graffiti) or more serious (e.g., slashing of tires), the response by you as the parent must be one of quick and decisive action. In PST, we recommend that a child who has engaged in vandalism be subjected to a psychological procedure known as "overcorrection." In this technique, the child must correct (or undo) not only what he has sabotaged, destroyed, or damaged, but a great deal more, as well. If, for example, your child's vandalism consisted of spray-painting graffiti on a neighbor's building, he might be forced to re-paint that house first, and then to paint the sides of several of the nearby houses, as well. If he had pulled the bushes out from someone's garden, then he might have to replace those bushes and then plant new ones in other locations, also. Additionally, all of the steps to be taken in the event of stealing can be employed above and beyond the overcorrection procedure, so that any child will learn quickly that vandalism simply does not pay.

Truancy: The Endless Vacation

Children in the late 1980s are careful to make the distinction between "skipping" and "cutting" school, with the former meaning that school was not attended at all that day and the latter serving to indicate that particular classes were missed. In any event, the very existence of school seems to inspire children to develop ways of avoiding it. Your child must learn quickly that such behavior leads to consequences that actually seem worse than school itself.

Truancy is a problem that exists simultaneously on several different levels, not the least of which is that for each day or class that a child misses, his education indisputably is being damaged. From a completely different angle, truancy is an insidious behavior which tends to worsen over time, allowing children to learn that they can escape from responsibility without consequence and setting them up for a lifetime of irresponsible behavior.

Don't Be a Stranger at School

In PST, we suggest that you check frequently with your child's school about his attendance and about the quality of the work that he is doing. Report cards are issued no more than four times each year, so a child's behavior can change drastically, yet go unnoticed for as long as two months. In many cities, parents are not notified when their children skip or cut classes; therefore, a quick check with your child's school or teacher each month could help to prevent more serious long-term problems.

Since truancy is a behavior in which a child attempts to garner greater freedom than he usually is permitted to enjoy, it is important that the consequences for such behavior take this into account. A truant child not only is damaging his own education, but is misrepresenting himself to you in that he is leading you to believe, directly or indirectly, that he is attending classes. Since punishment often works best when it is related to the misbehavior itself, a truant child should find that his behavior leads to a loss, rather than to a gaining, of freedom.

As soon as you discover that your child intentionally has missed classes (assuming that this is not a one-time-only occurrence), you should inform him that freedom is a privilege that is not to be taken for granted. As such, his behavior no longer warrants the trust that existed behind the freedom, and therefore changes need to be made in his lifestyle until he has given you reason to believe that he once again can be trusted.

Parent: Jason, your teacher told me today that you've missed school four times in the past two weeks.

Child: Well, a bunch of my friends went to the mall, and they wanted me to go with them.

Parent: We've already discussed the reasons why you have to go to school, but you've violated the trust that I placed in you.

Child: I won't do it anymore, I promise.

Parent: I know that you won't, Jason. And the reason I'm so sure is that I'm going to be sending a daily report form with you to school and your teacher is going to sign it at the end of the day. If you come home without it, you will be grounded for the weekend. As of now, you are grounded each weekday after school. That means that when you get home, you cannot leave the house or have friends over, nor can you watch TV, listen to records, or do anything except your homework.

Child: No, Dad, that's not fair! I promise that I won't skip school anymore, really!

Parent: After a month or two, if everything's okay, you can go out again after school. But you will be bringing home daily report forms with your teacher's signature for the rest of the school year. Trust has to be earned, Jason. You'll have to work hard to regain the trust that you've damaged. You had lots of freedom before, but that wasn't enough for you. This will help you to put everything into perspective.

In this example, the parent has set clear limits for the behavior that he is willing to tolerate from his child. Not only will his child learn that missing class can lead to unpleasant consequences, but he has learned a valuable lesson about trust, as well. Note that this behavioral modification was done without anger and without any inadvertent reinforcing of the wrong behavior. Clear, concise, and consistent limits were set for the child. The consequence was adversive enough to serve as a true punishment and yet was completely reasonable in nature. When utilizing the principles of PST, you should always strive for effective and realistic responses to your child's behavior.

Drug Abuse: An Epidemic

Let's start by being candid. There is no magical solution for the drug abuse problem that is rampant in America today. Children are being exposed to drugs virtually everywhere that they turn, and there is no single technique that you can use that will even come close to guaranteeing that your child will remain drug-free. However, there are things that you can do to minimize the problem, and thus PST would be incomplete without at least a brief examination of those alternatives. Because PST is focused upon children 12 years of age and younger, you can set the groundwork that, it is hoped, will aid your child in avoiding drug abuse as he enters adolescence and faces increasing pressure from his peers.

Why Some Children Resist Drugs

There are two main characteristics which distinguish those children who resist experimenting with drugs from those who engage in drug use. The first is education: The more that your child knows about drugs and the ways in which they affect the human body, the more likely he may be to avoid becoming involved with them. Read any of the many books that have been published on the effects of drugs so that you can simplify and teach these facts to your child. In our office, nearly every child over the age of 10 is taught enough about the effects of cocaine, for example, that they can offer a surprisingly detailed explanation of that drug's effect on complex brain functions such as neurotransmission and re-uptake. Many of the children that we see can talk at length about the side effects of marijuana, describing the lowering of testosterone levels and sperm count, and can point out that its use can damage the cilia (tiny hairs) that line the lungs. Education is a powerful weapon, and its impact on drug abuse should not be minimized.

On another level, there is a particular type of child who is somewhat more resistant than average to drug abuse. Such a child has a good, positive self-image, is fairly independent in thinking, and has no significant personal problems which would make the escape provided by drugs seem to be particularly attractive. It is not really too much of an oversimplification to say that drugs appeal to those people who need something to make them feel better. Happy, well-adjusted people, whether children or adults, don't need chemical means to feel good. Instead, drugs offer a quick and rather easy method of relieving pressure (yes, children face pressures of their own) to those children who do not like themselves or their lives very much and can help to obscure those things that interfere with relaxation and "feeling good." You can help your child to boost his self-image by finding things at which he can excel; sports, hobbies, scholastics, or anything that he can enjoy and in which he can feel a sense of pride. The happier your child feels about *himself* (as opposed and in contrast to how happy he is about privileges, for example), the more likely he may be to refrain from seeking a temporary way of feeling better.

Peer Pressure Takes It Toll

The pressure exerted by children upon one another concerning drug abuse seems to be continuing to increase. At parties, many children feel left out if they are not smoking marijuana or drinking alcohol, and you might be surprised at the age group where such behavior tends to begin. It is for this reason that we suggest that drug abuse be treated very differently from other sorts of antisocial behavior. Do *not* punish your child for experimenting with drugs, because to do so would be to teach him that if he feels pressured about drugs, you are the last person with whom he can discuss the problem. Instead, make certain your child knows that he can always come to you for support and guidance in this area, and that even if he tells you he has already succumbed to the temptation to see what it feels like to be high, he doesn't have to be afraid to ask you to help him to sort out his feelings or to avoid such behavior in the future. If you notice signs of drug abuse in your child, however, you must take steps to ascertain whether such behavior is actually occurring.

Do What You Must

If you have any reason to suspect that your child is experimenting with drugs, the first thing to do is to discuss it with him. If you start off by explaining that you are not looking for a reason to punish him, you might get an honest answer. However, if your child insists that he hasn't touched drugs, and you continue to see evidence (i.e., coke spoons, plastic bags full of residue, child's eyes bloodshot for no apparent reason), then you may need to take the next step. Surprise the child in the morning by appearing at his bedside with a bottle and by telling him that he is to give you a urine sample immediately. Don't take "no" for an answer; this is too serious a matter to open for debate. Your family physician or pharmacist can tell you where to have a toxicology screen done on the sample; you'll then know whether your child has ingested any drug in the recent past. If the answer is affirmative, you must decide how serious a problem you and your child are facing. If it is necessary, don't hesitate to help your child by seeking outpatient psychotherapy, by enrolling him in a program designed to help him to combat drug abuse, or even by changing his environment through short-term hospitalization. If you have discovered that your child is using drugs even infrequently, monitor his urine samples unpredictably and make sure that he never knows when he is going to be asked for one. Stay on top of the situation, educate yourself and your child, and do whatever you must to solve the problem.

Lying: The Pinocchio Syndrome

Most children lie to their parents at times. It would be unrealistic to expect otherwise, so what we are dealing with in this section is not the occasional white lie, but instead, a persistent pattern of untruths that is significant enough to arouse concern. Lying is an antisocial behavior that requires attention because it has the potential to worsen over time, and because, in a very real way, it interferes with a child's ability to communicate with others. There are three different types of liars, and each is profiled in the following subsections:

The Escaper

An *escaper* is a child who lies occasionally, with the lie serving to extricate him from some sort of trouble. Such a child may deny that he broke the vase, may claim that he was nowhere around when the dog got loose, or may tell you that he is not responsible for the long-distance telephone call to the weather service in Uganda. Most often, escapers are not serious liars, in that their lies do not interfere greatly with their credibility simply because they don't occur often enough. When dealing with an escaper, you are facing a child whose lying would probably cease if he were helped to behave more appropriately in the first place. Therefore, your best bet with an escaper is to focus on improving his behavior in other areas; when he learns to keep out of trouble, the lying will probably stop, as well.

The Controller

Another type of liar is known as a *controller*, so named in PST because of his tendency to avoid telling the truth—the ability to manipulate the beliefs of others is pleasurable to him. A controller is a child who wants you to think and to believe whatever he tells you, and if he is given the opportunity, he will eventually lead you to lose the ability to determine whether he is lying or not. You may remember the character Eddie Haskell on the "Leave It to Beaver" TV series; he was a classic controller. Taking pride in the ability to play games with the truth and with reality, a controller tells you what he thinks you want to hear, or simply decides what and how much you are going to know. When faced with a controller, you must tell him that his credibility has been lost. As a result, nothing that he says will be taken as valid unless it can be substantiated in some other way, or until he has re-established himself as a reliable child. Dealing with a chronic controller is a difficult task, because the only way that a child could have learned such behavior would have been through your previous tolerance (and reinforcement) of such actions. Teaching a child that the old game plan has been changed sometimes requires real dedication on the part of a parent. If you are going to alter the behavior of a controller, begin by teaching him that he will be rewarded for telling the truth, and will be punished for lying.

Parent: Okay, Brad, we're going to do things a little differently around here from now on. Whenever I ask you something, or whenever you tell me something, I want it to be the truth. Anytime that it is a lie, you will be punished. I might take away TV privileges or ground you, or do something else, but I will find some punishment for you.

Child: What about when I tell the truth?

Parent: Well, every time that you tell the truth you will be gaining back some credibility. If you tell the truth long enough, there will come a time when I don't have to doubt every word that you say. Plus, for every week that you go without telling a lie, we'll find something special to do. It might be bowling, or fishing, or a movie, or whatever, but it will depend on your telling the truth all of the time.

Child: Okay, I understand.
Parent: Do you really?

Like any other behavior, lying will persist only when it is reinforced. By removing the reward from lying, you can make the behavior seem much less attractive to your child. Teaching a controller not to lie is like giving him a lifelong gift.

The Confuser

The third and last type of liar is called a *confuser*. This child has lost the ability to distinguish between the truth and the lies that he tells, so that over a period of time he has little understanding or ability to differentiate between reality and his fabricated stories. Note that there is a difference between a controller and a confuser: The controller may leave you confused about what is true and what is not, but he knows exactly what is going on; the confuser is different—he's lost in his lies himself. Sometimes known as a chronic liar, a confuser may need professional assistance to deal with the emotional problems that have led to such a severe form of inappropriate behavior. Such a child is often ostracized by his peers, because children characteristically withdraw quickly from those that they cannot trust. If you see such a pattern in your child, don't hesitate to help him obtain the help that he needs.

Some Final Remarks

Antisocial behavior can take many forms, and not all of them can be addressed in this book. There is, as you have seen, a great deal that you can do about many of these behavioral problems. By adhering to the principles put forth in PST, you should have success in helping your child to overcome inappropriate behavior. If things do get out of hand, especially with some of the more severe problems, talk with a professional so that you can be assured that a bad situation won't be permitted to become any worse.

Question:
"You suggested that a child should not be punished for telling

you that he has been experimenting with drugs. Do you feel the same way about cigarette smoking?"

Answer:

No, cigarette smoking needs to be treated differently. When a child feels comfortable enough to confide in you about drug use, it means that your relationship with the child is a good, solid, and comfortable one. We see it as essential that a child be able to discuss drugs without the fear of consequences because drug abuse is so dangerous as to make other considerations pale by comparison. Admittedly, if a child is punished for other inappropriate behavior, the same should hold true (in theory) for drug use, but it would be foolish to risk having a child hide that behavior from you when intervention might save his life. As far as cigarette smoking goes, there is obvious risk there, too, but not an immediate risk, and not one so pressing that exceptions need to be made for the acceptance of that behavior without punishment. If your child has been told not to smoke cigarettes, then he must comply with that direction or face whatever consequences you choose to set up. On another level, cigarette smoking is actually more difficult to conceal than is drug use. Any child who smokes consistently will reek of tobacco and will eventually leave packs of cigarettes where they can be found. Most children would not fear the consequences of being caught with cigarettes nearly as much as they would with drugs, but that fear of being discovered experimenting with drugs could work to their detriment, because you may discover it too late.

Question:

"I've started trying to curb my eleven-year-old daughter's use of obscene language with the technique that you described, but she's starting to do the same thing back to me. How can I get her to stop trying to make *me* feel foolish?"

Answer:

There is only one possible reason your daughter could be doing such a thing to you, and that's because you are using obscene language while telling her not to do so. If you throw four-letter words around in front of her, how are you planning to teach her not to do the same thing? Remember: You are always a model for your children, and they will mimic whatever examples you choose to set for them. If you would like your daughter to clean up her act, then start speaking properly and leave the obscene language to someone else. In the meantime, consider this: It is a rather sad statement about you that your daughter has been able to find the opportunity to correct your inappropriate use of language.

Question:

"My son was recently involved in the stealing of some food. A delivery truck broke down nearby, and a bunch of kids raided the contents. The other kids' parents aren't punishing them, so my son says that it would be unfair for me to punish him. Do you have any advice for me?"

Answer:

Sure. Don't permit other people to dictate what is right and wrong to you. Your initial instinct was correct; your son broke the law by stealing and antisocial behavior should not be ignored. The fact that the food was taken from a disabled truck, as opposed to a convenience store, a supermarket, or someone's kitchen, is unimportant. You have a good opportunity here to teach your son a valuable lesson, and you would be ill-advised to pass it up. Follow the directions in the chapter about approaching antisocial behavior (and stealing, in particular) and help to prevent such behavior from occurring again in your son. Be sure to point out to him that the behavior of a group does not relieve the individual members of that group from the same thinking. Just because the other parents have chosen to act irresponsibly doesn't mean that you can do the same thing with impunity.

Question:

"I'd like to have my daughter's teachers fill out those daily report forms that you mentioned because I've been having a truancy problem with her. I'm worried, though, that I'm asking too much of these teachers. What if they don't want to fill out these forms?"

Answer:

Most teachers take their work very seriously and would be quite willing to spend a few extra moments each day to help to curb truancy in one of their students. The forms to which we referred can be found in Chapter Eight and require, literally, just seconds of a teacher's time. In fact, many teachers prefer that parents take an active interest in their child's schoolwork and do a great deal to encourage that they do so.

Chapter Eighteen

The Teen Years: A Whole New Ball Game

Adults have a fascinating way of remembering things the way they would like them to have been, and so, as a parent, you probably remember adolescence as having been much more fun than it was. Consider, for example, the television show "Happy Days." The producers of that show would have us remember the late 1950s and early 1960s as wonderful times; but if you stop and think about it, you might remember them as the days of the Cuban missile crisis, of the cold war, and of backyard bomb shelters. It was a time of segregation all over America, of the Vietnam war, and of hippies and campus demonstrations. There was not even the pretense of equal rights for women. Wonderful, carefree times? Hardly. But your recollections probably prompt you to say things to your adolescent, such as "This is the best time of your life, and you should be enjoying it," as you forget that acne, drugs, and SAT's are but just a few of the stressors facing teenagers today.

Being an Adolescent Isn't Easy

We saw a 15-year-old girl in our office recently who said that she wanted to lose her virginity because she was tired of being the last girl in her history class to do so. A 16-year-old boy stated that he had spent the entire weekend shopping around for the perfect earring, because he was the only guy left in his P.E. class without one. Similarly, another teenager that we see was upset recently because he foolishly opened the refrigerator when one of his friends asked for coke. There's a great deal of stress involved in being an adolescent today, so the last thing that any teenager needs is unnecessary problems with his parents That's where you come in.

The More That You Understand, the Better

The children toward which PST is directed are presumed to be 12 years of age, or younger. Many of the principles of behavior management work best with younger children, and, of course, children below the age of 12 have little independence (of a real nature) with which to challenge a parent. By the time a child has reached adolescence, he is both set in his ways and too sophisticated to respond well to many of the strategies that work with younger children. Nevertheless, some of the PST principles can be applied effectively to teenagers, and this chapter is devoted to offering you an opportunity to consider how changes in the techniques will maintain their usefulness.

Adolescents Should Not Be Treated like Children

The real difficulty you are going to face in dealing with your teenager is that he or she is now approaching adulthood and is likely to begin expecting the same rights and privileges that you typically reserve for yourself as an adult. Although we stated clearly, earlier in this book, that children and adults must have different sorts of rights, the distinction becomes somewhat blurred when dealing with adolescents. Teenagers (especially bright, mature teenagers) often think on a level that is similar to that of an adult, and many of them fail to understand why they should be treated any differently. Facing a difficult time in their lives, in that they are beginning to look, sound, and feel more like adults than like children, teenagers, nevertheless, must tolerate rules and expectations that are set and held for them by their parents. For many, the desire to rebel becomes almost a way of life.

Parent: Chris, violating your curfew is something that you've already been warned about repeatedly. I have no choice but to ground you for next weekend.

Child: I tell you what, Dad. How about if I do some extra chores around the house to make up for it? I have an important concert to go to on Saturday night.

Parent: I'm sorry, Chris, but you know the rules. No concert.

Child: Just like that, huh? How come it's always *your* way? You *always* seem to have it your way. It's like living at Burger King.

In this example, notice the teenager's frustration with the making of a decision that is beyond his control. Having offered what he thought was a reasonable alternative, this adolescent is torn between his own ability to think and to negotiate on a near-adult level and the necessity of complying with the demands of an authority figure. By saying, "I tell you what, Dad," he has attempted to place himself in a position of power equal to that of his father, as if they were partners expecting to reach a mutually satisfactory conclusion. Such thinking is, by definition, a reflection of the teenager's belief that he and his father hold equivalent bargaining positions, when, of course, such a situation cannot and should not be the case. Note that when the teenager stated, "How come it's always *your* way," the message once again was, actually, "Why don't I ever seem to come out on top in our disagreements? I deserve to make decisions just as you do." Such a belief is a common one among teenagers, and the problem that it reflects is that adolescents do deserve to be treated somewhat differently than younger children. The dilemma, of course, is how to do so while maintaining the control that is a necessary part of parenting.

Adolescents Are Not Yet Adults, However

If you were to stop and think about it, you would probably conclude that nearly every problem that parents have with their teenagers is a reflection of a struggle for power. Curfews, phone privileges, choice of friends, study time, purchasing decisions, and even matters of personal appearance (along with many other situations) all involve the *power* to make decisions and to act upon them. Because many teenagers see themselves as quite capable of making such decisions on their own, they are resentful of the need for parental approval and input in decision-making situations and are even more dismayed about the veto-power maintained by most parents. Adolescents need to be able to make and to live with their own decisions if they are to become responsible adults. But therein lies the problem: Left to their own devices, with any real degree of freedom, most teenagers would get themselves into one sort of difficulty or another, thus paying too high a premium for the experience of learning. Additionally, one of the rights most prized by parents (and understandably so) is that of not having to live with all of the demands and inappropriateness of a typical teenager. That is to say, many of the decisions that teenagers want to be able to make on their own affect other members of the family as well and often represent a risk to the safety and well-being (both physically and emotionally) of the adolescent himself.

Child: Can I take the car tonight, Mom?

Parent: Rick, you have only a restricted license. You know that it's illegal for you to drive alone, especially at night.

Child: Yeah, Mom, but everybody's doing it. I promise that I'll be careful.

Parent: Not a chance, Rick. Not only is it against the law, but you are not insured to drive alone yet, and I don't think that you've even had enough driving practice.

Child: You *never* understand! Why can't you just let me do what I want, just once?

Finding a workable compromise between the unrealistic demands and perceptions of a teenager and his need to begin assuming independence and responsibility is a monumental task. The key is a three-step plan: You must gain some understanding of the ways in which teenagers think; you must make an accurate appraisal of the pressures with which they are faced; and, finally, you must consider the particular strategies that are most likely to succeed in altering adolescent behavior.

The "Me" Generation (Step One)

The 1970s saw the onset of a psychological phenomenon known as the "me" generation: Normally rational people began thinking that no other person, thing, or situation could possibly be as important as they, themselves, were, and these people behaved accordingly. In retrospect, of course, we can dismiss such individuals as completely self-centered, sometimes arrogant, and often thoroughly unpleasant to be around. While the 1980s brought an end to such behavior by all of those adults who wish to have relationships with other people, the fact remains that teenagers always have subscribed (and probably always will) to the very notions that made the "me" generation possible. Let's take a closer look at what such thinking involves.

Egocentrism: The World Revolves Around Me

Adolescents are often *egocentric* (completely self-absorbed) and seem to believe that they are the center of the universe. They see themselves as more important than those around them, and as deserving of whatever they wish to do and to possess. For many teenagers, it is difficult to see things from another person's perspective, because they are too wrapped up in themselves. Many teenagers engage in what is known as "magical thinking," wherein they believe that if they want something badly enough, somehow it will come about.

Parent: Regina, you failed English and math again. You know how important those subjects are in the eleventh grade!

Child: Mom, it's nothing to get all worked up about. Besides, I don't want anything to get me upset before my date tonight with Bart.

Parent: You're worried about a date? I'm talking about your future.

Child: It'll work out, don't worry. Employers don't really care about how you did in school. I'll get a great job, just you wait and see. Now, tell me, does my hair look better back like this, or combed over to the sides?

Hedonism: If It Feels Good, Do It

The typical teenager is a *hedonist* (one who is interested only in that which is pleasurable). Motivated by a desire to enjoy himself above all else, the average adolescent does not consider the long-term effects and ramifications of what he does. Instead, he seeks to feel good whenever possible. Stop for a moment and think about the things for which many adolescents get into trouble; nearly all of them involve hedonism as a foundation for their occurrence. Adults also seek pleasure from the activities in which they engage, but one of the hallmarks of mature behavior is that when the price for fun becomes too high, the behavior changes. Such is not always the case with teenagers.

Parent: Alex, your principal called me today. He said that you have been absent from school for the past three weeks. How do you explain that?

Child: I've been skipping, I guess.

Parent: Thank you, Alex. I certainly wouldn't have been able to figure that out without your help.

Child: I hate school, Dad. I've told you that before.

Parent: Well, I can appreciate that, Alex, because I wasn't too fond of school, either. Unfortunately, we have to do things that we don't like sometimes, because they'll be better for us in the end. Besides, you have only one term to go before you graduate, so it wouldn't make sense to drop out when you're so close to finishing. Now, instead of going to the mall, or to the beach, or to your friends' homes everyday, I trust that you'll be going back to school.

Child: Sorry, Dad, but no way. I hate school.

Confusion: No One Ever Understands Me

Teenagers typically hold the belief that adults exist largely to demand that they do unpleasant things (such as go to school, work part time, or do chores at home), and it is often difficult for them to see beyond the surface of what is being asked of them. You read earlier in this book that children do not always have to be happy, and that you do not need to feel guilty about doing what is good for your child, even if he doesn't like it. The chances are that these were difficult concepts for you to accept at first. Imagine, then, what a struggle the average teenager must face in trying to understand such thinking. Rather than accept that his parents are looking out for his best interests by monitoring his behavior and by punishing him for what is deemed to be inappropriate, the typical adolescent will conclude instead that his parents take some sort of perverse pleasure in ruining his good times and in robbing him of the independence that he so desperately seeks.

Child: Guess what, Mom? Cindy invited me to spend the weekend in her parents' cabin up at the lake.

Parent: That's wonderful, Carol. It must be a big cabin if it's going to accommodate all of you.

Child: Well, there's just going to be two of us. Cindy's parents aren't going.

Parent: Then, neither are you. You're not old enough to stay up at a cabin with another fifteen-year-old all alone.

Child: We won't be all alone, we'll have each other.

Parent: I'm sorry, but maybe next year.

Child: I *am* old enough to go, it's just that *you* don't think so. Why don't you ever let me have fun, like my friends? You always find a way to ruin my good times! I wish that I could just go and live by myself so that I wouldn't have to put up with your dumb rules all of the time.

Adolescence: The Fun Years (Step Two)

There is perhaps no greater contradiction in the history of civilization than that in this subtitle. Adolescence is many things, but *fun* is not one of the concepts with which it is associated. Adolescents face incredible stressors as they struggle through a period of self-doubt, confusion, relative helplessness, and peer pressure (to name but a few of the many difficulties faced during this period). Consider, for example, the simple concept of personal appearance (or, if you prefer, "attractiveness"). Adolescents are hyper-sensitive about their appearance, and yet at this critical point in their lives, they very often find themselves looking awkward as their bodies race through growth spurts that can cause height changes of several inches in a single year. Just when teenagers want to look their best because they are so concerned with attracting members of the opposite sex, they have pimples and blemishes with which to contend. As they seek the comfort of an accepted mode of dress or hairstyle, or even musical affiliation, their decisions are rejected by parents who "never seem to understand," and they are pressured to conform to the expectations of authority figures rather than to the expectations of the peers whose approval means so much to them.

Adults face pressure from peers in a different way than do adolescents. Not only are adults presumably better equipped to deal with such pressure, but they have areas of freedom in their lives that teenagers often lack. As simple a faux pas as wearing the wrong brand of sneakers to school can be a social problem for an adolescent, as can interest in the "wrong" sort of rock groups, a lack of proper usage of the latest slang terms, or an unwillingness to break the limits set by parents. The minor events and the trivial decisions and behaviors engaged in by adults can be of immense consequence in the life of an adolescent. The moral of the story here is this: Don't judge the aspects of a teenager's life by your standards, or he will be correct about your inability to understand him.

The social demands and expectations for adolescents involve a partial rejection of family ties, and yet many teenagers are frightened about independence. Adolescence is a period in which teenagers begin to move away from dependence upon their parents, and in which they begin to rely upon themselves and those that they consider to have taken on a new sense of importance in their lives. Teenagers adhere closely to group norms, even if those norms involve doing things that make them initially uncomfortable. Sex, drugs, and antisocial behavior are often inappropriate and inadvisable for particular adolescents, but these same teenagers feel compelled to participate because of the social reinforcement that they receive for doing so. Breaking away from the confines of childhood is an important part of growing up, but it is a frightening and intimidating process that often involves problems that need to be addressed by you, the parent.

What to Do About It All (Step Three)

The single most important point in dealing with an adolescent is *communication*. As a parent, you must be able to communicate with your teenager if there is to be any hope of an improved relationship. What we suggest in PST is that you set the stage for a real sense of openness by sitting down with your adolescent and by explaining that although there are undoubtedly differences of opinion between the two of you and that there are likely to be others over time, you will make every effort to understand and to appreciate how he or she feels and will listen to what is said to you with the hope that you can expect the same in return. Emphasize that there is a tremendous difference between understanding and agreeing, and that you will try always for the former, even if the latter eludes you.

Parent: I wanted to talk with you about some things, Matt. Now that you're a teenager, our relationship is likely to change a bit.

Child: What do you mean?

Parent: Well, as you get older, you're going to become more independent. I saw a little of that last weekend when you disobeyed me and went out after eleven o'clock on Saturday night.

Child: Yeah, Dad, but you were being unreasonable. I had a date.

Parent: That's sort of the point that I wanted to make, Matt. I'd like us to be able to sit down and talk about our differences, so that you know that I'm always here for you, even if we don't agree on everything.

Child: You can't understand how I feel. Only my friends really know me. You think that I'm just a kid.

Parent: It may seem like that sometimes, but I know that you have your own thoughts and feelings and that a lot of what I say doesn't seem like it makes much sense to you.

Child: Right, Dad, it doesn't. You'd have to be my age to understand.

Parent: I might have to be your age to agree with you, but maybe I can understand you even with the difference in our ages.

Child: Maybe.

Parent: Don't get me wrong, Matt. I'm still going to make the rules around here. But I'd like you to have a little more input as to how things get decided.

Child: You mean like about my curfew?

Parent: Right. It's been eleven o'clock until now, but you've been pushing for twelve-thirty. You can't just take matters into your own hands and stay out as late as you like, because that's the same thing as telling me that I'm not your father anymore. I'm just an older person who pays your bills and makes foolish rules that get ignored.

Child: I guess that's kind of unfair to you. I'm sorry. But you have to see things from my side.

Parent: No, I don't *have* to do anything. But I'll try. As time goes by, I'll give you more and more freedom and more and more decision-making power, *if* you prove to me that you're mature enough to deserve it.

Child: How can I do that?

Parent: By following the rules that are set for you. Whether it's school grades, curfew, telephone time, or anything else, we'll discuss it. But you must abide by what I decide. Until you're eighteen years old, I still set the rules.

Notice that in this conversation, the father is not giving in to the adolescent's behavior or demands. Communicating successfully with an adolescent involves letting him know that you are the boss and you intend to maintain such a position, but you do realize that changes have to be made in your relationship because he is no longer a child. Most teenagers respect parents who maintain a sense of authority; the problems arise when the teenager begins to feel helpless, as if he has no input or power at all. In such situations, the adolescent is confronted with a dilemma: If he cannot communicate with his parent, then he must live with blind obedience or must disobey and thus create a host of new problems in the process. Remember: We are not suggesting that you have to check with your teenager for permission before making decisions that affect him or you. On the contrary, we are advocating that you allow your adolescent to feel like a part of things by sharing his feelings, his interests, and his views with you as you make the decisions.

Tolerance and Compromises Are Critical

Adolescents can be rebellious, frustrating, unpredictable, illogical, contradictory, and irrational, but you must be tolerant. Distinctions need to be made between what is important and what is trivial, and usually only the former should be addressed. For example, if a 9-year-old child were to refuse to straighten up his room, he might find himself restricted to that room for the weekend. If a 14-year-old were to do the same thing, a different response would be in order. In such a case, the first thing that you should do would be to ask yourself this question: "Is this really important, or am I being led into a power struggle that could and should be avoided?" Probably, careful consideration of this question will lead you to conclude that many of the things that upset you previously simply are not in your best interests to insist upon any longer. Instead, in this particular example, you might say, "Since you have made it clear that you want to keep your room in a manner that is unacceptable to me, you must keep the door closed when you are not home so that I do not have to deal with the mess. You have one month in which to clean it up, and as long as it's done by then, that's fine. At the end of a month, if it's still dirty, you will be responsible for cleaning the rest of the house instead of just your room." Note that by giving the teenager a month in which to comply (in a situation that clearly does not warrant immediate action by an adolescent), he is likely to be left with the feeling that a compromise was reached and that he was given some decision-making power (he is going to decide when during the month the room is to be cleaned).

Looking further at the question of what constitutes trivial issues in which the adolescent's right to some degree of choice should be respected, let's consider the following as an example.

Parent: Ralph, I want that earring out of your ear this instant.

Child: Mom, every guy at school is wearing one. I don't want to be different.

Parent: I'd be ashamed to be seen in public with you while you're wearing that thing. What would people think?

Child: Maybe they'd think it's cool that I have a mother who respects my right to wear what I want. I only wish that you did.

Parent: Ralph, it's not that I don't respect your rights. But you are insisting upon something that makes me feel uncomfortable.

Child: You're always talking about compromises. Let's try one.

Parent: Okay, Ralph, I'm open to suggestions.

Child: How about if I wear the earring only outside the house, and only when I'm not with you? That way, I can still wear it to school and when I'm with my friends, but you won't have to see it or feel embarrassed by it.

Parent: I still don't like it, but that sounds like a fair compromise. Each one of us is getting some of what we want.

Note that this issue had the potential to be a major family conflict, but instead was resolved in such a way as to give each party a sense of satisfaction. The adolescent felt that his mother made an effort to understand him, and he felt that he was being treated as an individual with some right to make decisions in matters that affect him. The mother, on the other hand, was left feeling that her son was willing to recognize her discomfort and to go along with her refusal to face public situations that could prove embarrassing to her. She had the final power to vote for or against the proposed compromise, thus maintaining her stature as the parent and as the authority figure. In this case, everyone came out ahead.

In PST, we define a *compromise* as *everyone getting some of what he wants, all of the time.* The ability to find a healthy compromise with an adolescent is an essential part of dealing with members of that age group. Through a compromise, the parent maintains control, the adolescent feels as if he is included and his wishes are valued, and a control battle is avoided completely. More important, perhaps, the teenager is being given an opportunity to begin assuming the role of an adult—he is contributing to decisions that are being made. Ideally, through the technique of compromising, you will be maintaining final control over decisions and yet will still be allowing the adolescent to feel that he is not without some control of his own. You are likely to find that if you compromise, you can accomplish a great deal more in terms of changing your teenager's behavior than you can through any other single technique.

Ignorance Is Not Bliss

Many parents fail to realize that their teenager is involved in drug use, is sexually promiscuous, or is engaged in antisocial behavior. Although there are often clear indications that any or all of these problems are occurring, there are times when adolescents evidence a remarkable ability to conceal the things that would upset their parents. In PST, we suggest to you that if your adolescent cannot come to you and confide in you about the bad things as well as the good, you have failed to achieve the strong relationship that might otherwise be possible. To help to ensure that your own teenager can let you know when things are going wrong, we advocate that you form an agreement in advance. Fear is the one thing preventing many teenagers from being honest with their parents, so if that aspect of your relationships were to be removed, the odds of your adolescent opening up to you would be greatly increased.

Parent: Diane, I have a deal that I'd like to make with you.
Child: What have I done now?
Parent: No, no, that's the whole point. I know there must be times when you're afraid to level with me because you think that it'll only get you into trouble. Up until now, perhaps you've been right. What I'd like to do, however, is to let you know that from now on, if you need my help, or if you just want to let me know something, I'll be here for you without my judge's robe on.
Child: I'm not sure that I understand. Are you saying that I can't get into trouble with you anymore as long as I'm honest?
Parent: Not exactly. I can't promise that you'll never be in trouble. What I *am* promising, however, is that I will help you out of a problem first and worry about how to deal with things like punishment later.
Child: So how do I come out ahead here?
Parent: Well, let's say that you came home and told me that you were pregnant. You and I would sit down, discuss the situation, and explore the options open to you. Then I would help you to make a decision about what you were going to do. When everything is resolved and finished, then we might deal with the inappropriateness of what had happened.
Child: Okay, now I get it. It's kind of like you're saying that now that I'm a teenager you're going to be more understanding of *my* feelings and less concerned about how quickly you can punish me for something. I can talk to you without having to be afraid, just as all of my friends are with their parents.
Parent: It sounds as if you understood me perfectly, Diane.
Child: Thanks, Mom. It sounds as if *you* are starting to understand *me* a lot more, too.

In this example, a teenager and her mother came to an agreement that will benefit both of them tremendously. The adolescent came to realize that although her mother will never be just like a friend to her (nor *should* she be), she can and will try to treat her like the young adult that she is becoming. In exchange, the mother has asked for a degree of honesty that is atypical among teenagers and their parents. As these two individuals proceed, they are now likely to maintain a closeness that might otherwise have been lost forever.

At this point, it is essential that you understand we are promoting a degree and a quality of communication between you and your adolescent that may prevent problems before they occur. By opening the doors to compromise and understanding, many of the struggles and battles will never have to be fought at all. Of course, if you used the principles of PST consistently with your child as he grew up, we would like to think that as a teenager, his acting-out behavior will be held to a minimum, anyway. However, since it is unrealistic to assume that all adolescents will respond well (or even predictably) to behavioral intervention, let's take a look at what you might need to know when all else fails.

Punishing an Adolescent

One of the most frustrating situations that presents itself to the parents of a teenager is the determination of what should be done when that adolescent's behavior is so poor that some form of punishment is necessary.

"Grounding" a teenager is almost the ultimate punishment. Nothing is as likely to get a response as the denial of freedom to an adolescent. However, there are other strategies. One of the most effective is to ask the teenager for input on the nature of the punishment; you may be surprised to find that many adolescents evidence some sense of understanding (if not agreement) when confronted with the opportunity to analyze the situation in determining an appropriate punishment.

Parent: Roger, you were out with your friends until nearly midnight last night.
Child: So, what's the problem?
Parent: Today was your final exam in geometry. I thought that you and I had an agreement about studying before tests.
Child: It's okay, I think that I passed it. It wasn't so hard.
Parent: No, Roger, it's not okay, and passing isn't the point here. You broke an agreement and did just as you pleased. Now, what are we going to do about it?

Child: I don't know. It's up to you.

Parent: Why do you think that I wanted you home to study?

Child: So that I could do well on the exam, I guess.

Parent: Right. I had your best interests at heart. I tried treating you like an adult, but that didn't work. You disobeyed me, and the only way for you to learn not to do that is to be punished. What would be a fair punishment?

Child: Why are you asking me?

Parent: Because you keep expecting to be treated like an adult, and I keep trying to treat you that way. Unfortunately, you're not making it easy for me to do so I thought that if you're mature enough to understand why you deserve to be punished, we might be making a little progress.

Child: Well, since I came in late last night, I guess that I should be grounded tonight.

Parent: Good, Roger. That sounds fair enough to me, and at least I know that I won't have to listen to you complaining about how the punishment is too severe.

The ways in which adolescents are punished must differ significantly from those techniques that work well with younger children. For example, if you were to tell a teenager that he can have only a cold sandwich because he was late for dinner again, that statement would likely be met with laughter, followed by a quick trip to the nearest McDonald's. Teenagers want, need, assume, and, to some degree, deserve independence, and they can be expected to make such a desire an integral part of their daily lives. Give an adolescent enough room to grow, but not enough room to "hang himself."

If Things Get Serious

With the average teenager and his typical teenage problems, a great deal can be accomplished with good communication, realistic responses, and reasonable freedom. However, should things begin to get out of hand, you may need to take more extreme measures. Grounding a male teenager who is heavily involved with drugs is not going to accomplish anything, nor is banning use of the car from an adolescent girl who has run away for the second time. As we have advocated in earlier chapters, do not hesitate to do whatever is necessary in a situation where your child's well-being is concerned. If your teenager needs to see the inside of a police station, then by all means, arrange for him to do so. If hospitalization is the only way in which he can be prevented from obtaining drugs, then you must do that to protect him. If psychotherapy is needed to help the family to live together comfortably, then don't hesitate to seek family counseling. Remember: The longer you allow an inappropriate behavior to persist, the more difficult it is going to be to change that behavior.

Some Do's and Don'ts

- Do respect your adolescent's privacy.
- Don't nag in an effort to alter behavior.
- Do set realistic limits.
- Don't demand perfection.
- Do set good examples, without demanding imitation.
- Don't rob your teenager of a sense of independence.
- Do offer to help when you can, even when it's rough.
- Don't portray yourself as having been a better teenager.
- Do play the role of a parent, not of a best friend.
- Don't overdo it when offering your teenager freedom.
- Do promise to help first, and punish later.
- Don't forget that adolescence is a very difficult time.
- Do remember that your teenager is neither child nor adult.
- Don't be surprised by your adolescent's egocentrism.
- Do show sensitivity to your teenager's feelings.
- Don't claim that you know how your teenager really feels.
- Do communicate to the best of your joint abilities.
- Don't be intolerant of the things that you don't like.
- Do insist that your own rights not be violated.
- Don't allow your adolescent to "get away" with anything.
- Do whatever is necessary if things become serious.
- Don't feel helpless, even if things aren't going well.
- Do remember always that you are the adult, and act like one.

Some Final Comments

Adolescents can and should be expected to take on far more responsibility than younger children, and yet they will evidence a different set of problems in attempting to meet those expectations. As you have seen in this chapter, adolescents face pressures and stressors that can be quite intense, although the nature of the specific sources of stress may seem trivial to you, as an adult. Teenagers want freedom, seek independence, and need opportunities in which to mature, but must be given realistic limits beyond which they cannot go. As a caring parent, you must strive to find the compromise that is possible in nearly every area of disagreement, and there will be many of those. Allow your teenager to see that he can count on you in bad times as well as in good ones, and he will be more likely to treat you as you would like to be treated (instead of as the "enemy" that many parents represent to their teenage children). Trust and communication are inseparable qualities, and they form the foundation of adolescent behavior-management. Adolescents have different rights than younger children, but their rights are different still from those of their parents. If you can help your adolescent to explore his limits without breaking them, you will have done the best that any parent can be expected to do.

Question:

"You stated that adolescents are typically motivated by hedonism, but my fourteen-year-old son *likes* working at his after-school job. That doesn't seem to indicate that he likes only what feels good. In fact, doesn't it mean the opposite?"

Answer:

To begin with, the idea of hedonism was expressed as a very general sort of concept, which could be applied to many teenagers but not to all of them. The only statement that we could make about teenagers that would apply to every single one of them is that they are all under the age of 20. Again, the majority of adolescents are motivated by pleasure; most of the things that they choose to do are reinforcing in that they are pleasant activities. Why does any adolescent skip classes? Quite simply, because it feels good not to go to school. Why does a teenager speak in obscene language to a teacher? Again, because it feels good to say whatever one wants, without regard for the consequences. Why does an adolescent disregard his curfew and stay out two hours later than he is permitted to stay? Because he *wants* to stay out later—it feels good to do so. Keep in mind that hedonism is a trait that fits many adults as well, and that it is not something uncommon or even unhealthy unless it is taken to an extreme. On another level, your son earns money by working after school, and it is probable that he finds that income to be so pleasurable that it is another "feels good" sort of behavior. But then, we could say the same thing about most working adults as well.

Question:

"I don't remember being rude to my parents and to my teachers when I was a teenager, and I don't see why my daughter should be allowed to get away with it. What's wrong with good, old-fashioned punishment, like having her stay home every afternoon and evening so that she can cook and clean until she learns to show some respect?"

Answer:

No one ever suggested that your daughter be allowed to behave inappropriately and "get away with it," and it certainly wasn't suggested in this book. If your adolescent is speaking rudely to you and to her teachers, then unquestionably that problem needs to be addressed. Unfortunately, providing your daughter with hours of domestic work is unlikely to make her speak politely to you; on the contrary, she'll probably occupy herself during that time with the creation of all sorts of new expressions about you, none of which could be printed here. What might be far more effective and much more appropriate would be for you to sit down with her and try to determine what is making her so angry and so unhappy that she wants to say those things in the first place. She probably needs an opportunity to vent a lot of the frustration and helplessness that characterizes most adolescents, and you could help by giving her a chance to do so. If you were to ground her and force her to give up all of the things that she probably values, you would be teaching her to comply out of desperation, not to respect others. While such a scenario might be effective and even advisable with younger children, remember that teenagers must be approached differently. She is old enough to think and to reason on a fairly sophisticated level, and thus she should be given credit for such abilities. Try reasoning with her, explaining all of the logic behind your thinking. For example: "I figure that you must be angry about a lot of things, because it's coming out in your speech. I'd like you to be able to tell me when you're feeling that way, so that I can do whatever is necessary to help you to feel better. I promise to try to understand, even if I don't agree with whatever you may say. But, in exchange, I must tell you that your rudeness to others will not be tolerated. I hope that you won't put me in the position of having to discipline you, because it seems as if we could avoid that by talking openly to one another."

Question:
"Do you really believe that being an adolescent is any more difficult today than it was years ago? I liked your 'Happy Days' example, because that was the period in which I grew up. It was rough being a teenager then, but I don't see it as any harder now."

Answer:
Yes, being an adolescent today may well be more difficult than it was in the late fifties and early sixties. There is drug involvement on a much greater scale; there is pressure to perform sexually at an earlier and earlier age; there is a sense of competition among teenagers that is far more intense than before; and, because of the power of the media, there is peer pressure on a greater (actually a global) scale. Teenagers have always had difficulty with parents, and that's never going to change completely; it's a natural and expected part of becoming independent. But nowadays, adolescents are being asked to grow up faster, physically and emotionally, and many of them simply are unprepared to do so. The teen years are perhaps the most challenging phase of a person's life, and it really does seem to be the case that it has become an even greater challenge.

Question:
"My thirteen-year-old son just told me that he has become sexually active. I had a lot of difficulty following your advice about listening and helping first, and punishing later. I think that

this is way too early for him, and I can't think of any way to stop him except to ground him permanently. Any suggestions?"

Answer:
   You are fortunate that your son has enough trust in you to have confided such a thing in the first place. He is probably feeling both frightened and guilty, and may have been looking to you for support and guidance, both of which he hopes he will find. You are correct in believing that it would be unwise to encourage him to continue such behavior at his age, although it is no longer a rarity at the onset of adolescence. Your best bet may well be to explain to him the reasons for your concern, without making him feel that he made a mistake in trusting you. It is almost impossible for someone of that age to appreciate all of the ramifications of such behavior, and on some level, he has probably reached that conclusion already. Don't ground him, as you stated that you were considering doing, because such action on your part would teach him that you are not the person to whom he can turn when he is confused. Furthermore, it is naive to believe that you could remove the opportunity for sexual activity completely, unless you were to keep him a virtual prisoner in the house. Instead, you may want to use his apparent trust in you as a tool for helping him to understand what a serious step he has taken at an early age, and hope, by doing so, that he will change the behavior on his own because of what he has learned from you.

Chapter Nineteen

Putting It All Together

Wow! How can you ever do all of this? How will you ever remember which technique to use? PST may, at first, seem like a lot of work, but it really isn't as difficult to implement as it may appear to be, especially initially. As you begin applying the techniques, you will find that they start coming to you automatically. After all, we don't expect you to carry this book around so that you can look up the appropriate approach each and every time something happens with your children; you always will have to use your best judgment. So, to facilitate your recollection of what PST is all about, we would like to ask that, at this point, you go back to the first chapter and review the basic principles of PST. By remembering these principles, you are more likely to stay on track as things occur.

Too Rigid?

At a PST seminar, a participant commented that she felt that the techniques are too rigid because of the control that one might gain over a child. Unfortunately, this participant missed the whole point of the PST workshop. PST techniques contribute to increased warmth and love within a home. One of the many tasks that every parent should complete is that of teaching children to follow rules and to respect authority figures. If a child does not follow such social requirements, the result may be a confused, neurotic, and irresponsible child whose parent has to yell and to scream before the child will do what is expected of him. Yelling and screaming can result only in the child feeling nervous and even rejected by his parent. Parents who are in control of a household will not have to waste time in repeating things to their children, or in getting upset. Such parents will have more time to enjoy being with their children, since when anger is removed, mutual respect can flourish.

Affection

Parents need to display affection toward their children, as the parent-child relationship (as well as the child's emotional development) is dependent to a great extent on that affection. A child should be kissed "good night" by his parents regardless of how good or how bad his behavior has been. A child must sense that his parents' love for him is unconditional. One of the major goals of PST is to help parents to put their inappropriate emotional reactions on the side and to deal with the child's actual behavior, instead of attacking the child's personality. With this kind of thinking, parents will be able to communicate their love to their child even while the child is being punished.

When to Communicate

The communication skills of listening (hearing), dealing with feelings, and two-way discussions can and should be used under certain circumstances. We are not suggesting that there are limited occasions on which you should communicate with your child, but rather are pointing out that there are times when a child's inappropriate behavior requires a different sort of response. Communication is called for during each of the following circumstances. For example:

- When your child comes to you to discuss a personal problem ("The kids make fun of me when I play football.").
- When the child appears to be experiencing some strong feelings but hasn't talked about them (your child comes home from school looking angry, but does not say anything). You could open up the lines of communication by saying, "You look as if you are feeling angry. I wonder what could be leading you to feel that way."
- When the child expresses a positive feeling about something ("I made a home run today!").
- When the child needs help in decision making ("I'm not having any fun. I can't think of anything to do.").
- When the parent wants the child to explain something or to discuss something ("Would you like to tell me how your day was at school?").

Although there will, of course, be many other circumstances in which communication techniques would be appropriate, the short list above may give you a head start in identifying some of those situations where your child needs to communicate, rather than merely to talk with you. If he has broken rules and behaved inappropriately, be careful that you do not substitute *discussion* for *punishment.*

When to Punish

Consequences (specific situations of punishment) that are applied for inappropriate behavior allow the child to experience the direct result of his own actions. Always try to relate the consequence to the behavior (e.g., if your child stole money from you, you might refuse to spend money on him for one month, with the exception of buying food and school supplies). Punishment can be most effective when a child:

- Is forgetful.
- Doesn't do chores.
- Does not follow directions.
- Does not care for personal belongings.
- Breaks household rules.
- Breaks school rules or requirements.
- Is irresponsible.

Again, there are many other situations for which punishment is appropriate. However, as we have discussed throughout the book, punishment techniques are effective only when you do not display anger.

When Nothing Works

If you feel that you have tried your best to deal with a family problem, that things are not getting better, and that you are worried about your child's well-being, then you might need to think about securing the services of a mental health professional. As you search for services in your community, you may become confused because of the many different types of professionals that are available to help. Since these professionals have so many different approaches to therapy, what should you do?

First, you must decide what type of professional you want to see. Let's take a look at the various professionals with whom you might consider making an appointment, and determine how they differ from one another.

Psychiatrist

A psychiatrist is a physician (M.D.) who studied psychiatry for several years after completing medical school. Psychiatrists who have had extensive training and experience in treating children become board certified in child and adolescent psychiatry. You should always ask a psychiatrist if he or she has met this standard of certification. It is important to remember that psychiatrists have most of their training in hospital settings, and often are experienced in working with the most severe types of cases, especially those needing medication management (schizophrenia, autism, psychosis). Common childhood behavior, motivation, and emotional problems do not require this level of service.

Psychologist

Psychologists usually hold one of the following types of doctoral degrees in psychology:

Ph.D. —Doctor of Philosophy degree in psychology (the most common for psychologists)

Psy.D. —Doctor of Psychology

Ed.D. —Doctor of Education (usually held by school psychologists or counseling psychologists)

After completing undergraduate school, the typical psychologist spends four years in graduate training, which includes coursework, clinical internship, and dissertation. Most states require psychologists, after receiving a doctorate, to have one or more years of supervised clinical experience before they can be licensed. Additionally, psychologists in most states must pass a rigorous licensing exam. If you are considering seeing a psychologist, always ask the doctor if he or she is licensed as a psychologist in your state. Sometimes, degrees can be misleading, so always check. In order to work effectively with children, a psychologist should have had extensive training in child psychology and therapy. Although many psychologists are generalists and work with all ages, some specialize in performing therapy with children, adolescents, and families, and they do not work with other types of problems.

Social Worker

A social worker who does therapy usually has an M.S.W. (Master of Social Work) degree and has qualified for state licensing (not all states license social workers), or has earned the letters ACSW or LCSW to place after his or her name (Academy of Clinical Social Workers or Licensed Clinical Social Worker). These letters assure you that they have qualified with their professional organization for meeting the requirements to practice in their field. The D.S.W. degree indicates that the person has earned the highest degree in the field, Doctor of Social Work. Clinical social workers are usually trained to do counseling, but generally are not trained to do the diagnostic testing or more advanced assessment work that a psychologist would be able to do. With the proper training, a social worker should be able to help with most child and family problems. As with any other professional person, the social worker you may want to see should be able to demonstrate to you that he or she has been trained in child and family work.

Counselor

There are many types of counselors (mental health, human relations, marriage and family, guidance/school). To perform psychotherapy, a counselor should have a minimum of a master's degree in counseling (M.A., M.S., M.Ed.) and should be licensed if practicing in a state that requires such licensure (not all of the states require counselors to be licensed). If you are in a state where licensing is not required, be sure to check the credentials of the person whom you may want to see. Most counselors will have qualified for membership in a professional organization such as the American Association for Counselor Development, or the American Association for Marriage and Family Therapy. Inquire of a prospective counselor as to the professional organization with which he or she is affiliated.

Marriage and Family Therapist

This is a counselor who specializes in family and marital problems. The training and the credentials would be similar to that described under "Counselor."

Psychotherapist

In states where licensing standards are loose or do not exist for counselors or social workers, or both, almost anyone may call himself a psychotherapist. In some states, someone with a third-grade education and with no training at all in psychotherapy can call himself a psychotherapist simply because there are no standards for licensing or certification. It is very important for you to check the credentials of any practitioner who is not required to be licensed in your state. We have known many people who call themselves psychotherapists, but who have had no formal training in the profession. Psychotherapist simply means a person who performs psychotherapy (the use of psychological methods in treating clients).

What Kind of Therapy Do I Pick?

When selecting a therapist, it is very important to ask, "What mode of therapy do you practice?" Since there are dozens of types of approaches, you need to be sure that the professional whom you are going to see is trained to use techniques that will be effective with child and family problems. Often, a therapist will say that he or she is eclectic. This means that the professional selects the most appropriate approach for the client. Although the term *eclectic* is used commonly, most therapists do favor a particular kind of therapy. If a therapist tells you that she is eclectic, you might reply by asking, "How much time do you typically spend with the child, and how much time do you typically spend with the parents when doing therapy with problems similar to ours?" In PST, we emphasize that in order for therapy to be effective, the parents must be actively involved. This must include the therapist spending a good deal of time with the parent. Since the parent has the greatest influence on the child, he or she must learn strategies for helping the child to learn new behaviors, to respond differently to stress, or to become more motivated. Except in unusual cases, therapy that is focused on a one-to-one relationship between the child and the therapist is often useless. Some parents like this kind of therapy simply because they can leave the child at the therapist's office and feel good about having secured help for the child. However, without active parental involvement in counseling, significant long-term achievements may not be accomplished.

Below, we have listed some common problems, preceded by a number.

1. Behavior
2. Motivation
3. Family relationships
4. Fears
5. Habits
6. Emotion
7. Peer relationships/social skills
8. Abuse, abandonment

Commonly Used Types of Therapy

The following forms of therapy are followed by the numbers which designate each problem in the foregoing list. The numbers indicate the problems for which a type of therapy is likely to be effective. We could not list the dozens of different types of therapy that are available, so we included the approaches most commonly used with children.

Reality Therapy (1,2,3,4,6,7,8)

Reality therapy is a learning process. The child and the parents learn how to deal with existing problems. Emphasis is placed on the acceptance of the consequences that come with behavior, with being responsible, and with thinking in a realistic manner.

Rational-Emotive Therapy (RET) (1,2,3,4,5,6,7,8)

RET concentrates on the present. Since we have control over our ideas, thinking, feelings, and actions, what happens in our lives is a result of our own thinking. The idea here is that you *feel* bad because you are *thinking* irrationally. People are taught to think rationally, thus giving up the irrational beliefs that led previously to problems. Examples of commonplace irrational beliefs might include:

- It is necessary that others approve of me and love me.
- It is catastrophic when things don't go the way that I'd like.
- People have little or no control over their unhappiness or over the circumstances in their lives.
- Since my child has problems, I am a failure as a parent.
- I must be perfect.

In RET, people learn to take responsibility for their own thoughts and actions, as well as for the consequences that result.

Client-Centered/Humanistic Counseling

We do not feel that this approach, used by itself, will be helpful with most childhood problems. The goal in this style of therapy is to create a warm and accepting environment, so that trust can develop between client and therapist. This should allow the client to share thoughts and ideas and to achieve greater self-understanding. The counselor is like a mirror, reflecting to the client his own thoughts and feelings, with the idea that the client (or child, in this case) will see his own problems clearly in the reflected statements. Such techniques are good in establishing rapport between a client and his therapist, but often the therapist would need to incorporate other modes of therapy so that he can maximize the changes that must occur in the child's behavior.

Family Therapy (3,8)

The family functions as a unit, and when stress is applied to one member of the unit, all of the other members will be affected. To help the family function more effectively, the members are taught how to improve their communication, how to increase the self-esteem of each family member, and how to encourage responsible behavior. All of the family members are usually involved.

Behavior Therapy (1,2,4,5 and, when combined with other types of therapy, 3,6, and 7, too)

Behavior therapy is a learning process in that inappropriate behavior is presumed to have been learned. Thus, appropriate behavior is strengthened and inappropriate behavior is extinguished. After the problem is identified, a plan is made for its solution. Emphasis is placed on what is happening now—not on what has happened in the past. Related techniques (e.g., rational-emotive therapy, biofeedback) sometimes are employed to help the child to function more adaptively. There is more research to support the validity of behavior therapy than there is on any other type of therapy being used.

Psychoanalytic Therapy

In PST, we do not recommend this therapeutic style for use with children. Psychoanalytic therapy involves making the unconscious conscious, which is a process that often involves a great deal of time. We have found that looking deep below the surface for the solution to a problem is often unnecessary, as it can be addressed more efficiently through behavioral intervention. Play therapy is used often in psychoanalytic therapy and, in many cases, we feel that this is a waste of time, effort, and money. Although play therapy can be helpful in unusual circumstances (such as with an abused child or with a non-verbal child), it simply fails to address the situation with adequate speed or effectiveness.

Group Therapy (2,6,7)

Group counseling often serves as a supplement to family and child therapy. While it does not (by itself) represent an appropriate forum for the solution to serious emotional or behavioral problems with children, it can be an excellent adjunct to other forms of intervention. Group therapy can be very helpful in problems with peer relationships, as a child can learn and improve social skills while in a safe setting with children of a similar age.

What to Ask When You Call a Therapist

If and when you decide to seek professional assistance for your child, there are many things which are important for you to

know. When you call for an appointment, you might want to inquire about the therapist's fees, hours, and acceptance of insur-
ance. Even if you go to a family service agency or to a mental
health clinic which has a large staff, you need to be sure that you
will be matched with an appropriate therapist at that facility. To
help you in determining whether the therapist is, in fact, appropriate for your child or for your family, we offer the following
questions to guide you through the conversation:

- How much experience and training do you have in working with children and families?
- If there is a school problem, will you contact my child's
  teacher? Will you or a member of your staff go to the
  school and observe my child in class if it is necessary?
- Will you test my child to assess his level of functioning
  and to determine what special interventions might be
  necessary?
- How do you involve the parent in the therapy?
- Will you teach me what to do with my child to help in
  solving his problems, and will you give me specific tech-
  niques to use?
- If there is a crisis, can you be reached by phone within a
  reasonable amount of time?
- What kind of license do you hold to practice (e.g., psy-
  chologist, counselor, social worker)?
- If you are a psychologist, is your doctoral degree from a
  University program that is approved by the American
  Psychological Association?
- If you are a psychiatrist, are you board certified in child
  and adolescent psychiatry?
- What percentage of your caseload is child and family?

The answers that the therapist provides to the above questions
will help you in deciding whether that professional is the one
who is most appropriate for your family. When you need to
search for a therapist, speak to your school counselor, school
social worker or visiting teacher, pediatrician, or clergyman.
They are often the best people to ask, simply because they have

had contact with many mental health professionals in your community. They will know which professionals have had real success with children and families. Personal recommendations are often the best way to locate a good therapist. If you know someone personally who can suggest a particular professional with whom he or she was pleased, then you probably can feel comfortable about selecting that therapist.

PST Parent Study Groups

You might want to consider forming a PST study group, because it is very effective to study and to discuss these techniques with other parents. Several chapters could be discussed in weekly two-hour meetings, thus giving you an opportunity to share your experiences in using the techniques, in identifying modifications that you have found to be effective, and in helping each other with encouragement.

Because some parents prefer to be in a parent study group that is led by a mental health professional, the authors have been conducting training programs to certify various professionals as PST instructors. These certified trainers will have the highest level of skill in helping you to put PST into action. PST workshops also are presented by the authors throughout the United States each year, and you can add your name to the PST mailing list if you would like to be kept informed as to the dates of these programs, as well as of new materials. The authors welcome your comments, as well as your suggestions for future publications. Although we cannot guarantee a personal response to every question, you can write to Dr. Marvin Silverman and to Dr. David A. Lustig at P.O. Box 841405, Pembroke Pines, Florida 33084.

A Closing Comment

We hope that *Parent Survival Training* has helped to make life a little easier for you, and that it has contributed to your children's overall emotional and behavioral development.

Happy Parenting!

Chapter Twenty

Questions and Answers About PST

At our *Parent Survival Training* workshops, we have discovered that many parents have a tremendous number of questions to ask us. Because there are so many areas of concern, these questions run the gamut from A to Z, and the questions that you may have after reading this book could well be among them. We hope the sampling of questions that we have included in this chapter will be of help in resolving any uncertainty that you might still be experiencing.

It's Never Too Late to Begin

"Now that I know about the way in which PST works, how do I go about putting into action all of the things that I've learned? Do I announce exactly what changes are going to occur, or do I begin with no warning at all?"

Answer:

Putting PST into effect with children who are not accustomed to having limits set for them can be a challenge, especially at first. In most families, children whose behavior warrants correction have an excellent understanding of just what they can get away with, and they are likely to be quite displeased with any change you make in the "system" they have come to know so well. We suggest that you approach your children by saying, "Okay, we are going to be doing a lot of things differently around here, and I realize that in the beginning you may not like all of the changes. From now on, there will be certain rewards for proper behavior on your part, and certain consequences to face for failing to act appropriately. For example, you will do what you are told to do the first time, because I will no longer continue to nag you about things. If you behave well, that's great; if you ignore or disobey me, you will be punished."

As you explain in detail what aspects of PST you will be focusing upon, your children will be given an idea of what is to be expected of them. You cannot begin utilizing most PST techniques without warning, because your children would have no understanding of what changes you are looking for in their behavior, nor would they understand why they are suddenly being punished for the same things that they are accustomed to doing. Don't hesitate to make statements, such as "The game is over," when you need to emphasize that you are now going to be calling the shots instead of allowing your children to continue doing so. PST offers parents an opportunity to create a warm, nurturant environment that helps to prepare children for the real world. Interestingly enough, most children like PST once they become accustomed to the limits that are set for them, and the family is a happier one when the children behave appropriately and the parents assume the responsibilities that they should have taken on in the first place.

And the Winner Is . . . No One!

"When brothers and sisters fight, if you punish both of them without determining which child actually started the fight, isn't the system unfair to the child who was not at fault?"

Answer:

In PST, we recommend not only that parents not take sides in fights among siblings, but suggest also that if punishment is called for, it should be presented to all of the children involved. We can understand your concern that the innocent child may get punished and that such a situation may not be fair. Remember first, however, that it takes at least two children to have a fight; one child cannot fight by himself. Most of the time, each child involved in a conflict is at least partially at fault. We agree that, at times, only one child actually is guilty of having created the problem at hand. Unfortunately, though, you can almost never be absolutely certain about who started the fight, and if you question the children, there will be two sides to the story. By the very nature of the situation, you would have to believe one child's story and reject the other, and you would, of course, be listening to a distorted version of what really happened. Suppose that your 11-year-old boy punches his 8-year-old sister, and she comes to you, in tears, trying to let you know what happened. It is always possible that the 8-year-old could have bothered her older brother earlier, and that he is getting back at her now. If you were to punish the 11-year-old, it might be unfair to him, even though he is the one who did the hitting. You cannot and should not be a district attorney or a judge. Project to your children the attitude that when there is a fight, everyone involved is to blame. The children will soon learn that it is a waste of time to come to you and to tattle, and that they should start resolving conflicts by themselves or be prepared for the consequences. This approach may not be completely fair, but you may be surprised at how effective it can be at reducing the number of fights that occur among and between siblings. It is preferable to the taking of sides (with its inherent risk that one child will be made even more angry toward the other).

Go Ahead, Make My Day

"How do you go about getting a child to comply with a punishment? For example, what can I do to be sure that my child will stay in her room or remain in the chair, if that is what the punishment calls for?"

Answer:

The only reason that any child could have in violating the constraints of a punishment would be to test the limits, and that should indicate to you that your child does not yet know where those limits lie. When a child leaves her room after having been told that she must remain there, your authority is being challenged. If you fail to act immediately, then your credibility will be as damaged as your authority has been already. What you must do is to explain to your daughter, in advance, that the punishments that you assign are not being put up for a vote. They are mandatory, and if she chooses to disobey what you have designated, then there will be a significantly higher cost for her to pay. Make sure that she understands that if she were to walk out of her room during a two-hour punishment, for example, she would first have to go back inside and begin the entire two-hour period again, even if only a few minutes remained in the initial punishment (so she will learn that two hours means two consecutive hours). Afterward, there would be still additional punishment to compensate for the disobeying of the original directions. The idea here is that your child must learn that she will do what she is told when being punished, because the alternative will be worse. When she sees that you do not become upset, but that you administer further punishment calmly and systematically, she will know that she cannot get away with game playing.

My Child's Bedroom Looks Like "Toys R Us"

"Why should I send my child to his room as a punishment, when it looks like a big toy store? There are so many things there that will amuse him that he'll probably enjoy himself. How can I expect him just to sit there and do nothing?"

Answer:

If your child is told that he is being punished and that he is not to touch or to play with anything in his room, then he should be expected to follow your directions. If he does decide to do what he wants and touches some of his things, he must see that you will not tolerate such defiance. At that point, take whatever he has touched away from him and never return it. In PST, we suggest that the confiscated goods be donated to a charity, and that the child witness the parent giving away his possession(s). If the child touches a very expensive item that you are unwilling to give away (e.g., a television, a stereo, or a computer), then take away the privilege of its use for at least three months. The child must be told the length of time he will be without his possession and should be reminded that, regardless of how well he behaves or what he might say in the near future, it will not be returned until the date that you have identified. We suggest that you not actually remove valuable things from your child's room in an effort to keep him from enjoying them. Instead, give your son an opportunity to learn to resist temptation. If he cannot resist, he then will have to accept the consequence of losing what he has touched. Since you will not always catch the child touching his things, you can take away only those possessions that you have witnessed him misusing directly or even indirectly (e.g., a television set that is warm due to its recent use). Above all, don't feel guilty about doing these things; they are for your child's own good.

Ms. Lazy and Her Homework

"How can I make my daughter do her homework in a reasonable amount of time? She knows how to do her work, but she just stares at the wall. She writes down answers without really concentrating on what she is doing, and I want to see this behavior change."

Answer:

Try to have your daughter start her homework before she has access to privileges, such as television, or going out to play. Tell her that she will not be allowed to watch television, to play, or to do anything that she enjoys until the homework has been completed. If she comes home immediately after school, you can tell her that she will not sit down to have dinner until the work is finished. Your daughter should see that responsibilities must be assumed before she can expect to have access to pleasurable things. Also, make sure that she does not see that you are getting frustrated or upset as a result of her behavior. This type of reaction from you may actually reward her for malingering, since she would be gaining some satisfaction from seeing how easily she can get you to feel upset.

My Child Studied with Dr. Ruth

"What should I do about my child, who is far more sexually educated than is Johnny next door? His mother has already complained to me once."

Answer:

It sounds as if the problem is not that your child is sexually educated, but that he feels free to dispense his knowledge to any who are willing to listen. If we assume, hopefully with good reason, that your child's knowledge is appropriate for his age, then we are forced to conclude that you have given him a wealth of information about sex itself, while failing to include guidance about the times and places when such matters are to be discussed. You would get nowhere by suggesting to your son that he never discuss sex with other children, since such discussions among peers could be prevented only by raising children in isolation chambers. However, you may want to try telling your son that he is no longer to discuss sex with Johnny, as his mother has asked that he refrain from doing so, under the penalty of being unable to spend time with him should the behavior continue. Explain to your child that because this is a sensitive subject, some children his age will be made uncomfortable if he talks very much about it. Make sure he knows that he can always come to you for answers or information, and that you are an appropriate partner for such discussions.

Mr. Whiner Lives Here

"What can one do with a child who whines when he doesn't get his own way? It's a very irritating habit, and it is driving everyone in the family absolutely nuts."

Answer:

You should show your child that whining is useless so that he will learn that it's a waste of his time. In order to do this, you must never react to his whining. When he whines, do not look at him and do not speak with him. Try not to allow your dislike for his complaining to register on your face, since facial expressions can be as powerful as words. As time passes, your child will learn that whining will not result in any reaction from his parents. Eventually, he should stop. As with similar techniques discussed in PST, remember that his whining is likely to become more intense as you begin to ignore it. If this occurs, continue to ignore the whining and stick to those issues with which you need to deal. As far as you are concerned, the whining does not exist, and, therefore, you will not react to it.

Misery Loves Company

"We have trouble carrying out a punishment, and usually let our child off because we feel sorry for him when he misses something like a party. What can we do to be stronger?"

Answer:

To be stronger, you must tell yourself, "I know how miserable my child feels. He must learn that he cannot always feel happy. If he thinks that he must always feel good, he will be in for a shock when he gets older. If I feel sorry for him and let him get away without the punishment, I will have my hands full with his behavior later on. If he sees that I will go back on my word, then the next time that I have to tell him something, he will see me as a bag of hot air and my words will be meaningless to him." Keep reminding yourself about how important it is for your child to see that you will not feel sorry for him and that you will not take away a punishment. You will be opening up the door for many problems if you are too soft, because you will be permitting your child to escape from the very consequences with which he must learn to deal.

Family Talks: Geneva Revisited

"What place, if any, do you think that family heart-to-heart talks and meetings actually have? Are they necessary?"

Answer:

In certain kinds of families, heart-to-heart talks may be an excellent technique for keeping the lines of communication open among the different family members. Unfortunately, in many families, such talks and meetings can take on the air of another obligation or chore and create as much resentment as they purport to dispel. The key here is the desire of the family members in question to have such talks, as well as the ability of these individuals to discuss problems rationally, without using the meetings as "attack sessions" or as opportunities for aggravation or hysteria, or both. In response to your question, the answer is "no," they are not necessary, but they could be of great value if everyone involved is willing to participate constructively.

I Hate You, Mommy

"What about the child who always yells 'I hate you' when she doesn't get her own way? I have a real problem with my child doing that."

Answer:

Such a reaction is common when a child does not get her own way. The important thing here is for your daughter to see that such statements will not affect you. You know that she is saying such a thing because she is feeling angry and not because she really hates you. Too often, when a parent reacts to such a statement, the child learns that she can manipulate her parent into an emotional reaction. Therefore, your best reaction is no reaction. Don't say anything to her; you must avoid facial expressions of disgust or anger. If your conversation with the child is finished, then walk away. If you are still explaining or discussing something, then stick to the issue at hand while totally ignoring the child's statements about how she hates you. It is important that at no time do you give your child the satisfaction of seeing that she can make you feel upset with such statements.

Gifted Children, Special Problems

"No one ever seems to address the problems of dealing with a gifted child. My son is extremely bright and seems to have problems that differ somewhat from the mainstream."

Answer:

You have raised an interesting question; gifted children do have problems that differ somewhat from those of other children. To begin with, of course, a very bright child is likely to think on a more sophisticated level than his chronological age would lead you to expect, and so you may find yourself surprised often about his ability to reason things out. Such children sometimes confound their parents by challenging them with logic that is difficult to combat. On another level, gifted children sometimes set standards for themselves that are difficult to reach and become upset and dissatisfied with themselves whenever they fail to do anything perfectly. There is a self-image problem with many bright children; they have a great deal to be proud of, but often have trouble recognizing their own strong points. For many, it is difficult to make friends within their peer group because others of the same age are boring to them, and even, sometimes, rejecting of them ("Oh, he's just a geek . . . he gets straight A's. . ."). To make all of this worse, a gifted child may also have to contend with a parent who expects so much from him that a constant sense of pressure and stress is created within the home. We suggest often that the parents of a gifted child attempt to ensure that he has a well-rounded lifestyle, including participation in group sports (to help to build peer relationships), adequate time to pursue a hobby (to reduce the stress of challenging academic work, as well as to serve as a source of self-confidence), and realistic goals toward which to work (to prevent "child burn-out").

Keep Your Presents—See If I Care!

"I started rewarding my six-year-old son for every good grade that he earned, and his grades improved a lot. The last time that I asked him to make an effort to do better or face the discontinuation of the gifts, he told me that he doesn't need any more presents. What can I do now to motivate him?"

Answer:

A good behavior management program must consist of a combination of rewards and punishments. In the *real* world, we have rewards for good work (e.g., a paycheck) and punishments for bad work (e.g., getting fired). Since you want to prepare your child to live in the real world, you must have rewards and punishments in your household. When your child does work hard and earns good grades, he should be reinforced with extra privileges or special gifts. However, when he has acted irresponsibly, he must face the consequences for his inappropriate actions.

It is really difficult to punish a child for poor grades. You may not always know if the child was told about a test in advance, or even if the teacher actually gave him an opportunity to learn the skills needed for a test. You should use punishment only for those school-related tasks for which the child does have control. For example, if there is a weekly spelling test and your son knows that he must study the words, and then earns an "F" anyway, some form of punishment (e.g., allowance money deducted, television privileges suspended) would be appropriate. Since the child knew about the exam and had enough time to prepare but chose not to do so, he can be held responsible for the poor grade. Of course, these suggestions are based upon the assumption that the child is capable of achieving the grades in question. If he had a learning disability that would make it difficult or even impossible to remember how to spell the words, then punishment would be inappropriate. If the child earned a good grade, you would want to recognize it and allow him access to some extra privileges, or supply him with some other incentive (e.g., extra money added to his allowance).

I Need the Karate Kid
"How can I, as a parent, deal with the bullies who are frightening my child in school as well as in the neighborhood?"

Answer:
The whole problem is that you shouldn't be dealing with the bullies at all; your child must learn how to do that. If we assume for the purposes of this discussion that your child's safety isn't being threatened by much older, larger children who would pose a real hazard to his safety, then your help would only serve to prolong the dependence that your child will assume on you or on others. As we have recommended countless times to parents in similar situations, enroll your child promptly in a good karate school. Martial arts training will help your child to build self-confidence, self-discipline, and of course an ability in self-defense that he will carry with him throughout his life. The children who study karate frequently have a subsequent improvement in school behavior and even in their academic work, as the concepts of self-discipline extend beyond the physical training alone. Incidentally, we recommend such training for daughters as well as for sons; girls often have a need for self-defense in today's world. By giving your child an opportunity to learn karate, you will be allowing him not just a chance to experience the security of being able to defend himself, but the ability to become more self-sufficient and independent as his self-confidence grows.

This Is Going to Hurt You More Than Me
"I have trouble determining when it's okay to spank my child. How do you determine when it is appropriate to spank?"

Answer:
There are much better ways of altering behavior in a child than is offered by spanking. Spanking should be saved for emergency situations when other punishments cannot be given promptly, or

for those cases in which you are dealing with a very young child who cannot fully understand your explanations about his behavior (or comprehend the range of consequences). Let's assume for example that a 2-year-old child, despite numerous warnings, goes to the edge of a lake by himself. He should be spanked immediately, while the parent says, "No, you may not go near the water!" In such a case, the child should be spanked only on his buttocks and only with the back of the hand. Never spank a child with an object, never spank excessively, and be careful that you never spank while you are feeling extremely angry. If a very young child is to learn from experience, the punishment or reward must be given as soon as the behavior occurs, but, again, it is important that you not do so while feeling so angry that you could overdo it. The difficulty with spanking as a behavioral modifier is that in order for it to alter a child's behavior effectively, it must be unpleasant enough to motivate the child to behave. Ironically, if spanking is performed safely, it is neither painful enough nor long enough in duration to motivate most children to change their behavior. Accordingly, we suggest that its use be limited to emergency situations with a young child.

Get Your Own Toys, Daddy

"Is it a good punishment to take away a young child's stuffed toy? My four-year-old son likes to sleep with his little toy bear, so it would seem that taking it away would really teach him a lesson."

Answer:

It would teach him a lesson, all right: that his father is a cruel, vindictive man who is perfectly content to rob his child of a basic sense of security, as long as he makes his point. To a young child, a stuffed animal can be a friend, a protector, a confidant, and much more. Taking such a toy away from a child would serve only to frighten him, and that is the last thing that we would suggest in PST. Parents need to be able to discipline their children when such punishment is needed, but a real sense of fear is not a tool with which to make a point. There are dozens of other things that your son could have taken away (e.g., bicycle, television privileges, other toys), but none of these would endanger his sense of well-being and security. Try imagining how he might feel if you were to do such a thing, and then perhaps you'll be able to develop a long list of alternatives, each of which is likely to work far more effectively.

Daddy, Mommy Tried to Punish Me!

"What happens when one parent sets up a punishment, only to have the other parent lift the punishment?"

Answer:

If this were to happen, the child would learn from experience that he can do whatever he wants to do because his parents won't back each other up. If one spouse sets a punishment, the other spouse should reinforce it regardless of whether or not he or she agrees. Of course, if there were a very inappropriate punishment (e.g., "you cannot go out of the house for the next year"), some change would have to be made. If this were necessary, then both spouses should agree upon precisely what would constitute a more appropriate punishment. The mother and the father should both approach the child and explain (for example) that it has been discussed, and that it seems more appropriate for the child to stay in the house until he has completed one week of school without missing an assignment. If both parents tell this to the child, he will see that his mother and father are communicating and agreeing about how to raise their children. This will lead to development of respect by the child toward both parents, as well as to learning the lesson that "my parents will not allow me to manipulate them."

My Child Thinks That He's a Shadow

"What do you do with a child who follows you around, and who refuses to leave you alone even to do everyday household chores?"

Answer:

It sounds as if your child is experiencing a common and expected childhood phenomenon known as *separation anxiety.* What occurs in such a situation is that the child develops a fear of being separated from his parent, so that he becomes anxious whenever the parent is out of sight. Remember that young children do not think like adults, so that some of what they experience seems very illogical, at first. A young child may not realize that the parent is coming back, or even that the parent still exists when he or she cannot be seen. Hence, by following you around, the child can convince himself that you are present, safe, and accounted for. In all likelihood, your child will outgrow this stage, as does almost every other child, but you may be able to help to bring that about by practicing with him. Demonstrate that you can leave for a moment and return safely, and over a period of days or weeks, you should be able to increase the amount of time that you can spend away without eliciting a fear response. Since none of this is cause for concern with a young child, you can always wait it out and see that it changes as the child matures.

Can I Borrow a Pen?

"My son always seems to forget several of the directions that I give him, especially when I give four or five. Should I write them down so that he can't say that he forgot a few, and remembered only three of the five?"

Answer:

It would be difficult to write a list of instructions every time that you need your child to do a few things. However, such a list would be good for routine daily chores so that you could specify the time by which the chore must be completed, and so that the child can refer to the list when he needs to do so. On another level, with a very young child, it may be inappropriate to give more than one direction at a time. While a bright 12-year-old should have no problem handling five directions when they are presented verbally, a younger child may have difficulty. With any child, you must be certain that you have his attention when you give him any sort of directions. You can check on just how well your child attended to what you've said by asking him to repeat the directions to you so that both of you can confirm that you have communicated clearly to each other. Incidentally, as far as the written list goes, the problem with relying constantly on written directions is that the child may never learn to use his auditory memory abilities, and might have difficulty responding to oral directions given in school later on.

And in This Corner, My Wife, Weighing In at . . .

"My wife and I fight in front of the kids fairly often, and I'm wondering whether this could have a detrimental effect on them."

Answer:

There is a difference between arguing and disagreeing, and when you say "fighting," it's difficult to be sure exactly what you mean. Some amount of conflict is normal and expected in most relationships, so if your children see you disagreeing or even arguing, it could actually be a learning experience for them. They will see that their parents are human beings and, at times, may have disagreements and may become upset. The important thing is that the children see their parents resolve the conflict in a healthy and reasonable manner. If the fighting to which you referred consists of you and your wife throwing dishes at each other, screaming, swearing, or permitting the anger to carry on for days, then one could expect this to have a detrimental effect on the children. However, if you stick to the point of the argument, resolve it peacefully, and go on talking with each other and being friendly, your children will learn through observation that people do have conflicts which can be resolved in a rational manner; that people can go on with their relationship afterward. Therefore, the key issue is not whether it's all right for your child to observe you experiencing conflict, but rather, it is the sort of fighting and conflict-resolution approaches that they are witnessing.

Go Ahead, Mom, I Can Take It

"My daughter refuses to clean her room, and no punishment seems to work. Sundays in particular are horrendous days in our household. What can I do?"

Answer:

Any behavior will continue to occur as long as it is being reinforced. Clearly, your daughter has gained a large degree of control over you: Not only can she do what she pleases about her room, but she can interfere with your daily life and actually make your weekends seem unpleasant. By surrendering such control to your daughter, you have set the stage for further problems, as well.

We have yet to come across a child who wouldn't respond to some sort of behavioral intervention. It may be that with your daughter, whose behavior has been rewarded over a period of time, and who may well be obstinate to begin with, you will have to go a step or two farther than would be necessary with a different child. Nevertheless, it is important that you alter her behavior (as well as yours) as quickly as you can. We would suggest you tell her that you've had more than enough, and that she has two days in which to clean her room. At the conclusion of that time, you will inspect the room, and if it has not been cleaned, you will remove its contents. Leave her nothing more than a mattress on the floor, some pieces of her least favorite clothing (in that way, she can leave the house for school, but won't enjoy what she's wearing), and whatever supplies that she needs to do her schoolwork. Tell her that this time, and this time only, she will be given an opportunity to earn back the boxes containing her possessions. Give her no more than one per week, contingent upon good behavior, of course, and remind her that if this has to be done again, her possessions will be donated to a charity and you will not replace any of them. You may be surprised to find that even with your "nothing-seems-to-work" daughter, you get quick results with this technique.

I'm Gonna Tell on You!
"When a child is a tattletale, should this be ignored, or should it be addressed through some sort of behavioral approach?"

Answer:
Without question, tattletale behavior should be ignored. If you listen to what the child is trying to tell you about another child, she will learn that tattling is acceptable as a result of seeing that her parent pays attention to it. Instead, it is important to set up some guidelines with your child. She should know that if she sees someone doing something dangerous (e.g., playing with matches, using a dangerous tool), it is important to tell an

adult so that the other child can be prevented from getting hurt. However, for things that would not result in someone getting hurt, it is best for her to keep them to herself. Additionally, you need to leave some lines of communication open in the event that someone acts in an abusive manner to the child. Let the child know that telling you her brother ate an extra cookie is the type of thing that you can be left to discover for yourself; such information should not be told to you. Helping your child to stop tattletale behavior is important for other reasons, as well: Children who frequently tattle on other children often are rejected and picked on by their peers. Needless to say, you should do everything you can to make certain that you do not contribute to such a problem.

My Son Paid $500 for a School Lunch

"My seven-year-old son stole two valuable silver dollar coins from my bedroom. Each coin was worth about five hundred dollars. He brought the coins to school, and used one for lunch and the other to buy supplies at the school store. Eventually, the school realized that these were valuable coins, and they were returned to me. Other than actually killing my son, is there any punishment that would be appropriate for him?"

Answer:

The main issue here is that your son took something from you without permission. This act must result in punishment. First, tell your son that he is not allowed into your room for the next few months until you feel that you can trust him again. Tell him that you will not spend any money on him except for the essentials (e.g., food, clothing, and school supplies) during the next four weeks, because you will not spend money on someone who steals from you. If he gets an allowance, cut it in half for at least a month. If the family goes out to eat in a restaurant, have the child sit with the family and have only a glass of milk, and then serve him dinner as soon as you return home. Do not take him on any special family outings or activities. Even if you have to pay for a baby sitter so that you can take the rest of the family out without him, it will be worth it if your son learns he will miss out on all of the fun things in his daily life when he breaks rules as important as the one he ignored. It is also suggested that he be restricted to his room without privileges for at least one day, and that television privileges be removed for one week. He must learn that stealing results in unpleasant consequences, and that there are no circumstances under which it is worth doing.

Rip Van Winkle Lives in My House

"I cannot get my adolescent daughter to get out of bed in the morning for school, and I'm becoming more and more frustrated. What in the world should I do?"

Answer:
The crux of the entire problem was revealed in your first sentence. Why should *you* have trouble getting her out of bed, when she is old enough to assume that responsibility for herself? By nagging her each morning, you are teaching her that there is no reason for her to behave properly or to take on the degree of maturity one might expect of a teenage girl. After all, you're always there to make sure she gets up and does whatever it is that needs to be done, so certainly she doesn't have to bother herself with irritating concerns like the taking on of responsibility. If you continue to behave as you are, she won't need to look for a boyfriend, either, because you'll probably arrange that for her, as well.

If you want to do what is in your daughter's best interests, get her an alarm clock and tell her that from now on she is responsible for setting the alarm at night and for awakening and preparing for school each morning. You will no longer enter her room to awaken her. If she goes back to sleep, she will miss school, fail her classes, and be grounded each and every day until the behavior changes. That goes for use of the telephone, television, stereo, and other goodies, as well as for any freedom enjoyed outside the house. If she chooses to live the life of a hermit as the price for oversleeping, she'll be the first adolescent that we've come across who ever did.

My Child Is a Marriage-Buster

"How can I deal with a child who is turning my spouse against me?"

Answer:

No child can possibly make a husband and wife argue or have problems with each other. Although it may seem that way to you, do not blame your child for problems that you are having in your marriage. If your spouse is responding to your child's efforts to cause such conflicts, then your spouse is in need of counseling immediately. Also, the child is being burdened with carrying the responsibility for the marital problems. If, in the future, you should divorce, your child will feel guilty because he may believe that he actually had the power to cause these problems. No child has such power; however, an adult can allow himself to believe that a child could set up such a situation. In this case, the adult is the one with the problem because he is allowing a child to have such tremendous influence.

The Argument Syndrome

"How do I break the argument syndrome which has been in effect in my household for years?"

Answer:

You can break the argument syndrome regardless of how long this problem has been occurring. Just start following the PST principles and techniques. Whenever you feel that you are going to argue with your children, tell yourself, "I will not let my child have the satisfaction of seeing that he has the power to get me upset." Since you have now studied PST, you should realize that when you argue with your children, you are showing them that arguing with you is acceptable (after all, you're allowing it to occur). Thus, at this point, you should be ready to stop the pattern that has been established in your home and to let your children see that there is no way they can manipulate you into getting involved in an argument with them.

Is There an Echo in Here?

"My children are six and seven years old. When I tell them to do something, one will say, 'Well, Kyle doesn't have to!' In the same vein, when I ask one of them not to do something, I usually get, 'Well, Peter gets to do it!' How do I go about separating their behavior?"

Answer:

To begin with, you should be sure that the things you ask of them are approximately equal in scope. Because they are so close in age, they can be considered, to all intents and purposes, to be the same age (especially in most of the circumstances which probably concern you). Unless one is far more sophisticated than the other (and that would be a surprise given the age spread), their privileges should be comparable, as well. Assuming that you are not playing favorites, whenever you get a "you-treat-him-differently" sort of remark from one of them, point out that the other would be treated identically. Don't debate the point, because that would reinforce the behavior, but be certain that you do, in fact, keep your word. A remark, such as "If Kyle did that, he'd be punished just like you," should be all that is needed, and must be as much as you permit yourself to say in such cases. The only thing that you might add is something, such as "Kyle, isn't it incredible that Peter thought that I'd let you get away with something like this?" Over time, you should see a significant change in the behavior. If you want to hurry that along, however, you can explain that from now on, whenever one of the boys compares treatment with the other, both of them will have to be punished simultaneously. That should get the message through, loud and clear.

Watch Out, She's Got an Eraser!

"My twelve-year-old frequently loses her temper at school. She might throw a book against the wall, bang on her desk, or yell. I am not at school to deal with these things, so what can I do?"

Answer:

Arrange for your daughter's teacher to fill out and sign a daily note which would indicate whether your daughter controlled her temper or "exploded" at school. Set up consequences that your daughter will know about in advance. For example, on any day that she lost her temper in school, all privileges would be withheld (e.g., no television, no use of the telephone, no going out to play, and no friends coming to the house). The same consequence would occur on any day that she forgot to bring the note home, and you are not to accept any excuses. Unless she brings home a note from another adult at the school to confirm an excuse (e.g., the teacher had to leave early today), she cannot be excused for that day. Also, set up some special privileges for those occasions when your daughter does not lose her temper all week (e.g., going to a movie, getting a new sweater). You also must be certain that the adults in the house do not model this explosive temperament for her. If you or your spouse lose your tempers just as quickly as your daughter loses hers, then you must reduce this behavior, as well.

Heel, Boy! That's a Good Daddy!

"What can be done in this strange situation? My ex-husband encourages bad behavior in our children and has them licking people's faces, like dogs. They can mess up their rooms, throw tantrums, and do whatever they like."

Answer:

Your ex-husband is doing tremendous harm to your children, and, quite frankly, he may be in need of professional assistance. You might want to discuss this matter with your attorney, who can advise you about limiting his access to the children. In the meantime, there is the possibility that your husband is attempting to manipulate you by creating a nightmarish situation with parenting problems. After all, if he creates two children who behave like monsters, then you, of course, will have to live with that. There is a definite limit to what you can do, as he will probably undo whatever you attempt to accomplish. However, should you want to try, your best bet may be to rely on the ability of the children to differentiate between your limits and those imposed by your ex-husband when the children are with him. Explain to them that their father's ideas are very different than yours, and that you will not tolerate the behavior he is encouraging. Let them know that if you see behavior such as face licking, there will be immediate consequences to deal with, and that as long as such behavior is evident, they will continue to pay a price for it. What you need to do is make the children feel that the pleasure of engaging in such inappropriate behavior is not justified by the cost that is represented by the punishments that you set up. If you do not see a change in their behavior in the near future, then you may need to seek the services of a mental health professional so your children can be helped to understand that what their father is encouraging them to do is unhealthy.

Off to the Corner with You!
"When my eight-year-old daughter does something bad, I have her stand in the corner for three hours. That seems to be better than sending her to her room, since at least this way I can keep an eye on her. Do you agree?"

Answer:
Although it is easier for you to monitor your daughter when she stands in the corner, there are disadvantages. If other family members keep passing by, there is too much stimulation. For punishment to be effective, the child should feel uncomfortable and should not interact with other family members during the isolation. You should be aware that there is no need to have the child stand for so many hours, as this probably causes significant physical pain. If you use "restriction to a room" the way it is described in PST, the child should get the message that what she did was wrong.

But Mommy, Why Do I Have to Listen to You?
"When you tell your child to do something, and you are asked 'why' in response, is it best to explain, or would saying only 'because I said so' be a better response?"

Answer:
With an older child, or with a bright one, some explanation of your logic may be in order now and then, but the problem that you are likely to run into is the tendency of the child to expect explanations for everything. There is nothing wrong with telling a child that he is being punished *because* he has done something wrong, but when a child wants to know *why* he has to clean up his room, you have run into a very different sort of situation. What a child may be looking for in asking such a question is not an explanation at all, but rather a justification. Thus, at this point, you need to consider the distinction between an explanation and

a justification. With the former, you are helping the child to understand your reasoning, and thus promoting some intellectual maturation on his part. With the latter, however, you are going so far as to imply that you need your child's approval for the decisions that you make. If you limit yourself, then, to saying things, such as "You have to walk the dog now, Mitch, because it's one of your daily chores," you probably won't run into much difficulty. Be as careful as you can to avoid a second response in reference to the situation at hand, however. If your child questions you further (after your initial reply as to why he must do something), be sure to cut off the conversation so that his procrastination and his attempt at gaining control is not reinforced.

Funny, They Look like Shoes to Me

"My thirteen-year-old daughter seems to be having trouble telling the difference between her shoes and a pad of paper. She wrote the names of friends on the sides of her shoes. Do you think that she should pay me back for the shoes, since she wrote on them?"

Answer:

You daughter has to wear the shoes and she must live with their appearance. If a child destroys her personal property, a parent can take the attitude that "it is her property, and I will not replace it." Using this logic, you might remind yourself that your daughter will have to wear her shoes as they are, or she will have to buy a new pair of shoes with her own money. Since there are so many things that occur with an adolescent for you to be more concerned about, why waste energy on something insignificant? Of course, if she wrote on your shoes it would be a different story. She does not have the right to deface or to destroy the property of another family member. If that were to happen, she should pay for whatever she has ruined, or work out the money owed to you with extra labor around the house.

Presto, Change-O, Poof, You're Punished

"My adolescent son is obsessed with magic. He does tricks and shows, and loves to entertain. We made a deal recently in which he was told that as long as he passed all of his classes, he could keep doing magic. But he failed a couple of subjects because he wasn't trying, and I took all of his magic props away from him until he brings his grades back up. He's furious, and says that I'm being unfair. Am I?"

Answer:

Not at all. If your son knew in advance what the consequences for failing to comply would be, then he created the problem himself. Assuming that he is capable of doing the work that you're expecting from him, there is no excuse for spending so much time on a hobby while his academic work continues to suffer. It's easy to see, of course, why he is feeling angry; punishment only works if it's unpleasant enough to be worth avoiding. The chances are that in the next grading period, your son's academic work is going to improve significantly, because he wants his props back so badly. Don't allow yourself to feel guilty, because that will serve no purpose. Instead, remind yourself that what you're doing is for your son's own good, even if he doesn't like it. You're going to help him to change his behavior, presto, and to become a better student. Now, anything up your sleeve?

Chapter Twenty-one

The PST Quiz

If you are reading this, then you should already have completed reading the other chapters in this book. By now, you have gained (presumably) a far better understanding of your child's behavior and of the techniques needed to change that behavior than you had prior to learning PST. To help you in gauging just how much you have learned, and to offer you a final opportunity to learn even more, we now present the PST QUIZ, a multiple-choice test of your newly gained knowledge. To take the quiz, read each of the questions on the following pages, and in each case, choose the one answer that seems to fit best. Simply enter the letter representing that answer into the appropriate space on the answer form (which you will find printed below). There are fifty questions, each worth two points, and when you have finished the quiz, the correct answers can be found on page 306.

Good luck!

PST Quiz Answer Form

1. _____	18. _____	35. _____
2. _____	19. _____	36. _____
3. _____	20. _____	37. _____
4. _____	21. _____	38. _____
5. _____	22. _____	39. _____
6. _____	23. _____	40. _____
7. _____	24. _____	41. _____
8. _____	25. _____	42. _____
9. _____	26. _____	43. _____
10. _____	27. _____	44. _____
11. _____	28. _____	45. _____
12. _____	29. _____	46. _____
13. _____	30. _____	47. _____
14. _____	31. _____	48. _____
15. _____	32. _____	49. _____
16. _____	33. _____	50. _____
17. _____	34. _____	

1. Your 10-year-old son, Glen, has been asked to walk the dog each day upon returning home from school. For the past several weeks, he has been failing to do so, and you realize that something needs to be done quickly. Which of the following strategies is most likely to be successful?
   a. Glen should be grounded for the weekend because he didn't walk the dog for several weeks.
   b. Glen should be forced to clean up after the dog each time that the dog has an accident as a result of not being walked.
   c. Glen should be grounded for the weekend, and then again every day until he begins to walk the dog on his own.
   d. Glen should spend his entire day with the dog, so that he will be less likely to forget about his responsibilities.

2. Suzie, who is afraid of snakes, has asked her parents to help her to get over this fear. Which of the following is a legitimate PST technique designed for such problems?
   a. Suzie should be exposed to snakes gradually, so that her fear will fade away over time.
   b. Suzie should be asked to write a lengthy report about snakes, so that she learns more about them.
   c. Nothing should be done; Suzie will outgrow the fear.
   d. Suzie should be placed in a room that is filled with snakes, so that she can see for herself that they are not dangerous.

3. If you give a child a direction and he does not comply,
   a. you should give him a cookie.
   b. you should tell him a second time, and then if he doesn't listen, punish him.
   c. he must be punished, in a reasonable manner, for not following directions on the first request.
   d. you must avoid becoming angry, so do the chore yourself and save everyone a lot of trouble.

4. You've asked your child to come home for dinner at 6:00 P.M., but she's just walked in at 6:20. You should
   a. tell her that she cannot go out of the house at all tomorrow because she acted irresponsibly.

b. yell at her for being late.
c. avoid making a fuss over her behavior because you don't want to reinforce it accidentally.
d. tell her to hurry up and sit down, because the food is getting cold.

5. Melinda never gets dressed promptly in the morning and is frequently late for school. Her mother should
   a. ask Melinda why she insists on making her feel so frustrated by disobeying what she has been told to do.
   b. put a sheet around Melinda, put her in the back seat of the car, and make her get dressed on the way to school.
   c. point out to Melinda that if she continues to be late for her first class, her grades will suffer and she will have to be punished for that.
   d. help Melinda to get dressed so that she can get finished faster.

6. Mrs. Cohen wants her son, Wally, to clean up his room. The most appropriate way to present this request to Wally would be to say,
   a. "Wally, please clean your room."
   b. "Wally, please go to your room now, empty your garbage can outside, put all your toys in your toy box, pick up all those little pieces of paper that are on the floor, and then make your bed."
   c. "Go clean your filthy room, or you'll have to deal with your father when he gets home."
   d. "Wally, if you don't clean your room, I'm going to invite scientists from NASA to come over and study the life forms that are growing in there."

7. You've set up a system wherein your child's allowance is contingent upon his completion of household chores. Randy becomes very upset when he loses some of his allowance, and he lets you know that he will no longer participate in this program. You should
   a. stop the allowance program because the child is unwilling to participate, and follow up by starting another kind of program.

    b. let him have all of his allowance, but tell him that the next time he doesn't do his chores, he will lose the money.

    c. tell him that if he doesn't earn at least half of his allowance for the week, he will be restricted from all activities outside the house for the weekend.

    d. ask him how much money it would take to get him to cooperate fully with you.

8. Brothers and sisters who, as adults, have the closest relationships are the ones whose parents

    a. had the least interference in their fights and conflicts.

    b. never punished them for fighting.

    c. never were divorced.

    d. bought boxing gloves for them and let them fight it out.

9. As you walk into the playroom, you see 7-year-old Robbie hitting 5-year-old Wayne. You should

    a. tell Robbie never to hit his younger brother again, but to come and to tell you when there is a problem.

    b. have both children go to separate rooms in the house where they will be restricted without being able to touch or to play with anything for 30 minutes.

    c. question the children in detail so that you can find out what caused this to happen.

    d. punch Robbie, because he hit a smaller child, and he needs to learn just how that feels.

10. When a child (who has no learning disabilities or other handicaps) does not complete his school work and forgets to do his homework regularly, the parent should

    a. punish the child for failing to do the necessary work.

    b. explain to the child that he is going to ruin his future because he won't be able to go to college.

    c. set up a monitoring system with each of the child's teachers, and make the child's access to privileges contingent upon his school performance.

    d. let him fail the grade and keep failing others, so that he'll learn his lesson the hard way.

11. Which of the following can serve to reinforce and to encourage a child's complaints about physical pain?
   a. Getting attention from his parents.
   b. Being forced to go to school, even while he is complaining.
   c. Being ignored, as if he is not saying anything.
   d. Being scheduled for exploratory surgery.

12. Before attempting to use behavioral techniques to reduce bed-wetting, you must first
   a. wash the sheets and clean the bed thoroughly to give the child a "fresh" start.
   b. rule out the possibility that a physical problem is causing the bed-wetting.
   c. make sure that the child has nothing to drink during the four-hour period preceding bedtime.
   d. spank the child until he promises never to wet again.

13. Karate often
   a. increases a child's aggressive behavior.
   b. decreases aggressive behavior in highly aggressive youngsters.
   c. seems frightening to aggressive children.
   d. encourages a child to buy Japanese products.

14. Of the following, which method would be the most effective?
   a. Giving your child a flat $5 per week as allowance.
   b. Giving your child money as he needs it.
   c. Giving your child the opportunity to earn up to $5 per week in allowance.
   d. Giving your child a credit card so that you can take care of all of the bills for him.

15. Of the following, which method is the most likely to be effective?
   a. Carla's parents tell her that she must clean her room whenever she thinks that it has become really dirty.
   b. Carla's parents tell her that she must clean her room every Saturday.

    c. Carla's parents tell her that her room must be in order every night by bedtime. She is told that this means that she must hang up her clothes, put all of her toys away, empty her trash basket into the big basket downstairs, and have her desk straightened.

    d. Carla's parents tell her to clean her room the first and third Saturday of each month, unless the month has five Saturdays. If this occurs, she should clean the room on the first, third, and fifth Saturday, skip the following week, clean it on the second Wednesday of the new month, and then continue with the regular schedule. During a leap year, everything is moved up one day for the first three months of the year.

16. If you begin to ignore a child's inappropriate behavior,
    a. the behavior will get worse at first, and then start to improve.
    b. the behavior will improve at first, and then start to get worse.
    c. the child will ignore your attempts at changing his behavior.
    d. the child will make you sorry for what you've done.

17. When praising a child, be sure to tell the child
    a. how much you love him.
    b. that he is now a worthwhile person.
    c. exactly what he did that is worthy of praise.
    d. how he is taking after you.

18. As you enter a store, your 10-year-old daughter holds the door open for you. The most appropriate response to her behavior would be:
    a. "Good girl!"
    b. "Thanks a lot!"
    c. "Thank you for holding the door open for me. What a wonderful display of good manners!"
    d. "Hurry up and close that door. It's freezing outside!"

19. Jake writes a "bad" four-letter word on another child's paper at school. An appropriate consequence would be for Jake to

a. be told to write the "bad" word 5,000 times before he is allowed to have any privileges or fun.
b. apologize to the other child.
c. be suspended from school for one month.
d. explain to you what that word *really* means.

20. According to the basic principles of PST, behavior that is punished without anger will
a. occur more frequently.
b. occur less frequently.
c. never occur at all.
d. occur only on weekends.

21. If you are doing something that is for your child's own good, you should never feel
a. angry.
b. frustrated.
c. guilty.
d. hungry.

22. When setting up a "reward" that is to be used in helping to motivate your child to do something, you should
a. make certain that it is worth working for.
b. be careful to choose something unusual.
c. always let the child make the choice.
d. be sure to pick something that *you* would like to have.

23. If you allow yourself to display anger toward your child, you'll be teaching him that
a. he must always behave properly, or run the risk of upsetting you.
b. he can control your emotions.
c. you take misbehavior seriously.
d. he may be shorter than you, but you behave the same way.

24. When you attempt to eliminate a fear or a phobia by strengthening a new behavior that competes with the fear response, you are

a. counter-conditioning.
b. fear-fading.
c. modeling.
d. kidding.

25. The logic behind having an overweight child list in a memo book each item of food 15 minutes before consuming it is that
   a. he will be able to prove that he is trying to diet.
   b. after waiting 15 minutes, he is likely to resist the food entirely.
   c. he will take dieting much more seriously.
   d. he will learn that food doesn't grow on trees.

26. Your 9-year-old daughter, Carmen, has just brought her art project home from school. In which of the following examples is there negative latent content?
   a. "Well, we're certainly glad to see you enjoying your schoolwork so much."
   b. "Carmen, that's the best artwork that you've ever done. We're so proud of you!"
   c. "That's just beautiful, Carmen! If you keep doing work like that, you'll be as good as your sister in no time."
   d. "Is that a bird, dear? It's a little hard to tell from this angle."

27. When using a tape recorder as an aid to control your child's tantrum behavior, you should
   a. be sure to avoid recording every tantrum, or your child will know what to expect.
   b. keep requiring the tantrums until your child hates them enough to prevent recurrences.
   c. schedule the tantrums for a different time each day.
   d. send the tapes to a talent agent to see whether your child can begin a career in television broadcasting.

28. More than anything else, tantrums represent an issue involving
   a. control.
   b. attention.
   c. spontaneity.
   d. professional wrestling.

29. In PST, it is suggested that parents and children be given different rights and privileges because
    a. parents are older, and deserve to be respected.
    b. treating children and adults as equals makes no sense, and is bound to create havoc within the family.
    c. children are too concerned with frivolous matters to be able to make decisions.
    d. parents are taller and stronger, and, therefore, can do whatever they please.

30. In the statement "There is not one child on the face of this earth who cannot follow directions on the first request," the implication is that a child who doesn't do what he is told to do the first time around
    a. has not yet learned that laziness doesn't pay.
    b. is stubborn, and doesn't like being told what to do.
    c. has learned that he doesn't have to respond quickly, because his parent will keep repeating the directions.
    d. is from some planet other than Earth.

31. When teaching a child to follow directions on the first request, you must not offer reminders because
    a. reminders are the same thing as second requests.
    b. the child will perceive you as nagging him.
    c. you're wasting valuable time in getting the child started.
    d. you'll have to yell to be heard over the TV.

32. In setting up a poker chip system to help to motivate your child, you must explain that your child will get one extra chip every time that he
    a. does what is asked of him on the first request.
    b. lives up to all of your expectations for his behavior.
    c. earns ten chips or more in a single day.
    d. runs out of chips.

33. When siblings fight, you are best advised to
    a. stop them before the argument gets out of hand.
    b. let them solve the problem themselves, and if punishment is needed, apply it to both of them.

c. get involved so that they see that you care.

d. run for cover, and call out the National Guard.

34. Speaking, yelling, hitting, punishing, and rewarding are methods of
   a. parenting.
   b. reinforcing.
   c. communicating.
   d. attracting attention.

35. "I wonder why you look so down," is an example of
   a. goal-oriented communication.
   b. communicating through questions.
   c. latent content.
   d. nosey parenting.

36. In which of the following examples is the child correctly assigned responsibility for his own behavior and not for other family members' emotions?
   a. "Alan, I feel very angry about your attitude."
   b. "You've made me just furious, Alan."
   c. "Alan, you've gotten the whole family upset."
   d. "Don't be selfish, Alan; make the whole world happy."

37. The "disappearing choice" technique was discussed in detail in Chapter Five. Which of the following is a valid example of this strategy?
   a. "Are you going to clean up your room now, or would you rather be punished?"
   b. "Are you going to walk the dog after school, or will you be too busy?"
   c. "Are you going to finish your homework before you watch TV, or listen to your stereo when you're through?"
   d. "Are you still there?"

38. Habits can be difficult to break because the child
   a. is accustomed to engaging in the behavior.
   b. is reinforced by the behavior itself.
   c. may not realize that he has a habit.
   d. is probably imitating your behavior.

39. To help a child to stop thumb-sucking behavior, it is suggested in PST the child be told that thumb sucking
   a. is unfair to his other fingers.
   b. can mean that he will have to wear braces later on.
   c. is something that only babies do.
   d. is dangerous because it can cause his thumb to shrink.

40. The three characteristics associated with adolescence are:
   a. egocentrism, arrogance, and fear.
   b. egocentrism, hedonism, and confusion.
   c. hedonism, confusion, and arrogance.
   d. driving, dating, and curfew breaking.

41. Gina lies to her parents to keep out of trouble. In PST, the term for this type of liar is:
   a. controller.
   b. confuser.
   c. escaper.
   d. troublemaker.

42. With regard to sex education for children, most parents should
   a. make sure that the child's school does an adequate job of providing such education.
   b. start educating a child by the time he or she is 5 years old.
   c. review the basics, and be prepared to answer questions realistically as they come up.
   d. hire Dr. Ruth to teach the child properly.

43. In learning to curb your own runaway emotions, you need to understand the "three R's." The second of these, Response, refers to
   a. your tendency to overreact to the stresses of everyday life.
   b. the way in which you think or behave when confronted with Reality.
   c. the effect that the Result of your thinking has upon your behavior.
   d. your tendency to forget what the "three R's" stand for whenever you are asked about them.

44. An assertive child would
    a. ask a classmate to return the book that he borrowed.
    b. feel hesitant about requesting a different seat.
    c. hit any other child who got in his way.
    d. steal money if he needed it.

45. In comparing specific praise and critical praise, it can be seen that
    a. the two differ in content, but both work well.
    b. with critical praise, you can help the child to understand what he has done wrong.
    c. with specific praise, you avoid evaluating your child, and concentrate on what he has done well.
    d. with critical praise, you have a good excuse for hurting the child's feelings.

46. A kitchen timer is a useful device for helping a
    a. hyperactive child.
    b. shy and passive child.
    c. antisocial child.
    d. child who is making dinner.

47. A psychosomatic problem is one in which the child's
    a. medical problems are all imaginary.
    b. illness is directly related to his emotional state.
    c. symptoms are a result of his desires.
    d. mind tells his body that it's too sick to go to school.

48. One of the basic principles of PST is that occasional rewards work best. This is because
    a. the child can only guess when the reward is coming.
    b. the child will continue to behave well even at those moments when he is not being reinforced.
    c. constant reinforcement becomes boring.
    d. parents would go broke if they rewarded their children constantly.

49. With regard to fears and phobias:
    a. phobias are more common than fears.

b. children are more likely to have phobias, while adults more commonly have fears.

c. a phobia is far more intense than a fear and is irrational in nature.

d. if you were phobic, you might be afraid to answer this question.

50. "Past behavior is the best predictor of future behavior" is a statement that means

a. in any given situation (until you make changes), your child's behavior is likely to be similar to whatever it has been up until now.

b. future behavior will depend always upon the past.

c. if you can predict the future, you can change it.

d. if your child has a behavior problem now, he'll have one forever—even when he's elderly.

How to Compute Your Score

On the following page is the answer key for the quiz that you've just completed. Each answer is worth two points, so count up the number of correct answers that you have, and then multiply by 2 in order to arrive at your final score. In case you haven't figured it out by now, all choice (d) answers were false and were there strictly for your amusement.

We hope that you enjoyed taking the PST QUIZ.

94-100: You're extremely fluent in PST theory. Your children are in for quite a surprise.

86-92: You've read the book carefully and remembered much of what you read. You should be able to put the techniques into use without difficulty.

76-84: You've developed some mastery of the ideas, but are weak enough in some areas to warrant going back and re-reading those sections.

68-74: Your score is better than could be expected from some-one who hasn't read the book, but isn't very good for someone who has. If you want to use PST effectively, then you need a better understanding and recollection of the material. Try reading the book a second time.

<68:   Your score indicates that you neither remember nor understand much about PST. Come on—did you really read this book?

PST QUIZ ANSWERS

1.	c	26.	c
2.	a	27.	b
3.	c	28.	a
4.	a	29.	b
5.	b	30.	c
6.	b	31.	a
7.	c	32.	a
8.	a	33.	b
9.	b	34.	c
10.	c	35.	b
11.	a	36.	a
12.	b	37.	c
13.	b	38.	b
14.	c	39.	a
15.	c	40.	b
16.	a	41.	c
17.	c	42.	c
18.	c	43.	b
19.	a	44.	a
20.	b	45.	c
21.	c	46.	a
22.	a	47.	b
23.	b	48.	b
24.	a	49.	c
25.	b	50.	a

An Important Word from the Publisher

Dear Reader,

The child-rearing methods you have read about in this book have made the challenging task of parenting easier and more enjoyable for thousands of people. And their children have benefited, becoming increasingly more secure and responsible. All that is necessary to achieve the same gratifying results is for you to thoroughly understand PST and to put it into action.

To help ensure your success in this rewarding endeavor, we at Wilshire Book Company are very pleased to make it possible for you to hear, in your own home or automobile, the best of Dr. Lustig and Dr. Silverman's presentations recorded live at their renowned, nationwide PST workshops. This specially edited, 80-minute cassette tape program is packed with explanations, examples, and anecdotes that will enable you to immediately put PST to work in your household.

Learn how to:
- teach your child to follow directions on the first request.
- stop arguing with your child.
- put an end to tantrum behavior.
- teach your child to be responsible.
- avoid feeling guilty.
- set up an allowance system that works.
- reduce conflict between brothers and sisters.
- punish without becoming angry.

An investment in this cassette tape is an investment in your child's well-being and in your own peace of mind.

Send $11.00 for your PST cassette tape to:

Wilshire Book Company
12015 Sherman Road
North Hollywood, California 91605-3781

Melvin Powers, *Publisher*

INDEX